SUPERVISION

SUPERVISION

FOCUS ON INSTRUCTION

DON M. BEACH

Tarleton State University

JUDY REINHARTZ

University of Texas at Arlington

HARPER & ROW, PUBLISHERS, New York
Cambridge, Philadelphia, San Francisco,
1817 London, Mexico City, São Paulo, Singapore, Sydney

Sponsoring Editor: Alan McClare
Project Editor: Joan Gregory
Text Design Adaptation: Lucy Krikorian
Cover Design: Circa 86, Inc.
Text Art: ComCom Division of Haddon Craftsmen, Inc.
Production Manager: Jeanie Berke
Production Assistant: Beth Maglione
Compositor: ComCom Division of Haddon Craftsmen, Inc.
Printer and Binder: R. R. Donnelley & Sons Company
Cover Printer: N.E.B.C.

SUPERVISION: Focus on Instruction

Library of Congress Cataloging in Publication Data

Beach, Don M.
  Supervision: focus on instruction.

  Includes index.
  1. School supervision—United States.   I. Reinhartz,
Judy. II. Title.
LB2806.4.B43   1989   371.2'013   88-24418
ISBN 0-06-040558-9

88 89 90 91 9 8 7 6 5 4 3 2 1

This book is dedicated to teachers, who are the foundation and cornerstone of instruction, and to two special teachers, our spouses, Linda and Dennis, who provided the love, encouragement, and support that made this book possible.

Contents

Foreword

Supervision: Focus on Instruction is a very timely book. America is about five years into the latest wave of educational reform. Every ten years this nation seems to have another cycle of reform, always stressing either excellence or equity in alternative decades. International events and economic concerns caused a swing to equity as evidenced in the NEA's manifesto, *Education for All American Youth,* in the forties. *Sputnik* galvanized school reform for excellence (at least in mathematics, science, and engineering) in the fifties, while the Elementary and Secondary Education Act of 1965 brought the equity issue to the forefront in that decade. The seventies were uncertain times in many ways for the United States. Everything was challenged; many things were changed. Schools offered "pass-fail" courses, but students seemed to prefer "pass-pass"!

In the present decade, our nation apparently wants both equity and excellence. We are restructuring schools (or at least rethinking their roles in a post-industrial society), seeking ways to use K–12 schools to improve the economy and strengthen our nation's relative position amidst rapidly changing global circumstances.

A Nation at Risk and its companion reports have convinced educators, improvement-minded legislators, and citizens that a fresh round of school effectiveness initiatives are needed. Most states have legislated or mandated the same changes, many centered on using money as incentives for more effective teaching (or teachers), following the career ladder approach created by Lamar Alexander in Tennessee. Furthermore, this wave of school reform, probably because it is led by state officials rather than local school leaders, is an impatient one. No one seems to have any time for involvement of those to be affected, for considering alternatives, or for consulting the appropriate research bases.

Fortunately, this time we have many more findings on the nature of effective schools and how to produce them because of forces set in motion in the two previous decades, *viz.,* the research bases of teacher effect, school effect, instructional leadership, curriculum alignment, program coupling, and change processes in schools. It is from this rich and relatively young lode that professors Beach and Reinhartz have mined the resources to fashion *Supervision: Focus on Instruction.*

Today, the experienced and successful supervisor has had time to digest the myriad of books, articles, case studies, and handbooks about one or two of these research bases, most likely teacher effect. Unfortunately, almost none of us has had the time to learn all six. It is by filling in the missing pieces in all of the research bases that *Supervision: Focus on Instruction* promises to make a substantial contribution.

From acquaintance with research on teacher effect, we have come to know that teaching is complex, interactive, and contextual. Supervising effective teaching is even more so. Add to that the depth of understanding needed to use research on change and communication, effective schools, and curriculum development to really deliver excellence and equity simultaneously in the instruction of the 80s and 90s, and you have some grasp of the monumental task confronting first-line supervisors as well as those who would train those supervisors.

As the authors say several times, their central theme is the improvement of instruction, their focus is the role of the supervisor in the process, and the bottom line is increased student achievement. The supervisor in training, the young principal-to-be, or the future director of instruction will find the sections on foundations of supervision and the dimensions of supervision enlightening and invaluable. The authors' thirty-five years of combined experience help the rookie understand where we are, where we came from, and where, with luck and hard work, we might go. The seasoned veteran in the field will return again and again to Parts Three, Four, and Five, sampling from the many actions and strategies suggested for clinical coaching, curriculum planning, and program and performance evaluation. The "Your Turn" section at the end of each chapter affords readers an opportunity to use what they have read on hypothetical but very real problem solving.

Both groups of readers will come to understand that continued reliance on past practice will lead only to more bureaucratic rigmarole, while creative combining of theory, organizational development, and custom-tailored staff development programs can produce a *professionalism* of teaching via decision making from a scientific data base rather than from collective action.

Benjamin Bloom recently wrote, "Schools need to improve the life chances for most of the students." He asserts that it's a crime against mankind to deprive children of successful learning when it is possible for virtually all to learn at a higher level. The same can be said for supervisors and teachers. *Supervision: Focus on Instruction* improves our life chances!

Richard P. Manatt
Iowa State University

Preface

The purpose of *Supervision: Focus on Instruction* is to provide individuals who serve as instructional supervisors with the necessary concepts and skills needed to help teachers improve classroom instruction and increase student achievement. The central theme of the book is the improvement of instruction and the focus is on the role of the instructional supervisor in the improvement process.

Questions that provided guidance in the development of the text were: How can supervisors help teachers at a variety of professional levels improve instruction? How can instructional supervisors most effectively promote excellence in the classrooms? Clearly, in responding to these questions we view the teacher as the single most important factor in the improvement of instruction. Likewise, we view instructional supervisors and the instructional supervision process as critical to the continued professional growth and development of teachers.

This book has evolved from our combined experience of over thirty-five years in elementary and secondary classrooms, preservice teacher training, and in staff development programs and inservice training at the graduate level. The writing has been a collaborative effort in which the authors "speak with one voice," and we feel that the result is a unique blend of two viewpoints.

The text has been designed to provide an historical perspective of the supervisory process and the development of practices related to instructional supervision. It also has a sound theoretical base for practices within organizations and presents skills for effective instructional leadership. The authors cite and analyze theories and research of others and attempt to synthesize what is known about models and mechanics of supervision, supervisory style, teaching effectiveness, and the application of these elements to classroom instruction.

The text can be viewed as broad-based and eclectic in nature and rests on the belief that there is no single best way to supervise or teach. The models, skills, and procedures described in the text provide more results than some others. Multiple suggestions and options are provided for the instructional supervisor to consider and use, depending upon the role and title, the school situation, the teacher(s) involved, and the problem or need at that particular time. The options are designed to provide the supervisor with a variety of choices to pick and choose from in developing a supervisory repertoire.

The book is divided into four major parts. Part One, Foundations of Supervisory Practice, includes five chapters and provides an introduction to instructional supervision, an examination of the changing role of the supervisor, and an analysis of theories and principles related to organizations, leadership behavior, and communication. These chapters are designed to establish a theoretical foundation upon which the remaining chapters are based.

The second section clearly establishes the instructional dimensions of supervision. The emphasis in Part Two is on instructional planning and teaching and the role of the instructional supervisor in working with teachers in these two endeavors. For us, the sections on planning and teaching represent the pinnacles of instructional effectiveness. Focusing on instruction ultimately involves an in-depth analysis of both planning for instruction and the actual delivery of instruction.

Models and mechanics of supervision are the focus for Part Three. This section emphasizes the pragmatic aspects of the supervisory process. Where Part One emphasizes knowledge and understanding and is somewhat theoretical in nature, Part Three is designed to be very practical, for it emphasizes actions associated with the implementation of models with appropriate supervisory behavior. The various models of supervision are presented, along with the attendant supervisory behavior and technical skills associated with each. Several options are presented and discussed, further reinforcing the notion that a variety of approaches exist from which to select the one most compatible or appropriate to the situation and circumstances.

The final section, Part Four, includes other dimensions or aspects of functioning as an instructional supervisor. Such areas as evaluating teacher performance, working with teachers in staff development, making decisions, and bringing about change are included in this section. Part Four can be considered a crucial part of the text, for it focuses on those responsibilities supervisors are often required to assume to be successful.

For us, the "Your Turn" section at the end of each chapter represents our belief that in learning about procedures and practices, we should have an opportunity to become involved with the information. The tasks presented in these sections ask the reader to use the information presented in the chapter in a meaningful way in hypothetical situations. We view their use of information as an essential step in the development as instructional supervisors.

Finally, the production of this text has been a labor of love as we have incorporated most, if not all, of the information here in our classes over the past year or more. In a sense, you could say that the information has been "field tested." As new figures were developed or new activities created, our students were asked to respond to these materials.

As the title suggests, we view the primary focus of instructional supervision as an emphasis on instruction. Therefore, we have described practices and procedures that can help supervisors work more effectively with teachers with a clear focus on classroom instruction. As a result, we hope that what is included represents a significant contribution to a better understanding of the complex process of instructional supervision and will assist others in making the supervisory process more effective in helping teachers improve instruction. We are grateful to the following reviewers whose comments and suggestions were very helpful in developing the book: **Janet E. Alleman, Michigan State University; Robert T. Anderson, University of Alabama; Charles W. Funkhouser, University of Texas at Arlington; Edward Pajak, University of Georgia.**

Don M. Beach   Judy Reinhartz

SUPERVISION

one

FOUNDATIONS OF SUPERVISORY PRACTICE

chapter *1*

The Field of Instructional Supervision

The supervision of instruction is an important activity in promoting effective teaching in schools. The primary purpose of supervision, as presented in this text, is the improvement of instruction by fostering the continued professional development of all teachers. Such improvement and development rely on a supervisory system that is dedicated to helping teachers be successful in their classrooms. Instructional supervision, however, is a complex process that involves numerous people in different roles and situations, at multiple levels of the school organization.

Firth (1987) speaks of the complexity of roles and functions when he writes: "Despite countless attempts to identify, categorize, improve, and dignify the roles of . . . instructional supervisor[s], . . . [the roles] remain obscure and confused" (p. 2). He elaborates on the situation when he says that superintendents and principals have had their administrative roles defined by law or clarified in state school codes—but not so for others who function as instructional supervisors. "Such individuals may have different responsibilities but the same title, or identical responsibilities but different titles" (Firth, 1987, p. 2).

Regardless of the title of the person or persons involved, we see instructional supervision as a multifaceted process that focuses on instruction. It is the instructional supervision process that should provide both capable and less capable teachers with information about their teaching behavior so that they can continue to develop instructional skills and improve the quality of their performance.

In this chapter we will discuss some basic assumptions related to the supervision of instruction. In addition, we will provide several definitions of instructional supervision along with a description of the instructional supervisor and his or her function within the school organization. Finally, some of the advantages and disadvantages associated with the responsibility of being an instructional supervisor are presented.

ASSUMPTIONS RELATED TO INSTRUCTIONAL SUPERVISION

Instructional supervision is based on several assumptions regarding the process of how teachers are supervised. The assumptions serve to establish a mind set for those engaged in the supervisory process. According to Boyan and Copeland (1978), "Instructional supervision emphasizes both an open, collegial relationship between a teacher and a supervisor and a process for confronting instructional problems which uses reality-based data from classroom observation" (p. 2). The intent of such a process is to involve a supervisor who is concerned about people but is equally concerned about teachers delivering quality instruction. As a result, Boyan and Copeland (1978, pp. 2–3) have articulated several assumptions that have been associated with the instructional supervision process.

1. Many instructional problems encountered by classroom teachers can be resolved if the teachers change their behavior in positive ways. When teachers encounter instructional problems with students, the relevant questions to ask themselves are: "What can I do? What actions or behaviors can I exhibit that will bring about changes in my students so that the problem is resolved?" Many factors other than teacher behaviors have an impact on students (for example, home environment, peers, physical/physiological conditions), and teachers have little or no control over these. But teachers can control or modify what they know best, their own instructional behavior.

2. Recognition of needed changes in behavior is more effective when it comes from teachers, rather than being imposed from without. Video and/or audio taping can provide teachers with the opportunity to see and/or hear themselves objectively—an experience that is more likely to prompt an intrinsic desire to change.

3. Many behaviors exhibited during the teaching–learning process go unnoticed by teachers because they are not fully aware of how their behavior affects student behavior. When teachers focus mainly on student behavior, they miss an opportunity for improving their interaction with the class.

4. Increased awareness of teaching–learning behaviors can help teachers recognize needed change(s). As teachers become more aware of their own behaviors or specific actions in the classroom, they can begin to solve problems by pinpointing behaviors that need to be changed.

5. Existing teaching–learning behaviors can be revealed to teachers by using systematic observation techniques. The wide variety of observation techniques available can yield specific information about classroom behavior.

6. As a trained observer, the instructional supervisor can help teachers conduct systematic classroom observations. As the observer, the supervisor can objectively record relevant behaviors of both students and teachers. Such data are often helpful as the teacher and supervisor "relive" the lesson.

7. The trained observer (instructional supervisor) must present observational data to teachers in ways that will allow the teachers to accept the information as valid and accurate. When teachers recognize the validity of such data, they can identify the needed instructional changes.

8. Such acceptance and internalization are best achieved when the relationship between the supervisor and the teacher is collegial. The relationship should be based on cooperation, mutual respect, and reliance upon each other as a source of help in working together toward a common goal.

Instructional supervision is complicated further when supervisors work with teachers who are at different developmental stages and have diverse backgrounds and instructional abilities. The range of teacher performance behaviors (professional development), taken together, can be viewed as a continuum, with the less able teachers

Figure 1.1 Continuum of teaching performance behaviors.

at one end and the most able teachers at the opposite end. Figure 1.1 represents such a continuum of teacher performance behaviors that range from "Unacceptable" to "Clearly outstanding."

To accommodate such diversity in the range of teacher behaviors, the instructional supervision process must incorporate a variety of supervisory models. A more complete and detailed discussion of teacher developmental stages and supervisory styles will be presented in Chapter 8. Now that the focus of this text and the assumptions related to the process of supervision have been presented, the next section will discuss different definitions of supervision and will then provide a definition that will form the framework of this text.

WHAT IS INSTRUCTIONAL SUPERVISION?

Instructional supervision is composed of four interrelated elements that guide and shape supervisory practices and procedures. These interrelated elements are as follows:

1. the historical development of instructional supervision, including the body of knowledge that has been accumulated concerning what supervisors do
2. the theoretical base, including an understanding of organizations, leadership, communication, and teaching principles, that supports and validates supervisory behavior
3. the knowledge of how the models of supervision (particularly clinical and developmental) function
4. the specific techniques and procedures that supervisors need as they work with teachers

There is no single unifying definition of *instructional supervision*. There are almost as many definitions of the word *supervision* as there are of the term *education*. Definitions of *instructional supervision* have been largely dependent upon multiple forces at a given time, and the definitions have changed as the social milieu of schools has changed.

One of the earliest definitions of the word *supervision* comes from the Latin root meaning to "oversee" or "have oversight of." Dictionary definitions expand on this early generic definition and indicate that to *supervise* means to direct or manage the work of others. According to Pfeiffer and Dunlap (1982), instructional supervision

> is a multifaceted interpersonal process—dealing with teaching behavior, curriculum, learning environments, grouping of students, teacher utilization, and professional development. Also there are miscellaneous responsibilities which may include writing proposals for grants, providing public relations services, or fulfilling assignments which superordinates decide to delegate. (p. 1)

Other authors have defined *supervision* in the following terms:

1. a change process (Harris and Bessent, 1969; Lovell and Wiles, 1983)
2. a way of modifying teacher behavior (Wiles and Lovell, 1975)
3. a way of developing curricular materials for classroom instruction (Cogan, 1973)
4. a matter of human relations and the development of human resources (Sergiovanni and Starratt, 1979; Doll, 1983)
5. a leadership function involved with administration, curriculum, and teaching (Wiles and Bondi, 1980, 1986)
6. a management function within the school production system (Alfonso, Firth, and Neville, 1981)

We perceive instructional supervision as more complex than any of these single definitions. Before stating our definition of *supervision,* it is helpful to review additional definitions that emphasize the collegial, collaborative relationship between the teacher and supervisor in enhancing both teaching and learning. Glatthorn (1984) explains the term this way:

> Supervision is a process of facilitating the professional growth of a teacher, primarily by giving the teacher feedback about classroom interactions and helping the teacher make use of that feedback in order to make teaching more effective. (p. 2)

For Pfeiffer and Dunlap (1982), supervision is

> the process of interaction in which . . . individuals [supervisors] work with teachers to improve instruction. The ultimate goal is

better student learning. The achievement of this goal may involve changing teacher behavior, modifying curriculum, and/or restructuring the learning environment. (p. 5)

Building upon these ideas, we define the term *instructional supervision* as the process of working with teachers to improve classroom instruction. To be effective, supervisors must utilize knowledge of organizations, leadership, communication, and teaching principles as they work with teachers in classrooms and improve instruction by increasing student achievement. The emphasis in this text, then, is on working with teachers. Individuals who have the responsibility to help teachers do their best in the classroom are instructional supervisors.

WHO IS THE INSTRUCTIONAL SUPERVISOR?

School systems have long recognized the need for individuals to serve as instructional supervisors. Those who serve as supervisors occupy a variety of positions within the schools. The primary justification for utilizing instructional supervisors is to help teachers grow professionally in the classroom (Oliva, 1976). When the term *instructional supervisor* is used, we are referring to any individual, regardless of title, who functions in a supervisory position in the school system. Such positions may include, but are not limited to, the principal, assistant principal, department head, specialist-consultant, curriculum director, or assistant superintendent. It is the function, then, and not just the title, that defines an instructional supervisor (Wiles and Bondi, 1980). An instructional supervisor, therefore, is someone formally designated by the school organization who has the responsibility for working with teachers to increase the quality of student learning through improved instruction.

In examining a typical administrative structure for schools, even the superintendent, as the chief executive officer of the school system, serves in the top supervisory capacity. The superintendent generally supervises and evaluates the work of building principals and the staff of the central office. Accordingly, members of the central office staff also serve in supervisory positions as they work with teachers and other administrators in the district. At each school level, the principal serves as the supervisor in charge of instruction, and, within each individual school, there may be others serving in supervisory roles such as team leaders, department heads, or lead teachers.

When functioning as an instructional supervisor, the person in that position has responsibilities related to one or more of the following roles, duties, or functions:

1. formulating, implementing, and evaluating goals for the school and/or the teacher
2. developing, implementing, and evaluating curriculum
3. supervising and evaluating personnel and providing staff development opportunities
4. developing and managing resources for the teaching–learning process
5. evaluating instructional materials and programs for classroom use

Regardless of the title or position, supervisors are responsible for the delivery of instruction and the quality of that instruction (monitoring student progress on standardized and/or criterion-referenced tests). The instructional supervisors also should be concerned about the products or end results of the educational process (literate graduates and their ability to function in a rapidly changing society) and teacher morale (how teachers feel and function in their work environment). As supervisors strive to be successful in promoting effective instruction, they may have to rely heavily on their knowledge of the principles of supervisory practice.

ROLES OF THE INSTRUCTIONAL SUPERVISOR

As indicated earlier, instructional supervisors may have different titles or positions but perform many similar roles. The supervisory roles refer to the broader, general administrative or managerial behaviors, and the assistant superintendent of instruction has many duties that are similar to those of the building principal. The roles are specific and are in part dependent upon the expectations and job descriptions developed by each school system. Instructional supervisors are typically called upon to perform the following roles; the performance of one role often is related to others.

Planner. Within the operation of schools, planning is one of the most important roles for the instructional supervisor. Planning involves the ability to determine in advance what should be done and how it is to be accomplished. Whether the supervisor is helping develop a school calendar or a systemwide inservice program, planning is essential to the success of the endeavor. Planning is a prerequisite for supervisors, so that they can help teachers to be proactive (Jackson, 1968). For example, helping teachers with time management strategies as they build their lesson plans is crucial to effective instruction.

Organizer. The ability to organize is another role that is crucial if the instructional supervisor is to be successful. Whether the duties of the supervisor involve class scheduling or obtaining the necessary curricular materials, including textbooks, the ability to organize is essential. Linking people with the necessary resources is vital to the effective operation of the school.

Leader. In order to be successful, an instructional supervisor must be able to influence the behavior of others. For instance, the supervisor must be able to persuade teachers to modify their lesson plans or change their teaching behavior to accommodate individual differences in students. In addition, persuading teachers to adopt new curriculum, instructional programs, or instructional models is often a part of the supervisor's role. Being effective in leading others is therefore an important role for the supervisor.

Helper. The supervisor is charged with the responsibility of helping others. The primary objective for the supervisor is to help teachers develop and improve their instructional skills. As supervisors work in a variety of settings with teachers who have different needs and levels of professional competence, it is imperative that the supervisor function as a helper. The role of helper ranges from providing direct assistance to teachers in the form of observing and coaching to giving indirect assistance by listening to teachers as they think through their instructional sequence.

Evaluator or appraiser. While the building principal normally functions in the role of evaluator, other individuals, such as consultants or coordinators, are called upon to become a part of the teacher evaluation process. Although supervisory personnel have historically been associated with staff development, there is an increasing trend to involve individuals other than principals in teacher appraisal. The ability of the supervisor to appraise the instructional act is a prerequisite for the improvement of teaching and learning.

Motivator. One of the most important roles performed by an instructional supervisor is to motivate teachers. Motivation is enhancing a person's desire to do something. It is the supervisor's responsibility to work with teachers to foster an intrinsic desire to improve their instructional performance. The supervisor must use appropriate strategies that will motivate teachers to improve their performance, whether it is establishing set, providing input, or modeling. Being able to motivate is vital to the supervisor's ability to foster change and improvement.

Communicator. The ability to transfer information, ideas, or feelings within the school setting is an important supervisory role. Supervisors must be good communicators, and their ability to work with others effectively depends on their ability to communicate. It is imperative that supervisors be clear and concise when transmitting ideas and information to teachers and others in the school organization.

Decision maker. Instructional supervisors have to develop the skill and confidence to make split-second decisions. They must make decisions about programs, materials, and personnel, as well as clients (students and parents) and the school facilities. The supervisory process requires continuous decision making and involves working with teachers, parents, students, and other administrators to determine what is best for all involved. The ability to make a difference in the quality of instruction in a classroom may depend on the supervisor's ability to make sound decisions.

The roles—planner, organizer, leader, helper, evaluator/appraiser, motivator, communicator, decision maker—of an instructional supervisor are varied and clearly require an individual to be flexible, confident, and skilled in working with people. The roles also require supervisors who are knowledgeable about the teaching–learning process. With these varied and often difficult roles and requirements, why would anyone elect to become a supervisor? The next part of this chapter will discuss some of the advantages and disadvantages of becoming an instructional supervisor.

BEING AN INSTRUCTIONAL SUPERVISOR: ADVANTAGES AND DISADVANTAGES

Individuals often aspire to supervisory positions because they believe such positions will give them increased responsibility and an opportunity to expand their sphere of influence. Supervisory roles can lead to opportunities for advancement to other administrative positions. It is not uncommon for assistant superintendents, curriculum directors, or principals to have come from the ranks of those who first started in other instructional supervisory positions (such as department head, team leader, or elementary consultant).

Instructional supervisors may find the roles and the responsibilities to be personally and professionally rewarding. For some, additional intrinsic gratification is sought. After several years of classroom experience, some educators need greater stimulation beyond knowing that their students have done well. Another reason for seeking supervisory positions is to have greater autonomy and more flexibility in carrying out assignments. Finally, in helping teachers, supervisors find satisfaction in performing many roles that range from working with people on a one-to-one basis to planning staff development programs for an entire school district.

There are indeed many advantages of being an instructional supervisor; however, there is a need for a word of caution. Individuals who are interested in becoming instructional supervisors should be aware of some of the limitations. First, people who aspire to supervisory positions must be prepared to deal with the mismatch they may experience between their expectations and the reality of the performance on the job. Other limitations that supervisors must confront are the number of hours and long days they will have when there are projects to complete or deadlines to meet.

Supervisors can be further limited if they believe that they lack the necessary authority to implement change, enforce policies, or adopt new programs. Whether justifiable or not, many supervisors—regardless of their role—feel that they are given the responsibility to make changes or adopt new programs, yet are not granted adequate authority or support. Finally, instructional supervisors are confronted with the dilemma of moving from the role of helper (assisting teachers, by using a collegial, diagnostic approach) to a role of judge (making evaluations and decisions about instructional effectiveness that may affect a teacher's career). In the chapter on evaluation, this dilemma of helper versus judge will be discussed in greater detail.

Individuals who are considering a position that involves instructional supervision should be aware of the rewards and benefits as well as the possible limitations. The roles of the instructional supervisor within the educational system are challenging and provide professional as well as personal satisfaction.

SUMMARY

The supervision of instruction is important in promoting improved teaching and learning. There are eight assumptions presented which establish a framework for the supervisory process. Within this text, instructional supervision is viewed as a process of working with teachers to improve classroom instruction.

Any individual, regardless of his or her title, who functions in a supervisory position in the school system is an instructional supervisor. For example, superintendents, principals, consultants, and directors are a few of the titles used, and they have supervisory roles as a part of the job responsibility. Those who function in a supervisory capacity, regardless of the title, must be people-oriented as well as task-oriented to be effective in helping teachers improve instruction.

The instructional supervision process is complex and involves the following functions: formulating, implementing, and evaluating goals and objectives; developing, implementing, and evaluating curriculum; supervising and evaluating personnel and providing for staff development; developing and managing resources for the teaching–learning process; and evaluating materials, programs, and classroom instruction. Roles associated with supervisory personnel include planner, organizer, leader, helper, evaluator or appraiser, motivator, communicator, and decision maker. Supervisors perform these roles as they help teachers improve their instructional behaviors. Anyone considering a position as an instructional supervisor should be aware of the rewards as well as the limitations.

YOUR TURN

1.1 As someone who has been supervised, what comes to mind when you hear or see the word *supervision?* Write five words that you associate with the supervision process. Now that you have read this chapter, can you think of five additional words that might be used to describe the supervision process? Compare your two lists to determine if there are similarities and differences.

1.2 Using your experiences as a teacher and your understanding of the instructional supervision process, develop a list of suggestions that supervisors could use to help teachers be more effective in their classroom instruction.

1.3 Select a supervisory position (such as principal, curriculum director, elementary consultant, team leader) and describe a typical day in this position based on your understanding of instructional supervision and the responsibilities of this instructional supervisor.

1.4 As the elementary or secondary consultant in a district, you have been given the responsibility to coordinate all English/Language Arts instruction for the district. As you begin your new assignment, you discover that several teachers in one building will not work with one particular team member. What steps would you take to accomplish your assignment and get all the teachers working together to implement the English/Language Arts curriculum?

REFERENCES

Alfonso, R. J., Firth, G. R., and Neville, R. F. (1981). *Instructional supervision: A behavior system* (2nd ed.). Boston: Allyn and Bacon.

Boyan, N. J., and Copeland, W. D. (1978). *Instructional supervision training program.* Columbus, Ohio: Charles E. Merrill.

Cogan, M. L. (1973). *Clinical supervision.* Boston: Houghton Mifflin.

Doll, R. C. (1983). *Supervision for staff development: Ideas and applications.* Boston: Allyn and Bacon.

Firth, G. (March 1987). Recognition by professional organizations: A better way to clear up role confusion. *Update.* Alexandria, Va.: Association for Supervision and Curriculum Development, 2.

Glatthorn, A. A. (1984). *Differentiated supervision.* Alexandria, Va.: Association for Supervision and Curriculum Development.

Harris, B., and Bessent, W. (1969). *Inservice education: A guide to better practice.* Englewood Cliffs, N.J.: Prentice-Hall.

Jackson, P. (1968). *Life in classrooms.* New York: Holt, Rinehart and Winston.

Lovell, J. T., and Wiles, K. (1983). *Supervision for better schools* (5th ed.). Englewood Cliffs, N.J.: Prentice-Hall.

Oliva, P. F. (1976). *Supervision for today's schools.* New York: Thomas Y. Crowell.

Pfeiffer, I. L., and Dunlap, J. B. (1982). *Supervision of teachers: A guide to improving instruction.* Phoenix: Oryx Press.

Sergiovanni, T. J., and Starratt, R. J. (1979). *Supervision: Human perspectives* (2nd ed.). New York: McGraw-Hill.

Wiles, J., and Bondi, J. (1980). *Supervision: A guide to practice.* Columbus, Ohio: Charles E. Merrill.

Wiles, J., and Bondi, J. (1986). *Supervision: A guide to practice* (2nd ed.). Columbus, Ohio: Charles E. Merrill.

Wiles, K., and Lovell, J. (1975). *Supervision for better schools* (4th ed.). Englewood Cliffs, N.J.: Prentice-Hall.

chapter *2*

The Changing Role of Instructional Supervision

Current practices and procedures associated with instructional supervision have changed over time as American public education has grown and developed and as the conditions in American society have changed. The historical roots of supervisory practice are important because, according to Lucio and McNeil (1969), knowledge of the past "gives insight into the nature of supervision, for we are wedded in our practice to the thought of other eras" (p. 3). An understanding of current supervisory practice "requires knowledge of the way in which the process has evolved within the institution of American public education" (Alfonso, Firth, and Neville, 1981, p. 18). As indicated in Chapter 1, historical development is one of the interrelated elements of instructional supervision. It is therefore important to consider the past when analyzing present supervisory policies and conditions as well as when planning for the future. In noting this evolutionary trend, Tanner and Tanner (1987) state that

> the development of public education and the field of supervision are so completely intertwined. . . . Supervisors need to see their professional task in vital relationship to the great achievements already made in the field and the problems and difficulties that still face them. (p. 4)

15

Practices relating to instructional supervision are often in response to changes that take place in the social milieu. Further, supervisors should learn to view current supervisory practices and procedures in relationship to earlier events and conditions in education.

Schools, as social institutions, are not immune to shifts that take place within society. Historically, the schools have reflected the values and attitudes of each generation. In the late nineteenth and early twentieth centuries, schools were called upon to educate the waves of immigrants that came to this country. More recently, schools have experienced the impact of the social, political, and technological developments of the 1960s, 1970s, and 1980s. Alfonso, Firth, and Neville (1981), note that "Over the past thirty years, the American public school has been called upon to be an active instrument for social change" (p. 18). The dynamic nature of American culture has been fueled by domestic as well as international developments: the launching of *Sputnik,* the cold war, the nuclear age, the desegregation of the schools (and society), changes in the family structure, and local, state, and national tax revolts. Because of these and other developments that have taken place in society, the schools are frequently in a state of flux.

The context in which instructional supervision occurs is therefore a dynamic one. Depending upon the current social, economic, and/or political conditions, new educational priorities are established ranging from decisions made at the local level by school boards to actions taken at the national level by task forces, Congress, and/or the Supreme Court. As new educational priorities are established, practices related to instructional supervision are modified.

Because of recent changes in education, many brought about by the numerous published reports chronicling the less than satisfactory conditions of public education, the 1980s may become known as the decade of reform. The reform movement has created, almost overnight, a change in the schools and a resulting change in instructional supervision. Such changes are evidenced in the state-mandated reforms that have required that "basic skills" be taught, that minimum time requirements be adhered to for each subject taught in the elementary school, and that the required number of credits needed for graduation from high school be increased. In addition to providing greater structure in the curriculum, some states have implemented teacher testing (literacy skills), a career ladder for teacher advancement, and comprehensive teacher evaluation systems. As a result of these changes in the schools, the instructional supervisor has taken on new or different roles and responsibilities. For some instructional supervisors, emphasis has been placed on observation of classroom instruction and documentation of teaching effectiveness. Other instructional supervisors have been directly involved in helping teachers develop lesson plans with the "essentials" or "basics" and then actually teaching the lesson with the teacher in a process called "team coaching" (Joyce and Showers, 1982; Neubert and Bratton, 1987).

With numerous changes in education, the process of instructional supervision has taken on different characteristics. Recent conditions suggest that more attention is being given to comprehensive summative teacher evaluations and that supervisors will be taking a more active role as evaluators. To accommodate the current and future changes in education, additional adjustments will have to be made in the roles and responsibilities of the instructional supervisor.

When there are shifts in social priorities, the process of instructional supervision becomes one of purpose setting rather than routine maintenance. One of the functions of instructional supervision, at any time but especially during times of rapid change, is to give meaning to chaos. While our immediate social and educational focus seems to be frequently changing, a review of past practices will reveal that supervisory roles and responsibilities develop to meet the goals and priorities of each historical period.

There are many different timetables that can be used to identify major periods in educational practice. The periods within the timetable presented indicate that instructional supervision has evolved over time and has been influenced by the societal conditions of particular periods. To establish a historical perspective, Figure 2.1 provides a time line that traces the development of instructional supervision through different periods. The dates given are approximate time periods and not absolute benchmarks. Each period referred to is identified and described in greater detail in the sections that follow.

COLONIAL PERIOD (1600–1865)

The colonial period was marked by the establishment of schools in the local communities. According to Tanner and Tanner (1987):

> Throughout the colonies, supervision was by lay assessment. . . . Quite naturally, the responsibility fell on the town selectmen. They were instructed by the town to visit the schools and make reports to the town. (p. 5)

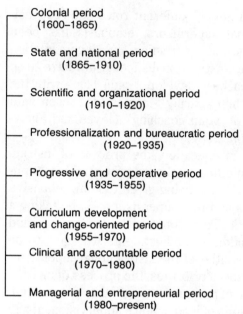

Colonial period
(1600–1865)

State and national period
(1865–1910)

Scientific and organizational period
(1910–1920)

Professionalization and bureaucratic period
(1920–1935)

Progressive and cooperative period
(1935–1955)

Curriculum development
and change-oriented period
(1955–1970)

Clinical and accountable period
(1970–1980)

Managerial and entrepreneurial period
(1980–present)

Figure 2.1   Time line: Development of instructional supervision.

Typically, then, each school was under the control of a lay committee that had general oversight for the schools. Supervision in the form of inspection was utilized to ensure community responsibility for the success of schools.

This lay committee, which included ministers, screened and selected teachers and established standards; it also visited schools to inspect the buildings and verify teacher and pupil performance (Burton and Brueckner, 1955). Characteristics of instructional supervision during this early period included (1) the authority of committee members over the educational process, (2) the inspection by and autocratic rule of committee members in supervising teachers and pupils, and (3) strict conformity to the rules and standards set by the lay committee. Although initially the emphasis was on local control, by 1860, toward the end of the early colonial period, state school systems had taken form and state responsibility for education was emerging (Alfonso, Firth, and Neville, 1981).

STATE AND NATIONAL PERIOD (1865–1910)

Beginning during this period and continuing in the subsequent decades, the growth of cities produced a marked increase in school enrollments (Pierce, 1935). There also developed a question as to who would control the schools. The district system of organization and control evolved to meet the needs of a sparse and rural population. Again, Tanner and Tanner (1987) note:

> It is not difficult to see why the district system was so popular. . . . The power and control of the state were kept distant. A community that wanted a school could organize a district, vote to levy a tax on their property, build a schoolhouse, hire a teacher and maintain the school. (p. 13)

The problem emerged when local districts failed to raise sufficient revenues to support schools and maintain standards. The result was a growing concern for the quality of education, and states engaged in a series of maneuvers that were related to the goals of the common school movement. One of the major aims of this movement was to establish some form of state control over local schools (Alfonso, Firth, and Neville, 1981). States began to institute systems of education, and took more responsibility for education by passing laws that gave general oversight for the operation of the schools to a state educational agency.

The growth of cities and the increasing enrollments in schools produced another change. The local management of schools was turned over to the principal (Pierce, 1935). A variety of titles such as *headmaster* or *head teacher* were used to designate leadership roles and responsibilities within a school; the specific period when all duties were first centralized around one individual called a *principal* cannot be determined precisely. When the title of *principal* did appear during this period, the supervisory duties, as identified by Spain, Drummond, and Goodlad (1956), consisted of the following:

1. maintaining discipline in the school
2. establishing rules and regulations for the performance of students and teachers
3. administering the physical plant (opening school, closing school, maintaining the building)
4. classifying pupils according to grade level or assignment
5. scheduling and regulating classes

With the development of the principalship during this period, instructional supervision became the responsibility of a single individual, and yet the authoritarian inspections, characteristic of the earlier colonial period, were still used frequently.

SCIENTIFIC AND ORGANIZATIONAL PERIOD (1910–1920)

During this period, advances in educational theory and practice were made as a result of educational experiments based on principles of psychology. Schools also applied information gained from time and motion studies (efficiency experts) to the daily classroom routines. School operations and procedures were influenced by the scientific management principles developed and implemented in business and industry. Because of the widespread adoption of an industrial orientation in educational settings, the influence of scientific management was pervasive (Wiles and Bondi, 1986).

During this time, a focus of instructional supervision was the more efficient use of time in the classroom and the routinization of various activities. The supervisor became somewhat of an efficiency monitor, checking to see that teachers were using time effectively and that the lessons were basically the same for all. Because of this preoccupation with efficiency, classes and schedules often became regimented. Teachers at each grade level were expected to be doing roughly the same activities at the same time each day. The regimentation and standardization of procedures were readily adopted, since the schools had to educate many different groups of immigrant children. The emphasis on regimentation can also be seen in the concept of the "melting pot"—children were "standardized" as they lost their ethnic identities and became "Americans."

PROFESSIONALIZATION AND BUREAUCRATIC PERIOD (1920–1935)

During this period, the educational bureaucracy became well established. The development of the school organization as a result of the earlier concern for efficiency led to divisions of labor and technical specialization. The trend to include specialized subjects in the school curriculum also brought forth supervisory specialists (Alfonso, Firth, and Neville, 1981). According to Bolin (1986):

> *The Superintendent Surveys Supervision,* which was published in 1930, was a landmark in thinking about instructional supervision because it represents an official turning over of supervision of classroom teachers to middle management personnel. (p. 27)

This transfer of supervisory responsibility and the development of multiple levels of supervisory professionals expanded the enforcement and inspection role.

As a result, the development of mid-management positions increased during this period. A typical school organization might include the school board, the superintendent, principal(s), other specialists, and teachers. State departments also developed appropriate hierarchies with multiple staff levels to create the state educational bureaucracy.

A word often associated with instructional supervision at this time was "snoopervision," because of the mechanical procedures and evaluative dimensions of the supervisor's observation and reports (Wiles and Bondi, 1986). Monitoring the progress of both students and teachers was an important function of supervision. As a result, teachers often had the feeling and sometimes the fear that they were being constantly "watched" by those holding positions in the educational hierarchy.

PROGRESSIVE AND COOPERATIVE PERIOD (1935–1955)

A significant change in the perception of instructional supervision occurred during this time period. The attitudes often associated with the previous era were authoritarian inspection and enforcement of rules; the attitude associated with this time period was one of help. Educators began to view supervision as guidance rather than as inspection (Lucio and McNeil, 1969). The 1946 ASCD yearbook, *Leadership Through Supervision,* described the supervisor as an educational leader who possessed such virtues as a love of children, a belief in people, vision, and the ability to be a friend. Instructional supervision was viewed as a process to help teachers improve their performance through classroom observation and cooperative problem solving.

An emphasis on "human relations" behavior emerged as a major theme in instructional supervision during the 1940s and early 1950s. The focus of this approach to supervision was on the instructional process rather than on the resulting product. Within this framework, the primary responsibility of the supervisor was to provide assistance to teachers in improving classroom instruction; less emphasis was placed on judging or evaluating.

The progressive education movement led by John Dewey also had a significant impact on this period in furthering the notion of providing assistance to teachers. Progressive education emphasized human relations, a humane educational environment for children, a view of teaching as a process rather than a product, and a "child-centered" school. Alfonso, Firth, and Neville (1981) indicate that

> innovative and creative schools struggled to promote the human-izing potential that the early progressives in education, particularly John Dewey, espoused. Dewey had an abiding faith in the child's creative spirit and potential for good. He warned teachers and others not to diminish this natural curiosity and creativity. (p. 28)

Because of rapid growth and diverse populations, the schools became more accommodating for students. As a result, the emphasis within instructional supervision changed from snooping, monitoring, and enforcing to helping teachers as well as students improve.

CURRICULUM DEVELOPMENT AND CHANGE-ORIENTED PERIOD (1955–1970)

Two historical events had a major impact on the operation of schools during this time period: the launching of *Sputnik I* by the Soviet Union and the Supreme Court decision *Brown v. Board of Education*. With the launching of the Soviet satellite in 1957, American education was seen as inferior to the Soviet system and was criticized for a lack of emphasis on math and science. There was a clamor for a return to the traditional subjects in the curriculum; as a result, the nature of American education changed rapidly. Schools began to emphasize science and math courses, and university programs were created to bring teachers to campus for the summer to attend science and math institutes. New educational programs were implemented, and curriculum development became the central focus of instructional supervisors (Ikenberry, 1974; Wiles and Bondi, 1986).

With the beginning of what has been called the "space race,"

American education reacted with a massive overhaul of the public school curriculum. In what has become known as the "alphabet soup" curriculum reform, each content area was carefully scrutinized by many of the most knowledgeable people in the field. Consequently, new curriculum programs such as the Biological Sciences Curriculum Study (BSCS); English 2000; Greater Cleveland Math Program; Man: A Course of Study (MACOS); and Science: A Process Approach (SAPA) were developed for elementary and secondary students. No content area was exempt from the scrutiny, and many new textbooks and educational programs were developed to help students "catch up" in math, science, and other areas.

Another event that shaped educational planning and programs was the Supreme Court decision in 1954 in *Brown v. Board of Education.* As a result of this decision, "separate but equal" segregation policies were invalidated and replaced by a Court mandate to integrate schools. The thrust of instructional supervision was to help teachers, along with their students, work with those from different ethnic backgrounds and with differing abilities. Schools established a variety of special programs to help socially and economically disadvantaged students succeed.

Primarily as a response to these two historical events, new curriculum guides were written and many individualized programs were developed. According to Bolin (1986), instructional supervisors were "looking at the curriculum as the focal point of school improvement and seeing the teacher as instrumental to curriculum implementation" (p. 27). Supervisors, therefore, were called upon to assist teachers in curriculum development, which often included writing curriculum materials or preparing learning packets for individualized instruction. Supervisors were also asked to help teachers in interpreting curriculum projects, collecting and organizing materials, and aiding in the transition to new materials and programs.

CLINICAL AND ACCOUNTABLE PERIOD (1970–1980)

The emphasis of instructional supervision during this period was on the application of a medical or clinical model to the public schools. Based on research from human behavior and guided by a desire to help individual teachers be more accountable, instructional supervisors adopted a clinical model for use in the schools. According to Wiles and Bondi (1986):

The supervision literature of the late 1960s and early 1970s was primarily concerned with the analyses of teaching–learning process and the new concept of "clinical supervision." Supervisors followed this theoretical lead to become proficient in videotaping, the use of interaction analysis instruments, and the use of "action research" to explore new possibilities for instruction. (p. 7)

The intent was to diagnose classroom problems and/or identify areas for improvement and then prescribe the appropriate course of action to correct the situation. This clinical model incorporated the ingredient of "objective" classroom observation to aid in the analysis or diagnosis of teacher–student interaction. The model was designed to help teachers "see" what needed to be done by providing a "mirror" of classroom data to look at. The clinical model, which is discussed in Chapter 8 in detail, also stressed accountability through the development of performance contracts, which grew out of classroom observation procedures. The aim of the clinical model was to help the teacher be aware of classroom results by diagnosing the problems interfering with teaching–learning and prescribing a "cure."

MANAGERIAL AND ENTREPRENEURIAL PERIOD (1980–PRESENT)

The influence of business practices has been seen in education in recent years. Clearly there has been a managerial tone in the operation of schools, and the ideas of the entrepreneur are being utilized at the building level within school districts. Consistent with business practices, individuals who serve as instructional supervisors have been given a variety of jobs with titles ranging from assistant superintendent for instruction to program facilitator. Regardless of the title, these supervisors speak a management language and are considered a part of the "management team" in many, if not most districts (Wiles and Bondi, 1986).

The influence of business literature and practice in the preparation of effective managers—who care about people, help them set and obtain goals, give praise and train winners (Blanchard and Johnson, 1982)—is being felt in schools. Likewise, the eight characteristics of excellent companies, derived from research conducted by Peters and Waterman (1982), can be applied to public schools. Certain characteristics may fit the school situation better than others, but each one should be given due consideration as a way of promoting excellence in education (Reinhartz and Beach, 1984).

These eight characteristics include the following:

1. *A bias for action.* The emphasis is on planning for action and putting an idea into practice, rather than spending an inordinate amount of time analyzing issues and consequences. The school organization should be fluid and flexible—giving value to an idea.
2. *Close to the customer.* Executives of well-run, large corporations are usually good listeners and seek input from their consumers. Educators are often too sensitive to their consumers—students, parents, and community leaders—but they need to be more consistent in seeking input and listening.
3. *Autonomy and entrepreneurship.* Successful companies value creativity and risk taking to maintain a competitive edge. Encouragement and rewards for teachers and supervisors who are problem solvers and creative thinkers are essential to a more effective school operation.
4. *Productivity through people.* Those employed by excellent companies feel they are partners in the day-to-day activities and are crucial to the economic success of these companies. Employee morale is greatly enhanced by programs and procedures that place an emphasis on the value of people. Successful schools, then, should treat teachers in ways that communicate that they truly make a difference.
5. *Hands-on, value driven.* Excellent companies have values that they live by, and these values are in a form that can be easily communicated to employees and customers. For schools, mission statements, goals, and objectives are essential, and these must be clearly articulated to provide unity and a common focus toward a common goal.
6. *Stick to the knitting.* Successful companies emphasize those things they do best—manufacturing a product or providing a service that is competitive. Faculty and staff of school districts need to recognize that they cannot be all things to all people. Therefore, to be more effective, schools should identify specific strengths and limit activities to those areas that help achieve the stated goals.
7. *Simple form, lean staff.* Successful companies have organizational structures that are basically simple and are guided by clearly stated goals. Simple form and lean staff translates into an organizational structure that would limit the number of central office or mid-management personnel in large districts and concentrate the workforce at the building level. To become more effective, schools may need to consider a sim-

ple organizational structure and operate with a limited staff. Such an organizational pattern promotes efficiency and economy and encourages reorganization as needed to solve problems.

8. *Simultaneous loose–tight properties.* This last characteristic is a synthesis of the previous seven. Companies that exhibit this trait have local control for appropriate decision making, yet there is a central monitoring process to make sure that the goals are still driving the operations of the company. If we apply this principle to schools, the idea of site-based management and collegial groups provides greater autonomy to the school faculty and staff and encourages decision making at the building level. At the same time, a decentralization plan would hold each school campus accountable for supporting the district's goals and objectives.

These eight characteristics may be the mechanism to keep schools viable and foster instructional excellence. Instructional supervisors seeking to improve teaching and learning can find these general traits helpful as they work with teachers and staff within their districts. Effective schools as well as companies are dependent upon people, and "if schools are to improve the quality of instruction, it will be at the local building level (loose–tight properties) with the teacher at the heart of the improvement process (productivity through people)" (Reinhartz and Beach, 1984, p. 29). As schools enter the last decade of the twentieth century, the corporate model may prove helpful to supervisors as they become the architects for achieving instructional excellence.

In noting the influence of business in working with people, Olson (1986) says:

> What the writers of excellence in industry are calling for is a 180 degree change in direction in supervising people—one that changes the role of the supervisor from that of inspecting, policing, and inhibiting to one that helps, coaches, facilitates, builds, and improves people. Should we in education do anything less? (p. 61)

It is too soon to tell how long the business influence and managerial emphasis will continue. There is every indication that supervisors will become even more involved with teachers in the improvement of instruction and that such involvement will require classroom observations and may involve coaching teachers or training teachers to coach each other, or the assessment of lessons through script taping or other coding devices that record teacher–pupil behaviors. Such practices demonstrate the effect that the developments in personnel policies and other areas of business have had on the schools.

Supervisors in the next decade will have to be multitalented individuals who clearly know good instruction and can coach teachers or work in other collaborative ways to help teachers develop their instructional skills. If the current trend continues, supervisors may also be called upon to assess or evaluate classroom instruction as one of the ways of helping teachers be more effective or improve instruction.

SUMMARY

As indicated in Chapter 1, knowledge of past trends in supervision provides a foundation for current practices and procedures. This chapter has identified major historical periods that influenced supervisory practices. Each period had a unique set of political, social, and economic circumstances that affected education and instructional supervision.

Although there is no single best grouping of periods, the major historical periods identified in this chapter include the following:

1. colonial period (1600–1865)
2. state and national period (1865–1910)
3. scientific and organizational period (1910–1920)
4. professionalization and bureaucratic period (1920–1935)
5. progressive and cooperative period (1935–1955)
6. curriculum development and change-oriented period (1955–1970)
7. clinical and accountable period (1970–1980)
8. managerial and entrepreneurial period (1980–present)

Each period identified has shaped the instructional supervision process based on the particular political, social, and economic characteristics of the time. The school does not exist apart from society, and the conditions existing at the time guide and shape supervisory practice in the schools. Clearly the trend during the past decade has been for school personnel who serve in supervisory roles to become more directly involved with helping teachers improve instruction. Lessons of the past and current trends suggest that supervisors will need to develop a repertoire of skills as they work with teachers at different professional levels within the school district. This historical analysis suggests that in the future, supervisors will have to be *super* individuals.

YOUR TURN

2.1 You have been asked to speak to a group of principals, consultants, and other supervisory personnel who are attending a three-day workshop on "Being an Effective Supervisor." You have been given the topic "Our Historical Roots: Being an Effective Supervisor." At first you think, "Oh, no. How dull! What does history have to do with being an effective supervisor?" As you prepare for your presentation, you decide to look at various periods and examine the effect that supervisory practices have had on present instruction. Outline your thoughts as you prepare for your session. Good luck as you identify past practices that have influenced present instructional procedures.

2.2 The members of your local school board have expressed frustration and confusion about all the educational reports and reforms. They have asked the staff to write a position paper that addresses two issues:

a. What are the changes in society that will impact programming for teachers and students (for instance, latchkey kids, values, and an older society)?

b. Devise a five-year plan that supervisors and teachers can use in adjusting to the current political, social, and economic realities. Identify trends in the areas of funding or budget development, instructional facilities, curriculum materials, instructional technology, and educational personnel.

2.3 Based on the following quotation by Olson (1986), which was included in the chapter, how would you respond and what specific suggestions would you have for supervisory personnel?

What the writers of excellence in industry are calling for is a 180 degree change in direction in supervising people—one that changes the role of the supervisor from that of inspecting, policing, and inhibiting to one that helps, coaches, facilitates, builds, and improves people. Should we in education do anything less?

2.4 Your school district is looking for an additional instructional supervisor for the central office. Your district is located in the heart of a large metropolitan area that has an active teachers' union/organization, collective bargaining, a large minority enrollment (57 percent), a growing Hispanic population, and a growing illiteracy rate. Write a job description for this person (1) based on the current social and educational circumstances and (2) in light of what his or her duties will be by the mid 1990s.

2.5 You are a firm believer that educational practices and procedures occur in cycles. Based on this belief, identify recurring trends that have taken place or are taking place in instructional supervision.

REFERENCES

Alfonso, R. J., Firth, G. R., and Neville, R. F. (1981). *Instructional supervision: A behavior system* (2nd ed.). Boston, Mass.: Allyn and Bacon.

Blanchard, K., and Johnson, S. (1982). *The one minute manager.* New York: William Morrow.

Bolin, F. (1986). Perspectives on the definition of supervision. *Wingspan, 3,* 1, 22–29.

Burton, W. H., and Brueckner, L. J. (1955). *Supervision* (3rd ed.). New York: Appleton-Century-Crofts.

Ikenberry, O. S. (1974). *American education foundations.* Columbus, Ohio: Charles E. Merrill.

Joyce, B., and Showers, B. (1982). The coaching of teaching. *Educational Leadership, 40,* 2, 4–10.

Leadership through supervision. (1946). Washington, D.C.: Association for Supervision and Curriculum Development.

Lucio, W. H., and McNeil, J. D. (1969). *Supervision: A synthesis of thought and action.* New York: McGraw-Hill.

Neubert, G. A., and Bratton, E. C. (February 1987). Team coaching: Staff development side by side. *Educational Leadership, 44,* 5, 29–32.

Olson, L. C. (1986). In search of excellence in supervision. *Wingspan, 3,* 1, 58–61.

Peters, T. J., and Waterman, R. H. (1982). *In search of excellence: Lessons from America's best-run companies.* New York: Harper & Row.

Pierce, P. R. (1935). *The origin and development of the public school principalship.* Chicago: University of Chicago Press.

Reinhartz, J., and Beach, D. M. (1984). In search of educational excellence: Will the corporate model work? *Teacher Education and Practice, 1,* 2, 51–54.

Spain, C., Drummond, H. D., and Goodlad, J. (1956). *Educational leadership and the elementary school principal.* New York: Holt, Rinehart.

Tanner, D., and Tanner, L. (1987). *Supervision in education: Problems and practices.* New York: Macmillan.

Wiles, J., and Bondi, J. (1986). *Supervision: A guide to practice* (2nd ed.). Columbus, Ohio: Charles E. Merrill.

chapter 3

Organization Theory for Supervisors

Even though it may not be apparent from the title, this chapter is about people and how they work together in groups to achieve goals and objectives. As individuals work to accomplish particular tasks, a rudimentary organization is formed. Because we have all had some experience in working within a group to achieve a goal, the concept of an organization is not foreign to us. Organizations are a part of our daily existence; they are an integral part of society. Civic clubs, corporations, governmental entities, and special interest groups are just some of the organizations that we come in contact with in our communities. Schools are also organizations in which the public is involved on a regular basis. Etzioni (1964) comments on how organizations, including schools, are a part of our total existence:

> Our society is an organizational society. We are born in organizations, and most of us spend much of our lives working for organizations. We spend much of our leisure time paying, playing, and praying in organizations. Most of us will die in an organization, and when the time comes for burial, the largest organization of all—the state—must grant official permission. (p. 1)

Organizations, however, do not exist independently of the society in which they operate. Like other organizations, schools are the products of society. "Hence, the nature of an organization's management system will be determined both by the larger sociocultural system and the organization's production technology" (Alfonso, Firth, and Neville, 1981, p. 56). As products of society, schools can be viewed as multifaceted organizations that are both similar to and different from other organizations. It is not surprising, then, that the organizational structure of schools mirrors the complexities of other organizations.

Organizations may be thought of "in terms of social needs and as mechanisms to advance human conditions" (Alfonso, Firth, and Neville, 1981, p. 52). However, if its policies and supervisory practices are not carefully monitored, an organization may restrict its members rather than provide structure, and the organizational environment may be demeaning rather than supportive of individuals. In many organizations there is a constant struggle to accomplish tasks or turn out a product without alienating the people who actually perform the service or do the work. Unfortunately, some organizations forget that people are the core of production; such organizations apply rules and procedures in order to achieve maximum performance from their employees as they accomplish specific tasks. Ultimately, these regulations inhibit, restrict, and demean the people who make up the organization rather than encourage, enhance, and affirm what the members are doing. At their worst, such organizations become oppressive places in which the focus is on the task, the emphasis is on production, and there is a general disregard for people.

Schools, as service-oriented organizations, must constantly seek to affirm and enhance people and at the same time guard against developing too many restrictive rules and procedures that may result in a stifling environment. Supervisors within organizations must therefore walk a tight rope in their efforts to produce results and at the same time obtain a commitment from the members.

As organizations, schools have various designs and structures that range from simple to complex, depending upon the nature and function of the school. Since the instructional supervisor works within the context of the school organization, it is helpful, first, to look at other organizational structures, behaviors, and functions and then to compare these characteristics with the school organization. For the supervisor, the organization is the professional environment in which decisions are made and leadership is exercised. When supervisors understand their professional environment—the school organization—the more effective they are in their job (Owens, 1970).

Instructional supervision is more than simply an accumulation of skills and competencies associated with a given role or title; it involves working with people within an organizational context to achieve desired ends. It is important for instructional supervisors to understand the structure and conditions of the school organization and to identify what can be done to improve and strengthen the operations of the school. Critical to this process is the ability to work within the organization to link the behavior of others to the goals and structure of the school system. When there is a mismatch between a supervisor's style and the purposes and goals of the school organization, the supervisor becomes ineffective in the instructional supervision process (Wiles and Bondi, 1986).

To be more effective in working with teachers and other school personnel, it is necessary for instructional supervisors to study organizational theory, structure, and behavior and to analyze schools as organizations with their attendant bureaucratic operations. This chapter will provide the instructional supervisor with a definition of organizations, an overview of the periods of organizational development, various views of organization (organization theory), and principles of organizational behavior.

DEFINITIONS OF ORGANIZATIONS

Organizations come in many shapes and sizes and exist for a variety of reasons. Yet with all their diversity, there are some common characteristics that most, if not all, organizations share. According to Gross (1964), organizations may be regarded as a group or cooperative system that has the following features:

1. An accepted pattern of purposes—the members recognize the primary need or reason for the organization to exist.
2. A sense of identification or belonging—the management or administration as well as the other employees regard themselves as a part of the organization.
3. Continuity of interaction—the members of the organization interact with each other with a degree of regularity and continuity; there are patterns or channels of communication.
4. Differentiation of function—different members of the organization perform different and/or specialized roles.
5. Conscious integration of organizational goals—the parts of

the organization are held together by deliberate efforts to achieve the goals.

Parsons (1965) provides a definition of organization and then applies it to educational settings:

> An organization is a system which, as the attainment of its goals "produces" an identifiable something which can be utilized in some way by another system; that is, the output of the organization is for some other system an input. . . . [For] an educational organization, it [the output] may be a certain type of "trained capacity" on the part of the students who have been subjected to its influence. (p. 63)

Others have defined organizations in the following ways:

1. social units that seek the attainment of specific goals (Pfeiffer and Dunlap, 1982)
2. a system of cooperation (Barnard, 1938)
3. a grouping of personnel to accomplish established purposes through allocation of functions and responsibilities (Gaus, 1936)
4. contrived designs or arrangements that serve a specific function or meet a need while transmitting values and accomplishing goals (Alfonso, Firth, and Neville, 1981)
5. social units that are constructed and reconstructed to seek specific goals and that have (a) a division of power, labor, and communication; (b) one or more centers of power that direct the organization toward goals; and (c) substitution and recombination of personnel through removal, transfer, or promotion (Etzioni, 1964)

Although these definitions differ in various ways, some common themes can be identified. These themes portray organizations as groups of individuals who (1) work together within a structure or system, (2) seek the attainment of goals or objectives, (3) have differentiated roles, functions, and responsibilities, and (4) have a set of common beliefs or principles. If we take all these elements into account, a comprehensive definition emerges. For us, an organization consists of individuals who are united by a common set of values or principles and who work together within a system or structure to accomplish specific goals and objectives.

PERIODS OF ORGANIZATIONAL DEVELOPMENT

Historically, organizations have changed over time based on the situations and elements present during a particular era. Thus an understanding of organizational development comes from an examination of the structure, behavior, and function during particular periods in our history. Three major periods of organizational development identified by Owens (1970) are:

1. scientific management (1910–1935)
2. human relations (1935–1950)
3. behavioral approach (1950–present)

Scientific management, or the classical theory as it is referred to, was developed by Taylor (1911) to create better, more efficient organizations. As an organizational theory, scientific management contains two fundamental ideas:

motivation, the explanation of why a person participates in an organization, and *organization,* specifically, techniques for dividing up specialized tasks and the various levels of authority. (Owens, 1970, p. 46)

Taylor's view of motivation was primarily economic. He believed that people work for an organization because they need money to meet basic physiological needs and that pay periods should be short to maximize reinforcement. In terms of the structure of an organization, the emphasis was on the division of labor. The division of labor was organized into small-scale tasks, and each employee functioned in a highly specialized area requiring a specific skill. In such a structure, strong central control and close supervision were essential to keep activities and functions coordinated. The characteristics of organizations emphasized by the classical theory—specialization, control, hierarchy, and division of labor—comprise what today is commonly called the *formal organization* (Owens, 1970).

Taylor's work (1911) prompted schools to adopt an organizational structure that emphasized the work process, specialization, and functional organizational lines. Because the public schools lack "production lines" and factory-type pay schedules, the organizational rather than the motivational aspects of classical theory are still apparent in school operations. When we speak of organizations in terms of classical theory, "we emphasize concepts such as authority, clear-cut hierarchy with centralized control, a definite division of functions and responsibilities, and orderly channels of communication" (Owens, 1970, p. 47). An early result of the schools' concern with organizational behavior and structure was a focus on the functional lines of responsibility. In addition, there was an emphasis on the operation of the organization, with little regard for human factors.

The second period, the human relations era, draws support from the following basic concepts attributed to Mayo and cited by Owens (1970):

1. The production results of employees are determined more by their social capacities than by their physical capacities.
2. Money is a motivational factor for working in an organization, but employees may seek other, perhaps more important rewards.
3. A highly specialized division of labor is not necessarily the best way to maximize organizational efficiency.
4. Employees respond to the hierarchy, rules, and reward system of an organization not as individuals but as members of a group.

These principles guided the human relations era and led instructional supervisors to adopt a more democratic approach when working with teachers. Line supervisors (administrators), however, often found it difficult to deal with the realities of the hierarchical organizational structure, which emphasized power and central control, while at the same time trying to maintain a democratic style as they worked with teachers.

The third period, using the behavioral approach, regards the organization as a complex system with both a formal and an informal structure. The formal structure has identifiable organizational roles. People who occupy those roles "behave" according to established guidelines or job descriptions. That is, people are supposed to act in a prescribed fashion based on their role in the organization. The function of the role remains constant even though there are changes in the personnel.

The behavioral view of organizations also acknowledges an informal structure. The people who occupy roles in the formal structure interact with each other face to face as they communicate, plan, make decisions, and examine procedures. Because some degree of the human dimension is inherent in any social interaction, individuals seek social and friendship groups within the organization. Informal groups may be based on such characteristics as age, sex, personal interests, marital status, or work orientation. The evidence from research suggests that an informal structure is necessary to the proper functioning of an organization and that, within an informal structure, primary groups have great power (Owens, 1970).

The behavioral approach, within a school context, suggests, for instance, that an individual may have the role of teacher based on employment status and job description, but that the same individual also functions as a person. It is the human factor that causes people to associate with others within an informal organizational structure. In addition, such association is based on similar characteristics or common work experiences. To illustrate this informal organizational principle, Owens (1970) says:

> teachers of the same grade level or in the same department, or those whose work-places are close together tend to belong to the same primary groups. . . . it is almost impossible to think of a school organization today that does not recognize the need of its personnel to develop primary group affiliations that will reward them with universally sought social and psychological satisfactions. (p. 50)

The three major periods of organizational development—scientific management, human relations, and the behavioral approach—add to our present understanding of organizational structure, function, and behavior. Such background knowledge can be valuable to instructional supervisors as they function daily in their roles within the school organization.

OTHER VIEWS OF ORGANIZATIONS

There are ways to view organizations other than from a historical perspective. Four themes or threads, which include many aspects of the historical perspective, can be used as a focus to analyze contemporary organizational theory (Wiles and Bondi, 1986):

1. structure and bureaucracy
2. organizational processes and functions
3. organizational relationships
4. organizational influence

These four themes are discussed in detail to assist the instructional supervisor in understanding other interpretations and perspectives about the structures underlying schools as organizations.

Structure and Bureaucracy

According to this perspective, structure and control are the primary mechanisms for bringing about instructional changes within the school organization. The organizational structure of the schools has followed a pattern set by corporations. The corporations first followed the principles of scientific management advocated by Taylor (1911) and later the principles of bureaucracy advocated by Weber (1947). The bureaucratic structure became the ideal model for organizations, and, according to Pfeiffer and Dunlap (1982):

> Characteristics of bureaucratic organizations included division of labor, hierarchy of authority, written policies and regulations, impersonal basis for interaction, and longevity of administrative careers. Bureaucracy provides stability, efficiency, and orderliness; however, it is rigid and impersonal, often stifling creativity and perpetuating separate, rather than common interests. (pp. 114–115)

Fayol (1949) also developed a set of principles that emphasized scientific management and bureaucracy. He established a pyramidal, hierarchical structure and incorporated such concepts as the division of labor, subordination, central control, and remuneration.

A study of the structure of American schools, in terms of supervisory or administrative positions, reveals an affinity for the formal bureaucratic organization and reflects an organizational pattern characteristic of business corporations. While there are differences in the roles supervisors and managers play within the business setting, their supervisory functions can be viewed as somewhat parallel to those held by supervisory personnel within the school organization. Figure 3.1 provides an example of the similarity that exists between the organizational structures of corporations and of schools.

The administrative arrangement of the formal organization is usually expressed in a line chart that shows relationships between and among administrative and supervisory personnel. Line charts include only those individuals who function directly in the chain of authority. Other organizational charts are expanded to include both

EDUCATIONAL POSITION   CORPORATE POSITION

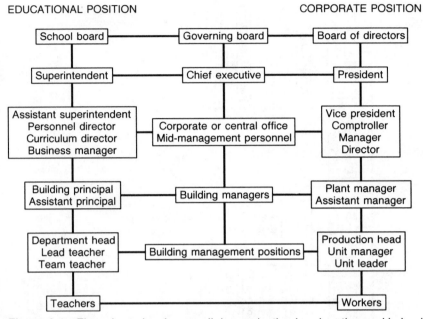

Figure 3.1 Flow chart showing parallel organization in education and in business or industry.

direct line relationships (authority) and other (indirect) staff relationships. Most school line/staff charts identify direct administrative authority along with other advisory, auxiliary, and technical staff members who may have input in the operation of the school organization but who lack direct authority. Figure 3.2 provides an example of the layers in the hierarchy of a suburban school organization chart. In this example, the central office positions include the superintendent and directors. In many urban districts, the directors would have the title of associate or assistant superintendent.

Today, most school districts and state educational agencies have some form of bureaucratic organizational structure that shows the direct lines of authority as well as indirect advisory relationships. Modifications are often made in the organizational structure to reflect changes that occur in society and the educational community. In large urban districts, where bureaucratic structures still exist, technical specialists, such as computer programmers and statisticians, transcend the monocratic structure based on their technical expertise (Wiles and Bondi, 1986).

Perhaps the school organizational structure will slowly begin to change and incorporate new ideas related to corporate structure,

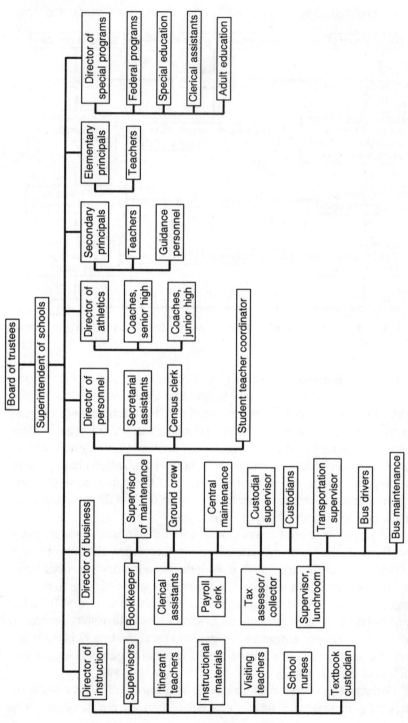

Figure 3.2 The hierarchy of organization in a typical suburban school.

function, and behavior. Townsend (1984), in his book *Further Up the Organization,* suggests ways to prevent management from stifling people and strangling production; he believes it is time to change organizational structure and behavior so that people can work together when given an opportunity. He advocates that organizations begin "treating everybody from top to bottom as respected adults rather than children or criminals" (p. x). He further says that organizations should ask for ideas, try them out, reward employees as groups, and even single out individuals in front of their peers and say, "Thanks!" Using such an organizational approach in schools should improve teacher morale and result in greater student achievement.

Organizational Processes and Functions

Within this framework, the construction and reconstruction of social units or systems are designed to improve organizational processes such as decision making, communications, and the allocation of resources. This perspective examines the way organizations operate and the instructional effectiveness that can result as supervisors study the processes that occur in the social units or systems of the school.

The use of a social systems theory provides for two types of organizational systems: open and closed. A school is an open system because of its input–output relationship with the community or environment (Owens, 1970). The input–output relationship is a process the school uses to interact with the community. The school as an organization responds to inputs of energy, resources, and stimuli from the community, and in turn affects the community by the quality of the outcomes in the form of programs and student progress.

The systems approach is also helpful in analyzing the factors that have an impact on individual behavior within organizations. The Getzels–Guba model (1957) suggests that there are two dimensions related to organizational behavior; one is personal and the other is institutional. Figure 3.3 presents a model illustrating the concept of the organization as a social system.

According to the model in the figure, the idiographic, or personal, dimension recognizes the influence of individual personalities, needs, goals, and values in shaping organizational behavior. The nomothetic, or organizational, role recognizes the impact of institutional expectations, status, and authority in shaping behavior. Such a model suggests that supervisors "realize that the behavior of . . .

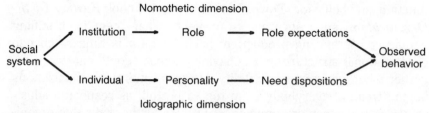

Figure 3.3 Nomothetic and idiographic dimensions of social behavior. (*Source:* Getzels, J. W., and Guba, E. G. [1957]. Social behavior and the administrative process. *School Review, 65,* 429. Used with permission.)

members [both teachers and supervisors] is influenced by both organizational expectations and personal needs and dispositions" (Campbell et al., 1985, p. 239).

In elaborating on the systems/process approach, Wiles and Bondi (1986) suggest that, for schools, a system can be viewed as any set of components that are organized to result in the attainment of a goal. For schools, systems include teachers, materials, buildings, and funds, as well as many other contributing factors that serve to provide an education for children. A systems perspective is valuable to supervisors in that it provides a way of identifying essential as well as nonessential elements in organizational productivity.

One of the greatest potential uses of the systems approach is the opportunity for organizational development. Using this perspective, schools would identify key organizational processes (such as developing budgets and evaluating instruction) and then apply behavioral principles in a planned and sustained effort to improve the entire educational system.

Organizational Relationships

A third way of viewing organizations is based on a study of relationships, both formal and informal. Iannacconne (1964) describes the complexities of the struggle that exists between the legal power and authority of the formal organization and the extralegal power and influence of informal groups within the organization. The earlier view of scientific management emphasized structure and bureaucracy within formal organizational relationships. The informal dimension of an organization is more concerned with the human factors and interpersonal relationships that affect motivation, morale, and communication. Mayo was an early proponent of the human relations approach because an overemphasis on the scientific method of operation had alienated workers and there was a need to have more small group interactions to overcome the dehumanizing forces (Wiles and Bondi, 1986). Other investigators (Peters and Waterman, 1982; Blanchard and Johnson, 1982), in their research on organizational excellence and increased productivity, have added to the discussion concerning the importance of the human factor in organizational effectiveness.

Lewin (1951), in his "group dynamics" or "field theory," describes how relationships in organizations are based on the following elements: the needs, values, and desires of the individuals; the characteristics of the group; and the psychological environment or cultural norms of the organization. These determinants form a field of forces that, when taken together, overlap. The individual behaves within this field. If there is to be a meaningful change in behavior, then both the group norms and the cultural norms must respond to and support the individual (Owens, 1970). This view suggests that as supervisors work with teachers to change instructional behavior(s), it is important for the supervisors to provide the necessary support and reinforcement for the change. However, additional support should come from the school environment or culture and from other teachers (group norms).

The influence of the school culture on teaching–learning behavior(s) has become central to our understanding of the operation of effective schools. We know from the work of Purkey and Smith (1982) that the organizational effectiveness of a school "is distinguished by its culture: a structure, process and climate of values and norms that channel staff and students in the direction of successful teaching and learning" (p. 68). In addition, Saphier and King (1985) suggest that effective schools have an organizational culture that (1) articulates expectations of students and faculty, (2) stresses excellence and academic effort, (3) views all students as capable of achieving, and (4) creates a safe, orderly, and respectful environment.

Argyris (1957) was particularly concerned about the dissonance, or lack of congruence, between the needs of individuals and the demands of the formal organization—a dissonance that could cause frustration, conflict, and failure. As individuals function in the formal organization, their needs are often ignored or neglected; they experience competition, rivalry, and insubordinate hostility, and they focus on the parts rather than on the whole. Instructional supervisors must work closely with teachers and be sensitive to their individual needs in order to provide assistance and reduce frustration and alienation.

Rogers (1958) carries the idea of support further by suggesting that counseling programs be established to provide "helping relation-ships." Owens (1970) says that within the helping relationship frame-work, efforts to produce more effective behavior should be

> educative, rather than coercive, and emphasize (1) the intrinsic satisfaction that the participant gets from being involved with deci-sion making responsibility and (2) the idea that, to develop maxi-mum satisfaction, individual participation must be varied accord-ing to a number of factors, including personalities, . . . values, and specific factors in the work-situation. (p. 87)

The helping relationship framework, or supportive view, recognizes that teachers' feelings, needs, and motivations are important factors that contribute to more productive relationships with other faculty and students at school. This cooperative, interactive approach has been emphasized more recently by Gould and Letven (1987) and by Glatthorn (1987). For example, in the Wisconsin Regional Staff De-velopment Center, educators from all grade levels and disciplines come together to learn with and from one another. It is in this collaborative approach that "members help each other maintain the spirit of inquiry crucial to the healthy intellectual life of all faculty members" (Gould and Letven, 1987, p. 51). In commenting further on this helping relationship framework, Glatthorn (1987) notes that "when districts provide supporting conditions, teachers can work together . . . , using a variety of collaborative methods, for their professional growth" (p. 31).

Herzberg's (1966) "job enrichment" or "motivation-hygiene" theory suggests that there are two views or sides to human nature. One side deals with fundamental needs such as safety, nourishment, and other basic drives. The other side of human nature has a "compel-ling urge" to be successful, to reach full potential through continuous psychological growth. This view recognizes that some organizational (job-related) factors can lead to job satisfaction while other conditions can lead to job dissatisfaction. Factors that can affect job dissatisfac-tion are called "hygiene factors" and include salary, work conditions, and job security. Elements that can contribute to job satisfaction are called "motivational factors" and include recognition, responsibility, and opportunities for growth.

This theory would suggest to supervisors that teachers whose greatest needs are met by salary, job security, and orderly work environment tend to get little satisfaction from their work per se,

show little interest in job performance, and are often chronic com-
plainers. Teachers who, on the other hand, are motivated by their
instructional activities and other professional accomplishments tend
to be less affected by hygiene factors and respond to opportunities
for professional growth and responsibility.

Organizational Influence

The fourth perspective examines the use of influence or the power
of persuasion in the operation of the organization. Such a view studies
the sources and distribution of power and influence and seeks to
answer the question, regardless of title or position, "Who is the really
powerful and influential person in the organization?" Using this organizational perspective, the supervisor is put in a political arena where
operational decisions and procedures are derived from powerful or
influential individuals and political actions.

   When we study the effects of influence in organizations, we
are looking at the behavior associated with power, authority, and
persuasion. These behaviors have their origins in the social and
behavioral sciences. Wiles and Bondi (1986) note that "the study of
influence is comprised of at least four subareas: studies of change,
of leadership, of decision making, and of the role of politics" (p. 36).
These subareas are important factors in the study of power and
influence, and three—change, leadership, and decision making—will
be discussed in detail in later chapters. Like other organizations,
schools constantly seek leadership, and are confronted with the
need to make decisions and implement changes. Schools must develop strategies for dealing with the pressures exerted by the politics of the environment. According to Bennis (1966), organizations
must monitor and respond by:

1. maintaining the internal system and coordinating the "human
   side of enterprise"—a process of mutual compliance here
   called "reciprocity";
2. adapting to and shaping the external environment, here called
   "adaptability" (p. 7).

Organizations such as schools must therefore devote energy not
only to maintaining the internal operating system but to dealing with
external pressures as well. The organization's response to external

pressures should involve planned change. According to Owens (1970):

> We know that significant change will come and that those organizations which can adequately adapt will be adjudged the most satisfactory. A glance at the current scene in the world of business organizations . . . and other organizations, including schools, confirms this view. (p. 62)

There are several different models available for directing organizational change, and these models range from complex and sophisticated to basic and functional. While a detailed discussion of the supervisor's role in the change process is presented in Chapter 12, a simplified model developed by Lionberger (1961) is outlined here. The following components of the model are:

1. an awareness of the need or pressure to change
2. interest in pursuing the change
3. evaluation of possible ramifications of the change
4. experimental or trial implementation of the change
5. adoption and full implementation of the change

Another dimension of organizational influence is leadership. The leadership role of the supervisor will be discussed in greater detail in the next chapter, but clearly leadership is an important force within an organization. Leadership is based on a number of factors, including (1) the nature of the situation, (2) the nature of the follower(s), (3) group management style and skill, and (4) communication skills. In influencing the school organization, instructional supervisors exhibit characteristics of leadership in (1) their ability to motivate, recognize, and reward performance, (2) their establishment of the work environment, (3) their communication style, and (4) their control techniques.

Another factor related to organizational influence is decision making. This factor will also be described in more detail in Chapter 12. However, it is important to note that decision making occurs within an organization at multiple levels as organizations move from the planning to the implementation stage. Developing policies that guide decisions provides supervisors with a way of stabilizing organizations through times of change.

The fourth and final factor in the study of organizational influence is the political arena and the use of power to influence the directions of an organization. The use of power to influence organizational decisions is clearly noted in the schools. Special interest groups have exerted power and influence on decisions that range from textbooks to teachers. The power structure within a given community is predicated on the relative distribution of social power among the citizens in determining the kinds of schools they want and will support. It is important to note, however, that the exercise of power by citizens is not equal and there is a resulting unequal distribution of influence in the school system (Nunnery and Kimbrough, 1971).

These four different views concerning the operations within organizations help supervisors recognize the importance of their professional work environment—the school as an organization. Knowledge of how organizations are structured and operate provides instructional supervisors with a basis for understanding how schools work. This understanding is critical because supervisors often function at a variety of levels within the school organization. As Wiles and Bondi (1986) state:

> Once the supervisor knows the [organizational] environment and understands how it works, he or she must then compare that purpose with his or her own conception of what schools should be doing. (p. 26)

The supervisor can then use this common ground of agreement to develop strategies to improve instruction for both teachers and students.

In order to be effective in focusing on classroom instruction and the improvement of instruction, it is essential that the supervisor understand the structure, function, and behavior inherent in a particular school or school district. Just as there are many different school districts or systems, there are many ways to organize education to meet the goals of the schools. Instructional supervisors can increase their effectiveness if they are aware of the major organizational structures or models and the different factors that operate in each. For instance, the behavior of a supervisor in a school district that operates within the general guidelines of scientific management would be quite different from that of a colleague whose school district adhered to the organizational relations model. Knowing the difference between the two organizational models and what factors influence the structure, functions, and behaviors of each model can determine the effectiveness of instructional supervisors as they work with teachers to improve student performance.

PRINCIPLES OF ORGANIZATIONAL BEHAVIOR

Our knowledge of organizational behavior is summarized in the following principles based on research data from a variety of organizational settings (Alfonso, Firth, and Neville, 1981; Lovell and Wiles, 1983). These principles can be used to guide supervisors as they work in school organizations:

1. For an educational organization to make a contribution to the community and function effectively, the organization's purpose must be consistent with the community's values and culture as the organization serves its members, students, parents, and the community residents.
2. An effective educational organization treats individual members as professionals with dignity and respect by maintaining an open, responsive, cooperative posture.
3. An effective educational organization encourages individual members to develop and capitalize on their creativity and potential, an effort that in turn increases effectiveness.
4. To be successful, an educational organization must have the necessary resources and talent, and the members of the organization must have a knowledge of organizational structure, an understanding of each member's role within the structure, and an awareness of how the organization operates.
5. Because of the dynamic nature of organizations, effective changes occur within an organization to meet changing societal conditions and circumstances and occur when members understand the structural integration and the continuous interaction within the group.
6. The morale of an educational organization will be enhanced when the members understand, perceive as important, and share a common set of values and goals.
7. An effective educational organization has members who behave in a predictable and reliable manner, based on shared values and clearly defined goals, and who periodically examine the stated goals in relation to the behavior of the organization and the organization's purpose.
8. Effective school organizations assist teachers by directly influencing the organizational subsystem of teacher behavior as measured by student achievement.

9. An effective educational organization has a clearly defined organizational structure with defined lines of authority and formally/informally established responsibilities with descriptions of requirements identified in each.
10. Effective educational organizations establish procedures and strategies for regular or frequent analysis of the overall effectiveness of the organization and have a monitoring system for assessing the degree of submission and alienation.

SUMMARY

Organizations are fundamental components of society. They are a part of our total existence, and schools are no exception. Schools share with other organizations many common characteristics. Chapter 3 focuses on the three major historical periods related to the development of organizational structure, behavior, and function. The three periods of organizational development, which are scientific management, human relations, and the behavioral approach, add to our current understanding of how organizations operate. In addition to studying organizations from a historical perspective, we can examine four other views or themes as a way of understanding organizations:

1. structure and bureaucracy
2. organizational processes and functions
3. organizational relationships
4. organizational influence

This chapter emphasizes those components that help to explain how and why organizations operate the way they do. By gaining information about organizations in general, and about schools as organizations more specifically, instructional supervisors will have greater insight about the environment in which they will be working. The chapter ends by listing 10 principles that synthesize research information about effective organizations.

An understanding of organizational theory provides supervisors with a frame of reference to guide their behavior as they work within the organization called *school*. Since organizations are composed of people, knowledge of the organizational setting can also guide instructional supervisors as they work with members of the school organization—namely, teachers. Like supervisors in the corporate setting, instructional supervisors walk a tight rope in an effort to produce results—student achievement—and at the same time obtain a commitment from group members—the teachers.

YOUR TURN

3.1 Schools as organizations function according to the tenets described in organizational theory. As an instructional supervisor, what environmental factors will you encounter that may hinder and/or help you as you work with teachers to develop and improve their instructional skills?

3.2 In what ways would the role of an instructional supervisor in a large urban or suburban school district differ from that role in a small, rural district?

3.3 Organizations share many characteristics in common. Cite three traits all schools share regardless of type, size, purpose, student population, and/or tax base.

3.4 Instructional supervisors function in a number of organizational roles. Name at least four informal organizational roles that supervisors fulfill.

3.5 Some administrators in the central office are making all the decisions while others appear to be advisors only. You have been asked to develop a line/staff chart that reflects your recommendations regarding the process of decision making relative to the reorganization of the central office. Your responsibility is to construct the chart in such a way as to clearly communicate lines of authority, duties, roles, and decision-making responsibilities.

3.6 In discussing organizations, Etzioni (1964) says:

> Most organizations most of the time cannot rely on most of their participants to carry out their assigned tasks voluntarily, to have internalized their obligations. The participants need to be supervised, the supervisors themselves need supervision, and so on all the way to the top of the organization. In this sense, the organizational structure is one of control, and the hierarchy of control is the most central element of the organizational structure.

Do you agree with this statement? Why or why not? What specific examples can you cite from school organizations to support your answer?

3.7 You have been hired to serve as a consultant who will focus on organizational and instructional effectiveness. Develop an organizational chart that maximizes the efficiency of the operations of the school district and promotes the instructional dimension of school.

3.8 As seen in Figures 3.1 and 3.2, most school organization structures are a top-down hierarchy. Develop a line/staff chart that shows a shared decision-making process and is not a top-down hierarchy of control.

REFERENCES

Alfonso, R. J., Firth, G. R., and Neville, R. F. (1981). *Instructional supervision: A behavior system.* (2nd ed.). Boston: Allyn and Bacon.

Argyris, C. (1957). The individual and the organization: Some problems of mutual adjustment. *Administrative Science Quarterly, 2,* 1–24.

Barnard, C. I. (1938). *The function of the executive.* Cambridge, Mass.: Harvard University Press.

Bennis, W. G. (1966). *Changing organizations.* New York: McGraw-Hill.

Blanchard, K., and Johnson, S. (1982). *The one minute manager.* New York: William Morrow.

Campbell, R. F., et al. (1985). *The organization and control of American schools.* Columbus, Ohio: Charles E. Merrill.

Etzioni. A. (1964). *Modern organizations.* Englewood Cliffs, N.J.: Prentice-Hall.

Fayol, H. (1949). *Administration industrielle et generale.* Trans. Constance Storrs, *General and industrial management.* London: Sir Isaac Pitman and Sons.

Gaus, J. M. (1936). A theory of organization in public administration. In *The frontiers of public administration,* by Gaus, J. M., White, L. D., and Demock, M. E. Chicago: University of Chicago Press.

Getzels, J. W., and Guba, E. G. (1957). Social behavior and the administrative process. *School Review, 65,* 423–441.

Glatthorn, A. A. (November 1987). Cooperative professional development: Peer-centered options for teacher growth. *Educational Leadership, 45,* 3, 31–35.

Gould, S., and Letven, E. (1987). A center for interactive professional development. *Educational Leadership, 45,* 3, 49–52.

Gross, B. M. (1964). *The managing of organizations.* New York: Free Press of Glencoe.

Herzberg, F. (1966). *Work and the nature of man.* Cleveland, World.

Iannacconne, L. (1964). An approach to the informal organization of the school. *Behavioral science and educational administration.* 63rd Yearbook of the National Society for the Study of Education, D. Griffiths, ed. Chicago: University of Chicago Press.

Lewin, K. (1951). *Field theory in social science.* New York: Harper Torch Books.

Lionberger, H. (1961). *Adoption of new ideas and practices.* Ames: Iowa State University Press.

Lovell, J. T., and Wiles, K. (1983). *Supervision for better schools* (5th ed.). Englewood Cliffs, N.J.: Prentice-Hall.

Nunnery, M., and Kimbrough, R. (1971). *Politics, power, polls, and school reform.* Berkeley, Calif.: McCutchan.

Owens, R. G. (1970). *Organizational behavior in schools.* Englewood Cliffs, N.J.: Prentice-Hall.

Parsons, T. (1965). Suggestions for a sociological approach to the theory of organizations. *Administrative Science Quarterly, 1,* Pt. 1, 63–85.

Peters, T. J., and Waterman, R. H. (1982). *In search of excellence: Lessons from America's best-run companies.* New York: Harper & Row.

Pfeiffer, I. L., and Dunlap, J. B. (1982). *Supervision of teachers: A guide to improving instruction.* Phoenix: Oryx Press.

Purkey, S. C., and Smith, M. S. (1981/1982). Too soon to cheer? Synthesis of research on effective schools. *Educational Leadership, 40,* 4, 64–69.

Rogers, C. (September 1958). Characteristics of a helping relationship. *Personnel and Guidance Journal, 37,* 1, 6–16.

Saphier, J., and King, M. (1985). Good seeds grow in strong cultures. *Educational Leadership, 42,* 6, 67–74.

Taylor, F. W. (1911). *The principles of scientific management.* New York: Harper & Row.

Townsend, R. (1984). *Further up the organization.* New York: Alfred A. Knopf.

Weber, M. (1947). *The theory of social and economic organizations.* Trans. A. M. Henderson and T. Parsons. New York: Free Press.

Wiles, J., and Bondi, J. (1986). *Supervision: A guide to practice.* (2nd ed.). Columbus, Ohio: Charles E. Merrill.

chapter 4

Leadership Theory for Supervisors

While the previous chapter described the structure of organizations as the professional setting of schools, it is the leadership behavior that occurs within the organizational setting that is critical to effective instruction. In fact, the impact of leadership, particularly that of the principal, determines the overall effectiveness of the school (Andrews, 1987). Without leadership, organizations become lifeless and ineffective, and, warns Fielder (1974), they are in serious trouble. It is no wonder, then, that the study of leadership is crucial to an understanding of organizational effectiveness. For schools, instructional leadership is essential to student achievement and the success of the total educational program.

The impact of leadership on school effectiveness has been the central focus of a number of recent studies. Andrews (1987) has found "a powerful relationship between leadership of the principal and student outcomes" (p. 15). In fact, the principal's leadership can so pervasively impact how teachers perceive the work environment that it can ultimately produce a measurable gain in student achievement. In another recent study, Mortimore and Sammons (1987) have identified 12 factors that distinguish effective elementary schools from less effective schools. Most of the factors that contribute to effectiveness are related to "purposeful leadership." For Mortimore and Sammons (1987), "Purposeful leadership occurs where the principal [instructional leader] understands the needs of the school and is actively involved in the school's work without exerting total control over the staff" (p. 7).

By accepting a position with instructional supervision responsibilities, an individual is accepting a job that involves leadership in the school organization. The importance of instructional supervision is enhanced when the supervision process is viewed as a general leadership function that links administration, curriculum, and teaching (Wiles and Bondi, 1980). Leadership, then, is a prerequisite for anyone involved in the improvement of instruction.

Since leadership seems to be a critical factor in most if not all effective organizations, this chapter will draw upon the research and scholarship available concerning leadership behavior in general and instructional leadership in particular. Included in this discussion of leadership are historical perspectives and theories of leadership, the dimensions and definitions of leadership, an examination of different styles of leadership, principles of leadership, an analysis of the use of authority and power, and a profile of effective instructional leaders.

HISTORICAL PERSPECTIVES AND LEADERSHIP THEORIES

Interest in leadership behavior seems ageless. As long as people have worked together in groups, leadership has been a factor in human history. Owens (1970) notes that

> much of the record of human experience which the civilized world has accumulated concerns leadership. If all the artistic, literary and scholarly works which deal with leadership were brought together we would have a collection of mammoth proportions. (p. 118)

One of the oldest perspectives on leadership behavior can be found in the writings of Machiavelli, in the early sixteenth century. Machiavelli viewed people as uncooperative, greedy, self-centered, and rebellious individuals; therefore his recommendations on how to lead, or govern, emphasized the need to control using whatever means necessary—lying, cheating, stealing, even committing murder—to establish order and maintain power. Centuries later, views of leadership behavior were based on Darwin's law of natural selection. Spencer (1927) universalized the concept of evolution by applying the principle of the survival of the fittest to human endeavors. In such a view of leadership, the fittest, or leaders, are "characterized by aggressiveness, the urge to dominate, and a desire to acquire material possessions; all of which makes conflict within organizations unavoidable" (Knezevich, 1984, p. 56). More recently, ethologists Lorenz (1952) and Bowlby (1980) have suggested the relevance of animal behavior to human activity in such phenomena as pecking orders, the struggle for dominance, the establishment of territory, and the expression of aggression as indicative of a leader's behavior within an organizational setting.

These views of leadership have been based on the belief that humans are motivated by strong emotions and selfish desires rather than by rational or social concerns. As indicated in the previous chapter, scientific management and Weber's view of the bureaucracy were organizational structures designed to compensate for the workers' limitations of self-centeredness and lack of motivation. McGregor (1960), however, coupled this limited view of human behavior to an opposing view and proposed two leadership theories based on differing patterns of behavior manifested by individuals in an organization. His Theory X and Theory Y help to explain contrasting views of motivation and other aspects of human behavior. Theory X focuses on a narrow view of human behavior and contains the following general propositions:

1. Individuals generally dislike to work and try to avoid it; people are basically lazy.
2. Most individuals, because of general dislike of work, have to be coerced, and even threatened with punishment, to work toward the goals set by the organization.
3. Individuals tend to favor direction and security and avoid responsibility.
4. Individuals are not very bright and lack creativity.

Leaders who view individuals this way base their decisions and their interactions with others on these propositions.

Theory Y provides a completely different view of people. The general propositions contained in Theory Y include the following:

1. The workplace and the work itself are pleasing and satisfying.
2. Individuals once committed to the organizational goals will be self-directed and will demonstrate self-control.
3. Job-related rewards come from satisfying the ego and self-actualization.
4. Individuals learn to seek and accept responsibility rather than to avoid it.
5. Individuals are creative and have ingenuity and imagination.

Leaders who view individuals according to Theory Y base their decisions and their interactions with others on these propositions.

Mondy, DeHay, and Sharplin (1983) suggest leadership styles that are based on a leader's views about the workers or group members (Figure 4.1). If the leader views individuals with distrust, as in Theory X, the leader will utilize a leadership style that is autocratic—directive, task-oriented, and even coercive. If the leader views individuals as contributing members of the organization who continue to grow and develop in their capacities, as in Theory Y, then the leader will utilize an open, participative or democratic style of leadership. With individuals who are considered experts or specialists, the leader can adapt a laissez-faire style of leadership (see page 62).

About the same time McGregor presented his Theory X and Theory Y, Likert (1961, 1967) developed a view of leadership based on a continuum of styles ranging from autocratic to participative. Along the continuum of leader behaviors are four basic leadership systems. System I is characterized by leadership that is exploitive-

Theory X workers	Theory Y workers		Expert-specialist workers
Autocratic: Leader tells workers what to do.	*Participative:* Leader allows and expects worker participation.	*Democratic:* Leader seeks majority rule from workers.	*Laissez-faire:* Leader lets group members make all decisions.

Figure 4.1 Leadership styles as related to types of workers. (*Source:* Mondy, R. W., DeHay, J. M., and Sharplin, A. D. [1983]. *Supervision,* p. 123. New York: Random House. Used with permission.)

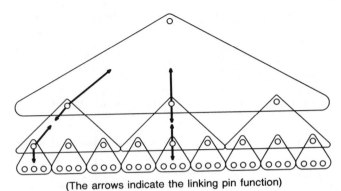

(The arrows indicate the linking pin function)

Figure 4.2 The linking pin concept of leadership. (*Source:* Likert, R. [1961]. *New patterns of management.* New York: McGraw-Hill. Used with permission.)

autocratic, with individuals being told what to do and taken advantage of for the leader's purpose. System II leadership is benevolent-democratic; the leader gives some directives but permits individuals to comment on the directives within a caring environment. System III leadership is consultative—that is, the leader establishes goals and objectives after discussing them with individuals in the organization; individuals, motivated by rewards, then decide how best to obtain the goals. System IV leadership is viewed as participative, since the goals and the implementation of decisions are agreed to by the group involved. Likert suggests that this leadership system is best because, as seen in Figure 4.2, the leader or supervisor is depicted as a link between the group and other management or administrative levels in the organization. In the figure, based on the linking pin concept of leadership, each triangle represents a work group, with the leader depicted by the "pin" at the top of each triangle. In this perspective, the primary behaviors of the leader are coordination and communication.

More recently, Blake and Mouton (1985) have developed the concept of the Managerial Grid® which identifies five general kinds of managerial or leadership behavior. Blake and Mouton suggest that in an organizational setting, managers or leaders must focus on two factors: concern for task or production and concern for people. The degree of concern for each determines the kind of leadership behavior that results. The two factors of people and production form the parameters of the Managerial Grid. Figure 4.3 shows the resulting leadership or managerial styles when plotted on the grid.

The concern for production forms the base of the Grid. On a

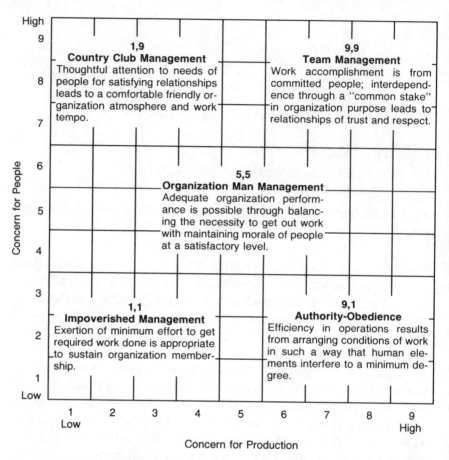

Figure 4.3 The Managerial Grid. (*Source:* Blake, Robert R., and Mouton, Jane Srygley [1985]. *The New Managerial Grid III: The key to leadership excellence*, p. 12. Houston: Gulf Publishing. Reproduced by permission.)

scale of 1 to 9, the leader has either a high (9) concern for task/ production or a low (1) concern. The concern for people is represented along the left side of the Grid on a scale from 1 to 9. A high concern for people would be (9) and a low concern (1). The point at which these two parameters intersect (1,1) forms the basis for a leadership behavior or managerial style that is called *impoverished* because it is marked by a lack of concern for either people or task/ production. The point on the Grid that represents a high concern for production and a low concern for people (9,1) is called *authority-obedience* leadership behavior. A high concern for people and a low concern for task/production (1,9) results in what is called *country club* leadership behavior; it emphasizes the morale and well-being of people. The behavior that is characterized by modifications or compromises in the concerns for task/production in order to help keep people satisfied (5,5) is referred to as *organization man* (or *organization person*) leadership. Finally, the leadership behavior advocated by Blake and Mouton that results in a high concern for both people and task/production (9,9) is called *team management.* This view of leadership suggests that the supervisor must attend to both production and people in a way that is optimum for both. When applied to the school setting, this means that the instructional supervisor must be knowledgeable about the technical aspects of teaching as well as sensitive and understanding toward teachers as people.

Hershey and Blanchard (1977) have proposed a leadership theory which suggests that an individual's leadership style will vary depending on the maturity level of individuals in the group or organization and the demands of the specific situation. Such a view is called a *contingency theory* because no particular kind of leadership behavior or style is appropriate for every situation. For Hershey and Blanchard, the important dimensions to consider in selecting leadership behaviors are the maturation of the individuals in the group and the specific task or assignment.

Finally, Maccoby (1981), in his book *The Leader,* provides a more contemporary theory of leadership behavior. According to Maccoby, today's leader should exhibit the following traits:

1. a tolerance of strangers and a flexibility about social arrangements
2. a willingness to experiment with new relationships at work and in the family
3. an orientation toward self-development and lifelong learning
4. an orientation toward the development of others and a willingness to support such development
5. a lack of loyalty in the traditional sense of submission and self-sacrifice to the organization
6. an unwillingness to follow orders blindly and an insistence on there being good reasons for orders
7. a willingness to be productively involved in organizations that demonstrate equity and a concern for human dignity and that foster cooperation

This new leader, as envisioned by Maccoby, has a sense of self, personal integrity, and a commitment to productive relationships within the family and the organization.

As our understanding of people and the way they behave in organizations has grown over time, so too has our understanding of leadership behavior. The contingency theories suggest that there is no single best way to lead. However, our historical perspectives on leadership behavior indicate that some leadership behaviors and styles are more appropriate than others. In order to understand various aspects of leadership behavior, instructional supervisors should be aware of the many theories of leadership that have developed over time. These historical perspectives can provide supervisors with a wide range of theories and behaviors to choose from as they attempt to develop their own leadership behavior profile.

DIMENSIONS AND DEFINITIONS OF LEADERSHIP

Leadership is an important facet of instructional supervision, but what is leadership? Clearly, there are individuals within the schools who are expected to demonstrate instructional leadership abilities (for instance, superintendents, principals, elementary and secondary coordinators), but their position and/or title alone does not ensure leadership capability. What, then, are the characteristics of effective leaders? These are important questions for instructional supervisors to pursue as they work with teachers to improve classroom instruction.

Like the term *supervision, leadership* has many definitions based on historical perspectives, circumstances, and the views of theorists and researchers. As Wiles and Bondi (1986) note, "There are some 130 different definitions of leadership in today's educational literature" (p. 43). As the number of definitions indicates, leadership is a complex process involving many variables. Of all the definitions of the word *leadership* presented in the literature, most can be classified according to one of two basic perspectives or categories. According to Owens (1970):

> Studies suggest that the things leaders do—the leadership behavior they exhibit—fall into two general categories called *dimensions.* Although no universally accepted labels for these two categories have yet appeared, the terms *structure* and *consideration* are . . . used. (p. 120)

The dimensions of structure and consideration are related to two basic perspectives. One is how the leader organizes and influences people to behave in ways that result in the attainment of goals. The other examines the ways leaders influence people regarding their feelings of importance, dignity, and commitment. In discussing the importance of structure and consideration in our understanding of leadership, Fleishman and Harris (1962) state: "Structures include behavior in which the supervisor organizes and defines group activities and his [or her] relation to the group" (p. 43). The role each member is to assume is defined along with the task(s), and members are pushed to produce. "Consideration includes behavior indicating mutual trust, respect, and a certain warmth and rapport between the supervisor and his [or her] group" (p. 44). The emphasis of this dimension is on a deeper concern for the needs of the people, to encourage them to participate in the decision-making process.

Halpin (1966), who conducted studies that apply the dimensions of structure and consideration to leadership in schools, explains the concepts in the following way:

1. *Initiating structure* refers to the leader's behavior in delineating the relationship between himself [or herself] and the members of his [or her] workgroup, and in endeavoring to establish well-defined patterns of organization, channels of communication, and methods of procedure.
2. *Consideration* refers to the behavior indicative of friendship, mutual trust, respect, and warmth in the relationship between the leader and the members of his [or her] staff. (p. 86)

Clearly, leadership requires a good working relationship with people within an organization. A comprehensive, people-oriented definition of leadership is provided by Knezevich (1984):

Leadership is a process of stimulating, developing, and working with people within an organization. It is a human-oriented process and focuses upon personnel motivation, human relationships or social interactions, interpersonal communications, organizational climate, interpersonal conflicts, personal growth and development, and enhancement of the productivity of human factors in general. (p. 60)

Stoops (1984) provides a unique list of leadership behaviors associated with the human-oriented definition of leadership. Figure

Ten Commandments for the Human Side of Leadership

1. Make followers feel important. Recognize their good deeds. Write complimentary notes. Compliment followers before their peers. Praise in public and criticize, if you must, in private.
2. Know and use your followers' names. Almost everyone likes to see his/her name in print, or hear it used favorably.
3. Know your followers' families, their names, their interests, their concerns, their successes. This is good salesmanship.
4. Be visible. Be available to your followers. Be seen on the assembly line, in offices, and classrooms each day.
5. Be sympathetic with followers' problems. Out of these problems grow opportunities. Give special attention to baffled youth who are victims of environment, and to lonely elderly associates.
6. Have faith in your followers. If you doubt them they will doubt you.
7. Involve followers in decisions and planning. If they help formulate plans, then it is their program—and they will follow.
8. Try to represent the needs and the desires of the majority of your followers. The "way-out" leader is soon displaced.
9. Avoid the temptation to feel tall by keeping followers down. Your task as a leader is to make every follower better than you. As Walter Lippman has said, "The final test of a leader is that he leaves behind him in other men the conviction and the will to carry on."
10. Practice sincere humility. Apply the Golden Rule to all leader-follower relationships.

Figure 4.4 Leadership as a human relationship. (*Source:* Stoops, E. [May 1984]. Ten Commandments for the human side of leadership. *Leader Letter.* Bloomington, Ind.: Phi Delta Kappa. Used with permission.)

4.4 identifies the "Ten Commandments for the Human Side of Leadership." The definitions and "commandments" provided in this section can serve as a guide for instructional supervisors in working with teachers to improve the overall effectiveness of classroom instruction.

LEADERSHIP STYLES

As indicated earlier in the chapter, one way to view leadership behavior is from the perspective of style. We have already referred to several leadership styles; we will now take a closer look at three leadership styles shown in Figure 4.1 (see page 56). These three common styles have been described by Giammatteo (1975). They are laissez-faire, autocratic, and democratic. While it should be clear that one style is not inherently superior to another, there are distinct advantages and disadvantages associated with each.

A *laissez-faire* leadership style is just as the term suggests—to let (other people) do as they choose. The laissez-faire leadership style typically ignores others, and so members go their own way. The greatest advantage of this style is that there is little work for the leader, and when group members are "self-starters," the leader has to do very little to look good. There are rare occasions when it might be advisable for the leader to adopt this style for a short period and take a "wait and see" attitude. Some of the disadvantages of this style include lower productivity or task accomplishment, poorer quality of work, and less satisfaction with work.

An *autocratic* leadership style is a directive approach in which the leader tells others what to do; all or most decisions are made by the leader, generally without considering the needs or wishes of others. A distinct advantage of this leadership approach is that quicker decisions can be reached and productivity tends to be higher while the leader is present. Disadvantages include greater hostility from group members, more dependence on the leader, and decreased productivity and apathy, especially when the leader is absent.

A *democratic* leadership style involves a participative approach to leadership, with individuals having input in decisions affecting programs and operations and the leader serving to help the group meet its needs and goals. The leader shows respect for group members; he or she offers direction but does not take total control. Generally, the advantages outweigh the disadvantages. Benefits include greater individual responsibility, more motivation and individual growth, higher morale and more efficient implementation. A clear disadvantage is the length of time it can take to make a decision or arrive at a clear consensus.

As can be seen, the basic styles are very different in their approach to leadership. Surely one would have to be judicious in the use of the laissez-faire style, but, as indicated, there might be times when it would be appropriate. And, depending on the situation, it might be appropriate for the leader to assume an autocratic style if a task needs to be completed very quickly. Generally, the democratic style would result in a greater sense of cooperativeness and accomplishment. Each style, however, could be appropriate in a specific situation.

PRINCIPLES OF LEADERSHIP

To be effective in their interaction with teachers and others as they function in leadership roles, instructional supervisors should be knowledgeable about the general principles of leadership that research has yielded. These general principles provide insights into the individual, group, and organizational dimensions of leadership. The list provided is a compilation of research from a variety of studies (Lovell and Wiles, 1983; Alfonso, Firth, and Neville, 1981).

1. Leadership is not a result of any single personality trait or combination of traits.
2. Leadership is widespread and diffuse throughout the group; it is a group role and is largely determined by the expectations of the group.
3. Leadership is a function of the frequency of interaction with members of the group.
4. Status and position do not necessarily guarantee leadership, but leadership will be enhanced if the leader has status and power in the organization.
5. Leadership can be enhanced by maintaining some degree of psychological distance from members of the group.
6. Leadership styles generate different and predictable responses and patterns of achievement among group members, and the leader should be aware of his or her dominant leadership style.
7. Leadership qualities and follower qualities are interchangeable.
8. Leadership is situational and is affected by a number of variables, including the feelings that individuals have about the leader, norms of the group, organizational conditions, ability to perform needed group functions, and the sex of leader and members.
9. Leadership is perceived differently by subordinates (group members) and superiors (bosses).
10. Leadership will be enhanced through the provisions of rewards and the satisfaction of the needs of group members.
11. Leadership should reflect the needs of people as well as provide for structure and is enhanced when it provides for active participation in decision making.
12. Leadership will emerge from a group when a member fulfills the needs and expectations of the others, or when the formal leader does not meet the group's expectations.

These 12 principles provide a conceptual framework that serves to guide instructional supervisors as they consider appropriate leadership behaviors for their situation.

THE USE OF POWER AND AUTHORITY

Leaders have at their disposal various kinds of power and authority they may use. The intent of both is to ensure that the organization works properly and that the rules and regulations are followed. According to Alfonso, Firth, and Neville (1981), "The authority of leadership can be expressed by various members of a formal organization and is not restricted to those holding formal offices. Through the expression of leadership authority, esteem is gained" (p. 65). The purpose of authority is to obtain from individuals voluntary compliance with requests. "Most teachers do what their principals ask of them because they feel that their principals have a legitimate right to make demands" (Tye and Tye, 1984, p. 321). Therefore, an instructional leader's authority is inherent in the position or associated with the responsibilities assigned.

Leaders, however, may be required to use various kinds of power to foster or obtain compliance with organizational rules and goals. Etzioni (1965) has identified three types of power that leaders can use. These include coercive, utilitarian, and identitive. The use of force or the threat of force is considered *coercive power.* In schools, the threat of nonrenewal of a contract or job is an example of the use of coercive power. Providing rewards of a material or service nature would be considered *utilitarian power.* Granting such items as an extra planning period, a teacher's aide, or a pay bonus would be an example of the use of utilitarian power. The use of symbols and prestige would represent *identitive power.* For a teacher to be selected to teach an honors course or to be recognized as the teacher of the year would be an example of the use of identitive power. All three types of power are designed to shape behavior in a way that meets the goals and objectives and complies with the rules and regulations of the organization.

French and Raven (1959) proposed five types of power available to leaders:

1. *reward power*—the ability to provide members with rewards such as higher salaries or released time
2. *coercive power*—the capacity to punish, by such means as dismissal, lower evaluation ratings, or poor teaching assignments
3. *legitimate power*—the use of power based on position within the organization such as superintendent, principal, or supervisor

4. *referent power*—the tendency to be associated with persons in leadership positions and the use of that association to promote certain behavior
5. *expert power*—special knowledge or skill that is beneficial to the organization, such as expertise in computer programming

Figure 4.5 lists the five types of power identified by French and Raven and cites examples of their use within a school context.

Categories	Examples
Reward power	"I believe that you are interested in. . . . Perhaps we can work something out, but before we do, you need to. . . ."
Coercive power	"I find your behavior unacceptable, and if it doesn't change . . ., I will have no choice except to suspend you."
Legitimate power	"Consistent with my responsibilities as principal, I am assigning you. . . ."
Referent power	"You have believed in me in the past, and I am asking you to trust me now."
Expert power	"This is an area in which I have background and experience, and therefore. . . ."

Figure 4.5 Examples of the use of different types of power. (*Source:* French, J. R. P, and Raven, B. [1959]. The bases of social power. In D. Cartwright (Ed.), *Studies in social power.* Ann Arbor: Institute for Social Research, University of Michigan. With permission of the Institute for Social Research.)

Mondy, DeHay, and Sharplin (1983) suggest that the supervisor's total power is the sum of the five forms available and that the only power actually conferred by the supervisor's position in the organization is legitimate power. Figure 4.6 shows that the supervisor's total power can be strengthened or weakened by the use ($+$ or $-$) of reward, coercive, referent, or expert power. Using this formula as an example, the instructional supervisor with little formal, legitimate power (position) might still have significant authority because of such factors as friendship with and respect from the teachers and expertise in the area. The opposite might also be true. A principal with considerable legitimate power might be virtually ineffective because of a lack of knowledge and on-the-job experience. As Figure 4.6

$$\frac{\text{Total}}{\text{power}} = \frac{\text{Legitimate}}{\text{power}} \pm \frac{\text{Reward}}{\text{power}} \pm \frac{\text{Coercive}}{\text{power}} \pm \frac{\text{Referent}}{\text{power}} \pm \frac{\text{Expert}}{\text{power}}$$

Figure 4.6 The constituents of total power. (*Source:* Mondy, R. W., DeHay, J. M., and Sharplin, A. D. [1983]. *Supervision,* p. 133. New York: Random House. Used with permission.)

suggests, legitimate power is only one element, and its effectiveness might be determined by the presence or absence of the four other types of power.

Closely associated with authority and power is the feeling of intimidation. Supervisors may feel intimidated when dealing with powerful individuals, or they may fail to take action because they are afraid of peers, superiors, or subordinates. The best shield against intimidation is competence and confidence. Supervisors who know their jobs and carry out their assignments with confidence should not feel threatened by others and should be better able to assert themselves.

PROFILE OF EFFECTIVE INSTRUCTIONAL LEADERS

Many characteristics of effective leaders have a direct bearing on instructional effectiveness. Leithwood (1987) provides a profile of the effective instructional leader (Figure 4.7). This profile identifies the

DIMENSIONS OF PRACTICE				
Level	Decision Making	Goals	Factors	Strategies
4 (High) Systematic problem solver	• skilled in the use of multiple forms: matches form to setting and works toward high levels of participation • decision processes oriented toward goal or education, based on information from personal, professional, and research sources • anticipates, initiates, and monitors decision processes	• selected from multiple public sources • highly ambitious for all students • transformed into short-term goals for planning • used to actively increase consistency among staff in directions they pursue	• attempts to influence all factors bearing on achievement • expectations derived from research and professional judgment	• uses a wide variety of strategies • criteria for choice include goals, factors, context, and perceived obstacles • makes extensive use of factor-specific strategies to achieve goals
3 Program manager	• skilled in use of several forms; selects form based on urgency and desire to involve staff • decision processes oriented toward school's program based on information from personal and professional sources • anticipates most decisions process	• selected from several sources, some of which are public • particular focus on exceptional students • encourages staff to use goals for planning • conveys goals when requested or as particular need arises	• attempts to influence factors bearing on the school program • expectations within factors are specific • expectations are derived from personal and staff experiences and occasionally from research	• relies on limited number of established, well-tested strategies • choice based on student needs, (especially special students), desire to be fair and consistent, concern to manage time effectively • uses factor-specific strategies that are derived largely from personal experience and system direction

(Continued)

	DIMENSIONS OF PRACTICE (*Continued*)			
Level	Decision Making	Goals	Factors	Strategies
2 Humanitarian	• uses primarily participatory forms of decision making based on a strong motivation to involve staff so they will be happy • tends to be proactive concerning decisions affecting school climate but largely reactive in all other areas unless required to act	• derived from belief in the importance of interpersonal relations to effective school • goals may be ambitious but be limited in focus • goals not systematically used for planning • conveys goals to others if requested	• attempts to influence factors bearing on interpersonal relations • expectations within factors ambitious but vague • expectations are mostly derived from personal experiences and beliefs	• chooses strategies that focus on interpersonal relationships • choice based on view of good school environment, view of own responsibilities, and desire to make jobs of staff easier • makes little use of systematic factor-specific strategies
1 (Low) Administrator	• uses primarily autocratic forms of decision making • decision process oriented toward smooth school administration based on personal sources of information • decision processes are reactive, inconsistent, and rarely monitored	• derived from personal needs • focus on school administration rather than students • pursuit of instructional goals considered to be responsibility of staff not principal • conveys goals to others if requested	• attempts to influence factors bearing on school appearance and day-to-day operations (mostly non-classroom factors) • expectations within factors are vague • expectations are derived from personal experiences	• chooses strategies based on personal need to maintain administrative control and remain uninvolved in classroom decisions • strategies mostly limited to use of vested authority and assisting staff with routine tasks • attends to factor-specific strategies in a superficial way if requested to do so

Figure 4.7 The profile of effective instructional leaders. (*Source:* Leithwood, K. A. [September 1987]. Using the principal profile to assess performance. *Educational Leadership, 45,* 1, 64. Used with permission of the Association for Supervision and Curriculum Development. Copyright © by ASCD. All rights reserved.)

many dimensions of instructional leadership. While originally designed as the "Principal Profile," the chart also can apply to others who perform supervisory duties in the schools. In this profile, Leithwood identifies four levels of leadership growth and the dimensions associated with the practice at each level. Using this chart as a guideline, instructional supervisors can develop their own profile.

SUMMARY

This chapter focuses on leadership theory as it applies to instructional supervisors. By accepting a position as an instructional supervisor, an individual is also accepting the role of a leader within the school organization. It is leadership that serves to link the administrative and managerial functions with the curriculum and teaching functions through the focus on instruction. Leadership, then, is a critical component of effective schools.

In discussing the aspects of leadership, the chapter presents six factors: historical perspectives and theories of leadership, dimensions and definitions of leadership, leadership styles, principles of leadership, the use of power and authority, and a profile of effective instructional leaders.

In the section on historical perspectives and leadership theory, a brief overview of some fundamental theories was presented. Each theory describes leadership behavior and provides a perspective on the development of leadership as a part of human history. As our understanding of people and the way they behave in organizational settings has grown, so too has our understanding of leadership behavior. The theories of leadership devised by Machiavelli, Spencer, McGregor, Likert, Blake and Mouton, and Hershey and Blanchard all view leadership as the result of patterns of behavior and responses from members within an organization. It is evident that there is no one best theory of leadership, but it is also true that, under particular circumstances, some theories are more appropriate than others. By being aware of the range of leadership theories and behaviors, instructional supervisors will be able to develop their own leadership behavior.

There are many definitions of leadership; in fact, Wiles and Bondi suggest that there are over 130 different definitions. This chapter provides several important definitions for instructional supervisors to consider as they examine their own understanding of the leadership process.

In understanding leadership behavior, it is also important to discuss leadership styles. Common leadership styles identified in the literature include laissez-faire, autocratic, and democratic. Each of these styles is briefly described, and each may be appropriate for a given situation. Next, the chapter synthesizes the research done on leadership and presents a list of leadership principles to guide and direct the behavior of instructional supervisors. These principles provide insights into the individual, group, and organizational dimensions of leadership behavior.

As instructional supervisors interact with teachers and others within the school organization, they wield power and authority. It is important for supervisors to understand the uses of power in order to use it well. The intent of the use of power is to have individuals comply voluntarily with the rules and regulations of the organization.

Finally, in the last section, a chart is presented that identifies levels of leadership effectiveness. The instructional leader profile is offered as a guide to help instructional supervisors map their own leadership potential.

YOUR TURN

4.1 You may be curious about which leadership behaviors you share with effective leaders. Complete the following leadership inventory to find out.

Leadership Inventory*

Based on Characteristics of Effective Leaders

a. Are you sensitive to the feelings of your group?	Yes No
b. Do you listen attentively to group members.	Yes No
c. Do you refrain from ridiculing members of the group?	Yes No
d. Do you help each member of the group feel important and needed?	Yes No
e. Do you refrain from arguing with the group?	Yes No
f. Do you make sure that everyone understands not only what is needed but why it is needed?	Yes No
g. Do you recognize that everyone is important and needs recognition?	Yes No
h. Do you share your leadership by cultivating leadership in your group?	Yes No
i. Do you develop long-range and short-range objectives for the group?	Yes No
j. Do you share opportunities and responsibilities with group members?	Yes No
k. Do you communicate and interact frequently with group members?	Yes No
l. As you work to solve problems, do you break big problems down into smaller ones?	Yes No
m. Do you plan, act, follow-up, and evaluate with group members?	Yes No

Now that you have completed the inventory, see how you measure up. If you responded *yes* to 11–13 questions—you are an effective leader; 8–10 questions—you are a moderately effective leader; 7 or fewer questions—your leadership behavior needs improvement.

4.2 Audiotape a meeting between a teacher and yourself. The focus of the

Source: Adapted from Reinhartz, J., and Beach, D. (1983). *Improving middle school instruction: A research-based self-assessment system,* p. 44. Washington, D.C.: National Education Association. With permission.

meeting should be some disagreement between you and the teacher regarding the need for making changes in the teacher's instructional behavior. After the meeting, analyze the dialogue using the "Ten Commandments for the Human Side of Leadership" (Figure 4.4) as a guide. Before reading each statement, add "Did I . . . ?" Then summarize your findings.

4.3 You are working with an aide who provides support for teachers in revising the curriculum in elementary science. You tend to have a "laid-back" leadership style that has worked successfully with the teachers in your building, but this aide will not follow your directions, particularly if the aide perceives them as unimportant. Consequently, in order to have the job done correctly, you are doing all the work yourself. This has increased the stress, and you are beginning to be resentful and even "edgy" with the teachers. What action will you take? If your usual leadership style is not working, what seems to be the matter? How will you correct the situation? How will you become more autocratic? What authority do you have to take action? Develop a step-by-step plan to correct the situation.

4.4 How would you respond to this quotation: "Leadership style is an extension of one's view of people, task, power and authority"? Do you agree or disagree with the statement? Why?

4.5 Six theories of leadership are presented in this chapter. Using the Blake and Mouton model of leadership presented in this chapter, how would you characterize a supervisor who is theoretically a 1,5? Write a profile of this supervisor.

4.6 You are in a situation in which you have neither a budget nor a staff that is responsible to you. Your title is sufficiently vague to encourage a variety of interpretations of your role. Yet as an instructional supervisor you are expected to improve the overall climate for teaching and learning in the school district. You are told after you accept the position that about the only real power you have is "the power of persuasion." How will you meet the objectives of your assignment with this type of power and authority? As you develop short-range and long-range plans, use the principles of leadership outlined in the chapter to guide you.

4.7 You and several of the teachers in the school district attended classes together at a local university. Over the years, you have all become good friends. In fact, many of the teachers have developed the practice of playing pranks on each other. You are concerned because you have recently been promoted to a supervisory position and the other teachers have continued to play practical jokes on you. In an effort to maintain a cordial relationship with these teachers and at the same time establish your position and authority, what course of action will you take when you discuss this matter with your friends?

4.8 In your first meeting of district supervisory personnel, you were intrigued and impressed by the praise Terry received from the superintendent, who said that "Terry is a born leader who can get teachers to do anything." Based on your understanding of leadership, what do you think the superintendent meant by the phrase a "born leader"?

REFERENCES

Alfonso, R. J., Firth, G. R., and Neville, R. F. (1981). *Instructional supervision: A behavior system.* (2nd ed.). Boston: Allyn and Bacon.

Andrews, R. (1987). On leadership and student achievement: A conversation with Richard Andrews. *Educational Leadership, 45,* 1, 9–16. [Interview with Ron Brandt, editor of *Educational Leadership*].

Blake, R. R., and Mouton, J. S. (1985). *The new managerial grid.* III: The key to leadership excellence. Houston: Gulf Publishing.

Bowlby, J. (1980). *Attachment and loss* (vol. 3). New York: Basic Books.

Etzioni, A. (1965). Organizational control structure. In J. G. March (Ed.), *Handbook of organizations.* Chicago: Rand McNally.

Fielder, F. E. (1974). *Leadership and effective management.* Glenview, Ill.: Scott, Foresman.

Fleishman, E. A., and Harris, E. F. (1962). Patterns of leadership behavior related to employee grievances and turnover. *Personnel Psychology, 15,* 1, 43–44.

French, J. R. P., and Raven, B. (1959). The bases of social power. In D. Cartwright (Ed.), *Studies in social power.* Ann Arbor: University of Michigan Press.

Giammatteo, M. C. (1975). Training package for a model city staff. Field Paper No. 15. Portland, Ore.: Northwest Regional Educational Laboratory.

Halpin, A. W. (1966). *Theory and research in administration.* New York: Macmillan Company.

Hershey, P., and Blanchard, K. (1977). *Management of organizational behavior: Utilizing human resources.* Englewood Cliffs, N.J.: Prentice-Hall.

Knezevich, S. J. (1984). *Administration of public education* (4th ed.). New York: Harper & Row.

Leithwood, K. A. (1987). Using the principal profile to assess performance. *Educational Leadership, 45,* 1, 63–66.

Likert, R. (1961). *New patterns of management.* New York: McGraw-Hill.

Likert, R. (1967). *The human organization.* New York: McGraw-Hill.

Lorenz, K. (1952). *King Solomon's ring.* New York: Crowell.

Lovell, J. T., and Wiles, K. (1983). *Supervision for better schools* (5th ed.). Englewood Cliffs, N.J.: Prentice-Hall.

McGregor, D. (1960). *The human side of enterprise.* New York: McGraw-Hill.

Maccoby, M. (1981). *The leader.* New York: Simon and Schuster.

Mondy, R. W., DeHay, J. M., and Sharplin, A. D. (1983). *Supervision.* New York: Random House.

Mortimore, P., and Sammons, P. (1987). New evidence on effective elementary schools. *Educational Leadership, 45,* 1, 4–8.

Owens, R. G. (1970). *Organizational behavior in schools.* Englewood Cliffs, N.J.: Prentice-Hall.

Spencer, H. (1927). *Education: Intellectual, moral and physical.* New York: Appleton-Century-Crofts.

Stoops, E. (May 1984). Ten commandments for the human side of leadership. *Leader Letter.* Bloomington, Ind.: Phi Delta Kappa.

Tye, K. A., and Tye, B. B. (1984). Teacher isolation and school reform. *Phi Delta Kappan, 65,* 5, 319–322.

Wiles, J., and Bondi, J. (1980). *Supervision: A guide to practice.* Columbus, Ohio: Charles E. Merrill.

Wiles, J., and Bondi, J. (1986). *Supervision: A guide to practice* (2nd ed.). Columbus, Ohio: Charles E. Merrill.

chapter 5

Communication Theory for Supervisors

Knowledge of organizational structure and leadership behavior is an important foundation for instructional supervisors. But the ability to communicate with teachers and others may ultimately determine the degree of success in improving instruction. Communication systems, which transmit information, are a part of all organizations, including corporations, families, and schools, and the ability to communicate effectively with others is vital to the success of any organization. Because of their various leadership positions in schools, instructional supervisors communicate with a wide variety of people, including students, teachers, parents, other school personnel, and members of the community. Barr, Elmes, and Walker (1980) suggest that

> without clear, direct communication . . . [the supervisor] could not possibly build with teachers the type of nonthreatening, healthy and fruitful relationship necessary to facilitate the teacher's growth as a professional. (p. 15)

Gorton (1987) believes that, to be successful as instructional supervisors, individuals must possess effective communication skills. Pfeiffer and Dunlap (1982) observe that the supervisor must be knowledgeable about the many aspects of the communication process, "since the supervisor deals with human relationships—working with an individual, a small group, or a large group to change behavior which will result in the improvement of instruction" (p. 179). Like these authors, we feel that the importance of effective communication practices cannot be overemphasized.

Recognizing the importance of communication skills in the overall effectiveness of the instructional supervisor, this chapter will (1) examine some definitions of communication and describe various aspects of the communication process; (2) discuss certain responses that encourage or inhibit good communication; (3) look at ways of communicating in behavioral language; (4) examine other forms of communication; and (5) identify principles of effective communication.

DEFINITIONS AND ASPECTS OF COMMUNICATION

The term *communication* comes from the Latin word *communicatus,* which means to impart, share, or to make common. The communication process, therefore, becomes a way of establishing common understandings, meanings, or purposes. According to Knezevich (1984):

> The many definitions of communication consider it (1) imparting or exchanging attitudes, ideas, and information through the use of human abilities or technology; (2) transmission and reception of ideas; (3) the broad field of interchange of thoughts and opinions among humans; or (4) a process of giving and receiving facts, feelings and ideas. (p. 75)

Perhaps one of the most commonly used definitions has been offered by Kelly and Rasey (1952), who define *communication* as "the process by which one individual can to a degree know what another thinks, feels or believes" (p. 78). Clearly there are similarities in all of these definitions that emphasize a common or mutual understanding or a sharing of information.

In working with teachers and others in schools, it is important for supervisors to have a clear understanding of the communication process. Good communication can be an effective tool for promoting learning and growth and can serve as a means of influencing the instructional behavior of teachers. Berlo (1960) and Seiler and colleagues (1982) have identified some basic components or aspects of the communication process that supervisors need to be aware of as they interact and communicate with others. These components of communication include the following:

1. the purpose to be achieved by the message
2. the source of the communication or person(s) sending the message
3. the encoding of the message and the ways or channels for sending the message
4. information or content of the message or the message itself
5. the receiver(s) or person(s) to whom the message is sent
6. the decoding or translating of the message
7. the need for a response to or feedback about the message

As noted from these different components, communication is clearly more than talk; more than words or sounds are communicated. As individuals communicate with each other, feelings and purposes are also communicated through expressions, gestures, posture, and overall physical attitudes. Communication, then, occurs in different ways at multiple levels.

In addition to these basic components of communication external factors such as ideas, feelings, suggestions, and descriptions help to shape and give meaning to the message. The communicator experiences a need to share such ideas and feelings in a form that will transfer a common meaning to the receiver. Therefore, the information and related factors must be encoded into a message through the use of symbols (oral language or printed words). The channel is the medium or method for transferring the message, which must then be decoded to the original meaning(s) by the receiver.

It is important to note that the communication process is seldom, if ever, 100 percent accurate. However, when the receiver has an opportunity to make a response to the message, the sender has a chance to verify that the receiver has accurately decoded the message. Figure 5.1 represents the communication process with the response/feedback component.

As Figure 5.1 shows, the response mechanism provides a means of clarifying the message and of improving on its accuracy. Supervisors may sometimes encounter situations in which the listener, or the receiver of the message, simply does not hear the message being sent. Without a response, it is difficult if not impossible to determine what has been heard. This results in what Barr, Elmes, and Walker (1980) refer to as a "problem in communication" (p. 16). Many in-

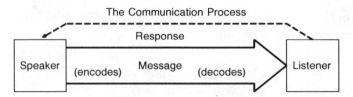

Figure 5.1 A schematic diagram of the communication process. (*Source:* Adapted from Boyan, N. J., and Copeland, W. D. [1978]. *Instructional Supervision Training Program,* p. 18. Columbus, Ohio: Charles E. Merrill. Used with permission.)

dividuals may recall the famous line in the movie *Cool Hand Luke* in which the prison warden, after severely punishing Luke for continuing to disobey, says to the inmate, "What we have here is a failure to communicate." What supervisors must carefully guard against is a failure to communicate with the teachers and others with whom they work.

SUPERVISOR RESPONSES THAT ENCOURAGE COMMUNICATION

In order to avoid such problems in communication and enhance the accuracy of the message, the supervisor should not only provide an opportunity for a response, as seen in Figure 5.1, but should encourage responses from the listener/receiver. Boyan and Copeland (1978) and Barr, Elmes, and Walker (1980) suggest five types of responses that supervisors can use to help ensure clear communication. These responses are designed for the supervisor to use in encouraging teachers and others to communicate openly and freely, not only to enhance the accuracy of the message but to verify the degree of understanding. The five response modes are (1) asking clarifying questions, (2) paraphrasing, (3) perception checking, (4) offering information, and (5) active attentive listening.

1. *Asking clarifying questions.* The intent of this type of response is to verify the meaning of the teacher's message. As the supervisor listens to what the teacher says, the message may appear to be vague or overly generalized, and to have multiple meanings. The supervisor's response should be to ask the teacher to repeat or clarify what was said. For example, the supervisor might say to the teacher, "I'm not sure I know what you mean when you say that Jerry is an active student. Is he disruptive?" Or the supervisor might respond by saying, "I'm not sure I understand the situation completely. Could

you describe her behavior again for me?" In using responses like these, the supervisor is asking the teacher to clarify his or her message and improve the degree of understanding on the part of the supervisor.

2. *Paraphrasing.* This kind of response helps the supervisor to avoid making assumptions about the situation and the message. By paraphrasing, the supervisor repeats the message in his or her own words and thus provides the teacher with an opportunity to verify the supervisor's understanding. For example, the teacher might say, "I can't get Sally to do what I ask her to do." From what the teacher says, the supervisor might assume that Sally is a discipline problem. In paraphrasing, the supervisor might say, "No matter what you do, Sally is a discipline problem because she won't mind you in class." Now the teacher can either respond "Yes, that is what I mean," or "No, she just sits quietly and daydreams and won't complete her assignments." The goal of paraphrasing is for supervisors to put the message in their own words so that teachers can clarify the content and verify the degree of accuracy of communication.

3. *Perception checking.* Use of this kind of response allows the supervisor to explore the meanings behind the message and to verify the feelings incorporated in the teacher's message. Often misunderstandings occur because the supervisor misinterprets the feelings behind the message; perception checking will help prevent this. For example, the teacher might say very little during the initial moments of an after-school conference the supervisor had requested. The supervisor might mistake the teacher's reticence as "pouting" and a way of showing displeasure at the conference. If these perceptions are not checked, or verified, they could lead to serious misunderstandings. Therefore, the supervisor might say, "I have the feeling or impression that you are upset at having this conference with me this afternoon. Am I right?" The supervisor's question gives the teacher the chance to say either, "Yes, I am very unhappy that I had to meet with you today when I had other plans," or "No, I'm not upset. I'm just tired and was thinking of all the work I have to get done between now and tomorrow." Such an interchange provides the supervisor with the opportunity to determine the feelings of the teacher.

4. *Offering information.* In this type of response, the supervisor can react to the teacher's message by offering relevant information. The teacher can then analyze the information to determine if it applies to the original message. The supervisor might say, "From what you

have told me about the student, it appears that we have two choices. We could either begin the diagnostic process to determine if the student will qualify for special education, or we could implement immediate intervention strategies to help overcome the academic deficiencies." A word of caution must be sounded, however, concerning the use of such a response. Often supervisors want to "tell" or offer information before they have given the teacher a chance to explain the problem fully. If not used sparingly and in conjunction with the four other types of responses listed here, offering information can actually become a hinderance to clear communication. The purpose of this response is to provide enough relevant information from the supervisor's perspective to enable the teacher to weigh the information and determine its appropriateness for a given situation.

5. *Active attentive listening.* This type of response may be the most critical in fostering open and free communication with teachers. It is often difficult for the supervisor to stay "tuned in" when, at the end of a long day, a teacher schedules an appointment to talk about an instructional problem. The key to success in developing good listening skills is to make some kind of response to the message that is being sent. Active, attentive listening is responsive listening and requires that the supervisor respond with "Yes," "I see," "Go on," or even "Okay" and "Uh-huh." However, the supervisor should guard against habitual and meaningless responses. Thus the supervisor can convey interest in the message through an alert facial expression, eye contact, and helpful spoken responses.

These five response modes are called "freeing responses" because they are designed to promote free, open communication. The supervisor can use the responses to foster clear communication and to increase understanding.

SUPERVISOR RESPONSES THAT DISCOURAGE COMMUNICATION

Not all the responses supervisors may employ are as helpful as the freeing responses. Other types of responses often serve to restrict or inhibit communication with teachers. Boyan and Copeland (1978) and Barr, Elmes, and Walker (1980) identify six response patterns that supervisors frequently use that result in discouraging or blocking clear and open communication. These six responses are (1) changing the subject, (2) explaining the teacher's behavior, (3) giving directions, (4) leveling the teacher's expectations, (5) denying the teacher's feelings, and (6) giving commands or orders.

1. *Changing the subject.* A response of this type serves to inhibit clear communication because it draws attention away from the teacher's message. For example, the teacher might say, "I really need help in motivating my low math group." But in changing the subject, and therefore the focus of the communication, the supervisor might respond by saying, "I'm so glad you came by. I needed to talk about your class achievement tests that are scheduled for next week." By changing the subject, the supervisor has cut off the message of the teacher and subsequently will not deal with the teacher's concern about motivating the low math group.

2. *Explaining the teacher's behavior.* This kind of response allows the supervisor to tell the teacher why he or she feels a certain way. For example, the supervisor might say, "I know that you are upset about the scores now, but remember you have been ill this past week. I'm sure you will see things differently when you feel better." A response like this communicates to teachers that their message was not significant and that time will take care of things.

3. *Giving directions.* This response pattern is related to offering information. A supervisor who tells a teacher what to do without first exploring all dimensions of the message, does not encourage the teacher to discuss the matter freely. For instance, after hearing only a few moments of the teacher's concerns or message, the supervisor may respond with a list: "Well, what you need to do to solve your problem is to develop a seating chart, post your classroom rules, and prepare more detailed lesson plans." Such a response will probably inhibit the teacher in continuing the conversation.

4. *Leveling the teacher's expectations.* Such a response can really serve to deflat a teacher and shut off free and open communication. A supervisor's statement like: "I hope you won't have any concerns about the new computer-assisted math program," or "I hope you won't disappoint me by being one of the last to review the new reading program," only serves to commit the teacher to a certain level of performance. Such statements do not encourage additional communication on the situations.

5. *Denying the teacher's feelings.* The attitude a response of this sort communicates to the teacher is that his or her feelings are not important. When a supervisor says, "Surely you don't feel that way about the new schedule," or "That's nothing to get upset over," the

message conveyed is that the teacher's feelings do not count. Such statements discourage teachers from further discussing their feelings with the supervisor and thus inhibit the communication process.

6. *Giving commands.* A response of this nature clearly limits further communication. When the supervisor says, "You will standardize all spelling lists by the end of the week," the teacher's autonomy has been taken away and the communication process is limited. The teacher is likely to feel that the supervisor would rather issue orders—regardless of their appropriateness to the teacher's classroom needs—than listen to and think about a description of the particular problems the teacher may be facing.

Supervisors, if their intent is to facilitate communication and promote a clear understanding of the message, should avoid these six types of "binding responses" and substitute the five freeing responses in their place.

COMMUNICATING IN BEHAVIORAL LANGUAGE

When communicating with teachers, instructional supervisors should understand the following prerequisites of communication. First, the supervisor should avoid making judgmental statements when describing classroom events and teaching behaviors. Second, the supervisor must communicate with the teacher in the most accurate and precise way possible. The teacher must be able to understand the supervisor's meaning, and the supervisor must likewise be able to understand the teacher's meaning. Only through a "mutual understanding will a healthy supervisory relationship grow" (Barr, Elmes, and Walker, 1980, p. 32). Finally, the teacher's area of instructional concern must be identified in precise and specific terms. As Barr, Elmes, and Walker add:

> To sum up, effective instructional supervision requires use of a language with three main characteristics. It must be (1) non-judgmental, (2) easily understood, and (3) specific. (pp. 32–33)

The tool used for helping the supervisor meet all three of these criteria is called *behavioral language*—that is, communication which describes classroom behavior impartially and factually rather than evaluatively, and which is precise, clear, and unambiguous.

In developing a behavioral vocabulary, the supervisor should focus on observable behaviors that occur within the teaching–learning process. For example, when observing in an elementary math class, the supervisor might note that the teacher called on only 3 of 22 students during the lesson but that those 3 students responded 18 times. Instead of saying to the teacher, "I don't think you did a very good job of questioning because you only called on 3 students," the supervisor would say, "I noted that you asked 18 questions during the math lesson and John, Mary, and Sam were the students who responded to the questions." This second statement simply describes what happened in the classroom and makes no attempt to judge or evaluate the actions.

In another situation, the supervisor might observe that "During a 20-minute lesson, 15 students (65 percent) were on-task, 6 students (26 percent) were passively off-task, and 2 students (9 percent) were actively off-task." The statements must be accurate, specific, and precise descriptions of observable behaviors in the classroom. Such behavioral statements contain information related to measurable quantities and observable events. This is not a judgment, for no value is assigned to the numbers; it is simply a statement or report of what happened. Figure 5.2 provides examples of behavioral and nonbehavioral statements. *Nonbehavior statements* are those that do not adhere to the principles of behavioral statements.

NONBEHAVIORAL STATEMENTS	BEHAVIORAL STATEMENTS
Your lesson didn't seem to go over very well.	Three out of 30 students responded to the questions. No student asked any questions about the lesson.
It looks like the kids hate to come to class.	Eighty percent of the time, half of the class is tardy. The absentee rate for the class is twice as high as for the typical class in this school.
The students in your class are poorly motivated to learn the new material.	None of the students volunteered to discuss the material. About 20 percent of the class completed the daily homework assignments.
Your teaching seems boring to a lot of the students.	Nine students fell asleep during class today. Also, six students were drawing pictures while I was observing.
Your students seem to understand the material well.	Two-thirds of the students in the class scored at least 90 percent on the weekly tests. Appropriate answers were given to all of the questions during the discussion today.

Figure 5.2 Examples of nonbehavioral and behavioral language. (*Source:* Adapted from Boyan, N. J., and Copeland, W. D. [1978]. *Instructional Supervision Training Program,* p. 39. Columbus, Ohio: Charles E. Merrill. Used with permission.)

Writing	Oral Face-to-Face	Oral Electronic/Visual
• Note	• Individual conference	• Telephone
• Letter	• Small group meetings	• P.A. system
• Memorandum	• Large group meetings	• Overhead or slide projector
• Community newspaper	• Social functions	• Radio
• School bulletin		• Television
		• Videotapes

Figure 5.3 Types of communication channels. (*Source:* Gorton, R. A. [1987]. *School leadership and administration* (3rd ed.), p. 39. Dubuque, Iowa: Wm. C. Brown. Used with permission.)

To communicate effectively with teachers, supervisors must learn to develop a behavioral language vocabulary. This will help in communicating clearly and concisely and is designed to influence the teacher's instructional behavior.

OTHER FORMS OF COMMUNICATION

Most of the discussion to this point has dealt with spoken or verbal communication. As indicated earlier in the chapter, communication is a multifaceted process that occurs on a variety of levels, with the sender using different methods or channels to convey messages. Figure 5.3 provides examples of what Gorton (1987) identifies as various channels of communication that can be used to transmit messages.

Two prevalent forms of communication that are used either by themselves or in conjunction with spoken messages include written communication and nonverbal communication. Both of these forms can be effective tools for the instructional supervisor in working with teachers and others in schools.

Written Communication

Nearly all organizations seem to have an affinity for written communication, especially in the form of memos and reports. Because of the various titles and positions instructional supervisors have and the administrative functions and duties they perform, it is often necessary to construct a "paper trail" of documents, especially when dealing with personnel matters. A paper trail verifies that important messages concerning specific behaviors have been communicated to the appropriate teachers. In addition, written messages can provide specific advantage over oral or other forms of communication. Pfeiffer and Dunlap (1982) consider the following to be the major advantages of written communication:

1. Communication (words) on paper provide a relatively permanent record.
2. Communication in written form contains valuable data that may be necessary for legal and/or political judgments.
3. Communication in written form can be affirmative, descriptive, and informative and can be distributed to infinite numbers of people in order to generate support or action.
4. Written communications often have a greater impact on the reader/receiver than spoken messages do, since written messages tend to be taken more seriously.

Clearly, there are times when the supervisor, in working with teachers to improve instruction, will find that a conversation will suffice. Frequently, in fact, a conversation will be preferable because it allows the teacher the opportunity to respond immediately. There are times, however, as noted above, when written communication is not only preferable but is called for because of the nature of the situation.

When preparing written communications, supervisors must guard against what Pfeiffer and Dunlap (1982) refer to as the tendency to "use words creatively" (p. 190) or engage in the kind of "wordsmanship" tactics that often plague organizations. Figure 5.4 provides, in the form of a game, an example of the kind of wordsmanship that supervisors may typically use in their efforts to sound more professional. In using the "wordsmanship" strategy, supervisors and other education professionals may construct sophisticated phrases that are, in fact, virtually meaningless. Supervisors must resist the creativity illustrated by the exercise in Figure 5.4, and provide forms of written communication that use clear and precise language. To win at wordsmanship, select any three numbers from 0 to 9, and then pick

How to Win at Wordsmanship

Column 1	Column 2	Column 3
0. integrated	0. management	0. options
1. total	1. organizational	1. flexibility
2. systematized	2. monitored	2. capability
3. parallel	3. reciprocal	3. mobility
4. functional	4. digital	4. programming
5. responsive	5. logistical	5. concept
6. optional	6. transitional	6. time-phase
7. synchronized	7. incremental	7. projection
8. compatible	8. third-generation	8. hardware
9. balanced	9. policy	9. contingency

Figure 5.4 Bureaucratic language at work—and play. (*Source:* Holcomb, J. [1987]. How to win at wordsmanship. Stephenville, Tex.: Tarleton State University. Mimeographed. Used with permission.)

the corresponding numbered words from each column and put them together (e.g., 140—total digital options).

In his book *Art of Plain Talk,* Flesch (1946) criticizes the use of "gobbledygook," or wordy and confusing jargon, and calls for forthright communication. The following guidelines, based in part on Flesch's ideas, should be considered by anyone preparing written communications:

1. Avoid writing up or down to the audience. Choose your vocabulary carefully, remembering that the *receptive vocabulary*—the one we use in reading and listening—is several times larger than the *expressive*—or written—*vocabulary* (Burmeister, 1974).
2. Do not use sarcasm or irony in written communications. Memos and reports are not the place to convey unfriendly remarks.
3. Use concrete words and illustrations. Avoid vague or abstract terms that might require lengthy elaboration.
4. Communicate in a direct and forthright fashion. Simply stated, do not beat around the bush; get to the point.
5. If possible, compose a draft of the communication for review before sending. Make sure the message you are sending is the one you want communicated.

These suggestions can help the supervisor communicate more effectively with teachers and others when written communication is needed.

Nonverbal Communication

Another form of communication that supervisors need to be aware of is nonverbal communication. Gorton (1987), in citing the work of Lipham and Francke (1966), states, "Whether we realize it or not, we communicate nonverbally through our facial expressions, our gestures, our dress, our tone of voice and the physical environment in which we communicate" (p. 40). Supervisors should be careful to match their body language, or nonverbal communication, with their verbal communication. Mixed messages and unclear communication can result when, for instance, the supervisor smiles while delivering unpleasant information or frowns when delivering good news. Pfeiffer and Dunlap (1982) describe six broad categories of nonverbal behavior: *haptic, optic, proxemic, labic, pedic,* and *chromic* communication.

1. *Haptic communication.* This form of nonverbal communication focuses on hand motion as a way of transferring a message or

meaning. Clearly, the handshake is the most universally accepted form of haptic communication.

2. *Optic communication.* This type of nonverbal communication uses the eyes to send a message to the receiver. Through the use of optic communication, the sender conveys a message that words cannot impart. The wink is one of the most common forms of optic communication; another form is eye contact, especially during a conversation.

3. *Proxemic communication.* Nonverbal communication of this type is concerned with personal territory or personal space. Proxemic communication relates to the placement or positioning of individuals in a social setting, normally while they are talking. Associated with proxemic communication are the placement of furniture and the physical layout of a room, because such factors may determine how individuals position themselves within the space.

4. *Labic communication.* This form of nonverbal communication involves messages, other than words, sent by the mouth. Smiles, frowns, and pouts are some common examples of labic communication.

5. *Pedic communication.* This type of nonverbal communication involves messages sent by the feet. Such behaviors as foot-tapping, swinging one foot while sitting, and even positioning the body on one foot and then the other communicate messages to others.

6. *Chromic communication.* This form of nonverbal communication involves the use of color. Color is such an integral part of our environment that we often take it for granted. Supervisors can use color to their advantage in the communication process in items ranging from personal clothing to colors of ink on paper (such as red marks to indicate a particular kind of response or comment).

These examples of nonverbal communication are included to help supervisors in their interactions with teachers. With an awareness of the various types of nonverbal communication, supervisors may be able to increase their effectiveness when they work with teachers in improving classroom instruction.

PRINCIPLES OF COMMUNICATION

As a way of highlighting what is known about effective communication practices, the following propositions provide a synthesis of research summaries cited in Alfonso, Firth, and Neville (1981), Lovell and

Wiles (1983), and Berelson and Steiner (1964). The list can guide supervisors as they communicate with teachers about classroom instruction.

1. Communication is never complete and never 100 percent accurate because of the nature of the communication process. The process involves a sender, a receiver, and other variables, and problems may arise in any of these stages in the process.
2. Effectiveness in communication can be increased by completing the communication circuit with immediate feedback that comes from two-way (oral or spoken) rather than one-way (written) communication.
3. Communication is affected by the positions the sender and receiver hold in an organization, and the message is more likely to be precise and accurate if it progresses in a downward direction (based on authority) than if it progresses in an upward direction within the organization.
4. The experience, expertise, and credibility of an individual affect the frequency of interaction and the degree of acceptance of the message (information) by others.
5. The message communicated is distorted by the types of personality (superiority/inferiority) of the sender and the receiver involved.
6. Communication is more effective when the sender and the receiver share common views and experiences and when the message is compatible with these views and is considered reasonable.
7. Communication verifies group norms, and the communication patterns affect accuracy, group leadership, satisfaction of members, and the efficiency with which the group carries out its tasks.
8. Communication is most effective when it is consistent with an individual's views.
9. Communication of factual information is not always the most effective in changing others' opinions, and the stronger the emotional and psychological factors, the less impact the information may have on the individual.
10. Communication effectiveness is increased when the sender considers his or her personality and style and then communicates the message, using channels (written, verbal, mass media) that are consistent with the expectations of the group.
11. Communication effectiveness can be improved if the sender

organizes the content of the message, determines the appropriate vocabulary for the receiver(s), and matches verbal messages with nonverbal cues.

SUMMARY

This chapter has focused on the need for supervisors to employ clear, concise communication when working with teachers to improve instruction. Effective communication practices are essential in working with teachers and others in school organizations.

Communication is more than talk; more than words or sounds are communicated. Most definitions of communication recognize some aspect of a common or mutual understanding and/or the sharing of information. Factors for supervisors to consider in the communication process include the sender, encoding of the message, the message, the channel(s) of communication, decoding of the message, and the receiver. To improve the accuracy of the communication process, an opportunity should be provided to the receiver to respond to the message. This form of two-way (verbal) communication is usually perferable to one-way (written) communication because it provides for immediate feedback.

There are several responses that supervisors can use to encourage and promote open and free communication. These freeing responses include (1) asking clarifying questions, (2) paraphrasing, (3) perception checking, (4) offering information, and (5) active attentive listening. In addition to these freeing responses, supervisors may sometimes find themselves employing responses that discourage open, clear communication. These binding responses include (1) changing the subject, (2) explaining the teacher's behavior, (3) giving directions, (4) leveling the teacher's expectations, (5) denying the teacher's feelings, and (6) giving commands. To develop open and clear communication practices, supervisors should focus on the freeing responses and avoid using the binding responses.

Supervisors may also employ other forms of communication, especially written and nonverbal, besides oral or spoken communication. Written communications are often necessary to document that a message has been delivered. Guidelines are provided that supervisors can follow to improve the quality of memos and reports.

Finally, communication principles are cited as a guide to help supervisors as they work with teachers and others in schools. These principles can serve as benchmarks for supervisors to use in their interaction with others.

YOUR TURN

5.1. Compose a memo to teachers describing the inservice/staff development opportunities that the school district has developed for the year. In this memo, identify any state policies concerning inservice, any local district policies concerning inservice, the titles of the programs, and the procedures, if any, for registering for the sessions.

5.2. A teacher has stopped you in the hall and wants to discuss his or her plans with you for a class field trip. On the basis of a few statements, you have concerns about the trip and feel that perhaps not enough advanced planning has been done for this trip to be a successful learning experience for the students. You do not want to say "no" automatically, and you feel that this is neither the time nor the place to discuss the matter. You would, however, like to keep the lines of communication open. How can you indicate a willingness to discuss the matter further and at the same time express your concerns that the planning may be inadequate and that the matter should be discussed in a more suitable setting? Write out your response.

5.3. Communicating in behavioral language is very important for the supervisor when working with teachers. This form of communication not only adds precision to descriptions of teaching–learning behaviors; it also helps supervisors avoid making judgmental statements. After observing in a classroom for several minutes (at least 15), develop five statements in behavioral language that reflect your observations.

5.4. Your school district has a practice of taking turns highlighting special or unique programs at school board meetings during the year. As a central office supervisor in charge of a special program in the district (choose one, such as talented and gifted, resource/special education, developmental reading, adult education), it is your turn to make a presentation at the meeting this month. What will you communicate to the board about your program? How will you communicate this information? What prior review or approval will you need for your presentation? What kind of response do you want the board to make? Outline your presentation and have a brief synopsis of your program to distribute to board members. In your outline, indicate the visuals you will use in communicating the information.

REFERENCES

Alfonso, R. J., Firth, G. R., and Neville, R. F. (1981). *Instructional supervision: A behavior system* (2nd ed.). Boston: Allyn and Bacon.

Barr, D., Elmes, R., and Walker, B. (1980). *Educational leadership for inservice administrators: Participant's manual for an experiential training program.* Omaha: Center for Urban Education.

Berelson, B., and Steiner, G. A. (1964). *Human behavior: An inventory of scientific findings.* New York: Harcourt Brace Jovanovich.

Berlo, D. K. (1960). *The process of communication.* New York: Holt, Rinehart and Winston.

Boyan, N. J., and Copeland, W. D. (1978). *Instructional Supervision Training Program.* Columbus, Ohio: Charles E. Merrill.

Burmeister, L. E. (1974). *Reading strategies for secondary school teachers.* Reading, Mass.: Addison-Wesley.

Flesch, R. (1946). *Art of plain talk.* New York: Harper & Row.

Gorton, R. A. (1987). *School leadership and administration* (3rd ed.). Dubuque, Iowa: Wm. C. Brown.

Kelly, E. C., and Rasey, M. I. (1952). *Education and the nature of man.* New York: Harper & Row.

Knezevich, S. J. (1984). *Administration of public education* (4th ed.). New York: Harper & Row.

Lipham, J. M., and Francke, D. (1966). Nonverbal behaviors of administrators. *Educational Administration Quarterly, 2,* 101–109.

Lovell, J. T., and Wiles, K. (1983). *Supervision for better schools* (5th ed.). Englewood Cliffs, N.J.: Prentice-Hall.

Pfeiffer, I. L., and Dunlap, J. B. (1982). *Supervision of teachers: A guide to improving instruction.* Phoenix: Oryx Press.

Seiler, W. J., et al. (1982). *Communication in business and professional organizations.* Reading, Mass.: Addison-Wesley.

two

INSTRUCTIONAL DIMENSIONS OF SUPERVISION

chapter 6

Models of Curriculum Development: Planning for Instruction

Perhaps, as you read the title of this chapter, you are perplexed and think, "What does curriculum development have to do with instructional supervision?" Because curriculum development is the foundation for effective instruction, supervisors should have an understanding of the instructional dimensions of curriculum development before they can effectively take on the role of helper or facilitator. Knowledge of the curriculum development process can help supervisors as they work with teachers in planning for teaching and learning. According to Pfeiffer and Dunlap (1982):

> Supervisory responsibilities in the area of curriculum are varied, but a general description of the supervisor's role in curriculum is that of facilitator. The development of curriculum requires planning and organization, . . . distributing curriculum materials, . . . [and conducting] inservice activities to prepare teachers to use the curriculum. . . . Supervisors . . . contribute in all of these steps. (p. 91)

The role that the instructional supervisor plays in curriculum development is an important one, for it assists teachers not only in planning the curriculum but in implementing it later as well. Supervisors are confronted with the problem of helping teachers continually refine and expand the curriculum so that it maintains a vital synthesis of knowledge that has a direct impact on the life and growth of each learner. As Tanner and Tanner (1987) note:

> The need for the professional staff to engage in curriculum development as a central responsibility and as a continuous process also becomes evident when one considers that the curriculum is always in danger of . . . subject matter being added. . . . (p. 421)

Many teachers as well as supervisors accept the curriculum just as they accept the air they breathe, without thinking about it. Teachers seldom question the development or content of their curriculum. For many, the curriculum is a given; it is seen as something developed by someone else, and those in supervisory positions are often considered the "guardians of curriculum" (Tanner and Tanner, 1980).

Curriculum has been integrated, fused, correlated, individualized, humanized, and the like; but it is generally agreed that curriculum development has two parts—a process part and a content part. This chapter will focus on the process of curriculum development. In examining the process part of curriculum planning and development, the chapter will provide several definitions of curriculum, describe some models that can be used in the curriculum development process, explore the task analysis process, and examine other resources for curriculum development. Before describing the models used in the curriculum development process, it is essential to answer the questions, "What is the curriculum?" and "Where does the curriculum come from?" Supervisors should be prepared to answer these questions as they work with teachers to guard against the prospect of taking the curriculum development process for granted. Teachers may accept the curriculum like the air they breathe, but they should recognize that curriculum is a vital ingredient for the instructional life of classrooms.

DEFINITIONS OF CURRICULUM

In order to help teachers focus on their classroom instruction, supervisors may need to assist them with a more complete understanding of what curriculum is and where it comes from. But before examining the complexities of the curriculum development process, it is important to understand what is meant by the term *curriculum*. Definitions of *curriculum* continue to evolve as our understanding of the instructional process increases. Based on educational conditions at a given time in history, *curriculum* has been defined in a variety of ways. One of the earliest meanings of *curriculum* was derived from the Latin root of the word, which meant a racecourse or a prescribed course to follow. Later the term was adapted, in education, to refer to a prescribed series of courses to take. Sergiovanni and Starratt (1983) use the following definition of *curriculum:* "that which the student is supposed to encounter, study, practice and master! . . . what the student learns" (p. 24). The Tanners (1987) view *curriculum* as

the reconstruction of knowledge and experience, systematically developed under the auspices of the educational institution, to enable the learner to grow in gaining intelligent control over subsequent knowledge and experience. (p. 342)

Each definition recognizes the role of the student in mastering or learning some prescribed or planned body of knowledge. The term *curriculum* may have different meanings for different people, but, for us, the most important element is knowledge or content as the foundation for effective instruction. Curriculum development involves careful planning, with the ultimate goal of student achievement.

MODELS OF CURRICULUM DEVELOPMENT

In working with teachers to plan for instruction, supervisors can follow one of several models, or paradigms, to guide curriculum development. Three models are presented here; each has a unique focus or emphasis which may be appropriate depending on the classroom situation.

The Taba Model

Taba (1962) stressed that teachers should approach curriculum development in a systematic way and proposed a five-step model. The five stages are (1) creation of teaching units by classroom teachers, (2) testing of the experimental units in the classroom, (3) revision and consolidation of the units, (4) development of a framework or overall curriculum design, and (5) dissemination of the units to others. This model was considered "inverted" because it started with the creation of units by classroom teachers rather than beginning with the dissemination from others. Perhaps the most frequently used component of the model involves the creation of the teaching unit. Taba (1962) advocated the use of the following eight steps to guide the unit development:

1. diagnosing needs
2. formulating specific objectives
3. selecting content
4. organizing content
5. selecting learning experiences
6. organizing learning experiences
7. evaluating
8. checking for balance and sequence

Taba was an ardent proponent of curriculum development at the "grass-roots" or teacher level. With some variations, her model has been widely accepted and used in schools as a tool for helping teachers structure the learning process as they develop their own classroom curriculum.

The Ohio State Department of Education Model

A more recent curriculum development model was designed by the Ohio State Department of Education (1980). This model has incorporated additional elements and is more comprehensive in its approach. The following outline identifies the various components of the model that can be used for curriculum development:

A. Course of study
   1. District philosophy and goals
   2. Program philosophy
   3. Program goals
   4. Program objectives
      a. Grade level
      b. Grade cluster
      c. Course objectives
B. Curriculum guide
   1. Materials and resources
   2. Instructional strategies
C. Implementation
   1. Inservice activities

2. Classroom objectives
3. Classroom lessons
D. Student attainment of goals and objectives

The Ohio State Department of Education also has an evaluation phase that cycles through the entire model and becomes an integral part of each teacher's curriculum plans.

The Tyler Rationale

For us, the *Tyler rationale* has been a most helpful guide in working with teachers in planning for instruction and in conceptualizing the curriculum development process and, therefore, it is discussed in detail. Popham and Baker (1970) note that the Tyler rationale is useful to supervisors as they work with teachers in analyzing and focusing on learner behaviors as well as on teacher instructional behaviors. As a planning tool, it is a process that supervisors can use with teachers to assist them "in systematically selecting and organizing curriculum content and materials for classroom application" (Funkhouser, et al., 1981, p. 4). The Tyler rationale provides a beginning point for working with teachers in identifying general educational goals that are later translated into specific instructional objectives. It is through the process of curriculum development that teachers articulate learner behaviors and develop new ways to provide students with more effective learning experiences.

Tyler (1949) identified four basic questions that supervisors and teachers should address when developing curriculum and implementing instruction. These questions are as follows:

1. What educational purposes should the school seek to attain?
2. What educational experiences can be provided that are likely to attain these purposes?
3. How can these educational experiences be effectively organized?
4. How can we determine whether the purposes are being attained? (pp. 1–2)

These questions form the basis of a rationale, or paradigm, that can help teachers plan for instruction, develop learning activities, and establish evaluation criteria and procedures.

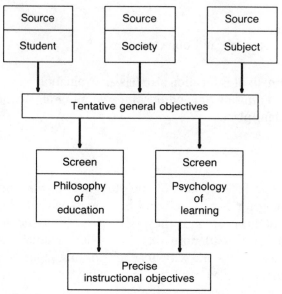

Figure 6.1   The Tyler rationale. (*Source:* Popham, W. J., and Baker, E. L. [1970]. *Establishing instructional goals,* p. 87. Englewood Cliffs, N.J.: Prentice-Hall. Used with permission.)

The schemata depicting the Tyler rationale in Figure 6.1 was developed by Popham and Baker (1970) and helps to answer the question "Where does curriculum come from?" According to the rationale, the three main sources of the curriculum are society's values, students' needs, and subject matter specialists. These sources provide data and help determine the educational purposes the schools should pursue. In addition, the sources suggest possible answers to the following questions:

1. What is society's philosophy of public education in the United States?
2. What goals should the public schools hope to achieve?
3. What types of jobs will be available for students graduating in the year 2000?
4. What knowledge and skills are needed for now and in the future?
5. What and how much are students capable of learning?
6. What type(s) of knowledge can students accommodate and assimilate?
7. How can schools provide an educational program (curricu-

lum) for students who have different interests, abilities and disabilities, skills, likes and dislikes, and socioeconomic backgrounds?
8. What is the structure of each content area or discipline?
9. Is the subject hierarchical, sequential, and/or spiral in nature?
10. What skills are inherent in the subject?
11. At what developmental level will the child or student best be able to assimilate facts, concepts, generalizations, and principles?

The answers to these questions are complex, but they come from members of society, the students themselves, and the structure of the content area, as well as from subject matter specialists; these sources provide a beginning point for determining the scope of the school curriculum. Tyler (1949) recognized the danger of asking subject matter specialists for suggestions for structuring the curriculum. He wanted them to focus on the question "What can your subject contribute to the education of young people who are not going to be specialists in your field?" (p. 26). In addition, he emphasized the need to differentiate general education from specialized education.

Sources of the Curriculum and Educational Screens It is from each source that general goals are developed that help determine what ultimately should be taught in school, how it should be taught, and how it should be evaluated. These general goals are usually expressed as a part of state and school district guidelines. Although the goals or aims are stated in very general terms, such as "knowledge and experiences to provide information and develop skills and values needed to perform daily activities in a safe manner free from injury or other losses" (Texas State Board of Education, 1979), such statements provide a basis for planning for instruction. These general goal statements, generated from the three sources of curriculum, are "sifted" through educational philosophy and educational psychology screens to produce instructional objectives expressed in more precise terms.

The screens, educational philosophy and the psychology of learning become filters through which the general goals pass. Tanner and Tanner (1987) note that "How these sources and influences [on the curriculum] are seen and acted on is determined by the philosophy of the professional staff" (p. 342). How does a teacher's philosophy of education or view of learning influence what will be included in the curriculum (ends) and how it will be taught (means)? The philosophy screen becomes important because it gives meaning and direction to actions taken by teachers regarding the curriculum. According to Wiles and Bondi (1984), "few educators hold a pure version of any of these philosophies. . . . Whatever the educator's philosophy or beliefs about schools, . . . it is critical that these values be clarified and understood in terms of their implications" (p. 79).

a. *Philosophies of education.* Ultimately, the philosophy governs the way in which we view the student, the scope (what) and sequence (when) of the curriculum, and the methodology used to teach the curriculum (Reinhartz, 1980). How teachers handle specific situations in a classroom will also reveal their educational philosophy (Ornstein and Levine, 1984). If teachers are not aware of the impact of their educational philosophy on classroom instruction, teachers may be vulnerable to externally imposed societal pressures, which may be fashionable at a given time but are not necessarily educationally sound.

The nature of the three sources of curriculum (values of society, needs of students, and the subject matter) should be examined in the light of educational philosophies. Entire books and courses examine the development and implications of educational philosophies in great detail. Our purpose here is to describe briefly three major philosophies and to show how they are used as a screen in the Tyler curriculum development model. Three widely accepted educational philosophies—essentialism, progressivism, and existentialism—give direction and focus to the general goals and objectives of the curriculum. As a result, these three philosophies have shaped American education (Ornstein and Levine, 1987).

The *essentialist* philosophy, a combination of idealism and realism, has several basic tenets, including support for the liberal arts— English, mathematics, science, history, foreign languages, and other traditional subjects. Essentialists believe that the curriculum is timeless and that, in the pursuit of basic truths, the intellect should be cultivated through "permanent" studies. According to Wilds and Lottich (1970):

> While . . . significant variations in philosophy existed among the essentialists, they are as one in prescribing the following rubrics for their educational programs:

1. a fixed curriculum;
2. certain minimum "essentials": literature, mathematics, history, and so on;
3. preconceived educational values;
4. education as individual adaptation to an absolute knowledge which exists independently of individuals. (p. 504)

The performing arts, industrial arts, vocational studies, and physical education are considered frills, or nonessentials. Educators holding the essentialist view believe that the school's main purpose is to equip students with intellectual powers. For them, the students' interests are secondary to the pursuit of academic excellence and the purpose of school is to teach basic skills through a uniform curriculum. Learning is measured by rigorous testing and, as a result, students are "sorted" (ability-grouped) based on the test results.

The second philosophy, *progressivism,* has a basis in experimentalism and pragmatism and views people as thinking beings who are capable of solving social problems. Progressivism, then, is an action-oriented philosophy that "sees thought as intrinsically connected with action. The value of an idea is measured by the consequences [results] produced when it is translated into action" (Rosen, 1968, p. 67). The architect of progressivism, also known as pragmatism, was Dewey (1902, 1906), who defined *experience* as the students' interaction with the environment and believed that the purpose of education is to cultivate problem-solving skills. According to this philosophy, schools, like society, require social interaction. Learning for the pragmatist is thus an active process in which all students participate. The learning environment is child-centered, and the teacher serves as a guide or project director.

For the progressive educator, experience is the best source of knowledge and, indeed, knowledge is gained only by means of experience. Therefore, progressives, according to Ikenberry (1974), are also pragmatists and experimentalists; as such, they subscribe to the following principles:

1. [People] can discover reality only through experience.
2. Since experience reveals that [people] society, and the universe are in a state of constant change there can be no absolute and permanent knowledge.
3. The mind of [individuals] enable [them] to think, to reason, to adjust to his environment, and to solve problems.
4. The scientific method should be used as the basis for problem solving.

> 5. Values change in a changing society. What is considered valu-
>   able today may be worthless tomorrow. Ethical values are
>   never universal because societies differ. . . .
> 6. Experimentalism as a philosophy recognizes change and prog-
>   ress in a democratic society. (p. 206)

For the progressive, then, education uses the scientific method
(identify problem, hypothesize, experiment, collect data, and draw
conclusions) to solve social problems. Thus the progressive teacher
tends to use an inductive approach to learning. Education involves a
series of process experiences in which students find themselves.
Using the scientific method, students can see problems and devise
methods for their solutions.

The third philosophy is *existentialism*. Tenets of this philosophy
include the view that individuals exist in a world in which they are
required to make choices within the context of the "anguish of freedom." It is through the choices individuals make that they give meaning to their lives and discover their personal worth and capabilities.
Individuals determine their destiny by the choices or decisions they
make. For the existentialist, the purpose of school is to help students
identify their strengths and weaknesses, and the goal of education is
to help each student achieve self-development and self-fulfillment. As
Ikenberry (1974) states:

> According to the existentialist, the school should not establish
> preconceived aims for the student. . . . The educational process
> should attempt:
> 1. To make each student aware of the meaning of life for himself
>   [or herself]
> 2. To encourage each student to develop his [or her] own ethical
>   value system and philosophy of life
> 3. To assist the student to recognize his [or her] own areas of
>   strength and weakness, and then develop his [or her] abilities
>   to their maximum potential
> 4. To impress on the student that freedom for decision making
>   requires him [or her] to accept a corresponding responsibility
>   for his [or her] decisions. (p. 219–220)

The existentialist would not advocate a structured curriculum,
because, in existentialism, little attention is given to systematic learning. The arts, literature, and social studies are included in the curriculum; however, they do not exist as a rigid course of study. When

existentialist ideas are implemented in a school, they take various forms, from totally student-run programs such as A. S. Neill's (1960) Summerhill School, to the use of individualized programs that utilize learning packets or learning centers. The teacher functions as a facilitator who guides students in making choices, thereby helping them to develop the confidence to think for themselves. Existential thought allows the student to search for personal identity and meaningfulness. Existentialists perceive science as cold and without morality; in an attempt to avoid science, the existentialist often confuses scientific thought with the political misuse of that thought and its products. For the existentialist, the use of nuclear power, which is a product of science, would not be justified because of the potential harm to people.

Tanner and Tanner (1987) summarize the influence of educational philosophy on practice when they state that

> the philosophy one subscribes to determines the uses to which the behavioral sciences are put in connection with (1) the nature of the learner, (2) the nature of society, and (3) the design of the curriculum. (p. 344)

Figure 6.2 provides an overview of each educational philosophy and outlines the implications on practice in classrooms. Using the philosophical tenets identified in Figure 6.2, supervisors and teachers can examine instructional goals filtered through educational philosophy. They can then seek to determine which of the conflicting views regarding the nature of the learner seems most helpful and, based on their findings, establish the type of educational experiences the curriculum should provide.

b. *A psychology of learning.* A psychology of learning serves as the second screen for the general goals of the curriculum. Many, if not most, of the things teachers do in their classrooms can be traced to a specific theory of learning. This second screen helps answer the questions "How do students learn best?" and "Are the goals appropriate for the level of the students?" While space does not allow for a complete overview of learning theories, two major areas of study or theories of learning are presented as examples of how this screen operates in the Tyler rationale. Two major fields of study regarding how students learn are the S-R (stimulus-response) theory, or behavi-

Philosophic Concepts

Educational Views

	Ontology[a]	Epistemology[b]	Axiology[c] Ethics	Axiology[c] Aesthetics		The Learner	The Teacher	The Curriculum	The Method	Social Policy
Idealism	A world of mind	Truth as idea	The imitation of the Absolute Self	The reflection of the Ideal	Essentialism	Learner as microcosmic mind	Teacher as paradigmatic self	Subject matter of symbol and idea (literature, history, etc.)	Absorbing ideas	The "trailing edge": Conserve the heritage
Realism	A world of things	Truth as observable fact	The law of nature	The reflection of nature	Essentialism	Learner as sense mechanism	Teacher as demonstrator	Subject matter of the physical world (mathematics, the sciences, etc.)	Mastering facts and information	The "trailing edge": Transmit settled knowledge
Experimentalism	A world of experience	Truth as what works	The public test	The public taste	Progressivism	Learner as experiencing organism	Teacher as research-project director	Subject matter of social world (social studies, projects, problems, etc.)	Problem-solving	The "growing edge": Teach how to manage change / Reconstructionism: The "Utopian Future"—Teach to reconstruct the social order
Existentialism	A world of existing	Truth as existential choice	The anguish of freedom	The revolt from the public norm	Existentialism	Learner as ultimate chooser	Teacher as provocateur of the self	Subject matter of choice (the arts, moral philosophy, ethics)	Finding the self	?

[a] *Ontology.* Seeks to answer "What is real?" to determine ultimate reality.
[b] *Epistemology.* Seeks to answer "How do we know?" to determine the truth.
[c] *Axiology.* Seeks to answer "What is of value?" Is composed of ethics (which provide guidelines for individuals to use to make life decisions) and aesthics (which determine what is beauty and art).

oristic learning theory, and the cognitive-field, or Gestalt-field, theory.

According to the *S-R theory,* or *behaviorism,* people learn through a conditioning process in which correct or approximately correct answers are reinforced. The reinforcement strengthens the bond between the "stimulus" (question or problem) and the "response" (answer or solution). As students practice or learn the task, each correct response they make is followed by reinforcement, so that appropriate behavior is encouraged or rewarded. In many classrooms, learning follows this mode and many activities tend to be confined to the lower end of Bloom's (1956) taxonomy of the cognitive domain (that is, recall and comprehension). According to Bigge (1982), within the S-R/behaviorist theory:

> Learning is considered nonpurposive habit formation. . . . Thus . . . learning is a more or less permanent change of behavior that occurs as a result of conditioning. . . . Consequently, the problem of the nature of the learning process is centered in a study of the relationships of processions of stimuli and responses and what occurs between them. (pp. 88–89)

Examples of classroom applications of the S-R/behaviorist learning theory include the use of the following:

1. assertive discipline (reinforcing/rewarding appropriate behavior with treats or free time)
2. behavior modification techniques (reinforcing appropriate behavior with praise)
3. questioning techniques (using many recall questions—informational or factual—that have a high degree of success)
4. computer-assisted instruction or CAI (using computers to provide questions, verifications of responses, and sometimes reinforcement)
5. motivational strategies (using rewards for students who complete instructional tasks)

The *cognitive-field,* or *Gestalt-field,* approach to learning is another theory of how students learn. The field theorist approach to learning takes into account the learner's attitudes, values, experiences, and interests and proceeds from whole to part. For Bigge (1982),

the key word of the Gestalt-field psychologists in describing learning is *insight.* They regard learning as a process of developing new
insights or changing old ones. . . . The noun learning denotes the
new insights or meanings that are acquired. (p. 96)

For the field theorists, the result (learning) is influenced by the
stimulus as well as by the sum total of what the person brings to
the learning situation. Reinforcements are not necessarily a part of
the learning process.

There are certainly classroom applications for cognitive-field, or
Gestalt-field, psychology. For example, problem solving is emphasized; mistakes are seen as opportunities to learn; unit planning is
encouraged; self-concept activities are used; and teacher questions
focus on higher-order cognitive skills (such as application, analysis,
synthesis, and evaluation).

After studying the three sources of curriculum, the general
goals of education, and the two screens, or filters through which these
goals are viewed, supervisors arrive at the final step in the Tyler
rationale—the identification of specific instructional objectives. Having taken into account all the information they have obtained, supervisors can now help teachers develop precise instructional objectives
that are incorporated into the unit planning process and that become
the central focus of each daily lesson plan.

Reducing Goals to Instructional Objectives   Writing and selecting
instructional objectives is the final step in the Tyler curriculum development rationale. The formulation of specific objectives, often called
instructional or *behavioral objectives,* clarifies and gives direction to
the general goals of education. "An instructional objective is an opera-
tionalized and evidential statement of an educational goal" (Beach,
Ryan, and Funkhouser, 1979, p. 41). Within the Tyler curriculum
framework, the general goals are translated into specific learning
outcomes which become the central focus for planning instructional
units and daily lessons, selecting strategies and activities, and developing assessment or evaluation procedures.

It is during this final step that teachers become the most directly
involved in the curriculum development process. More specifically,
this involvement occurs when teachers are asked to write precise
instructional objectives for their classrooms based on general goals.
Reducing goals to precise instructional objectives is a complex pro-

Goals for Public School Education

Student Development

The public schools should help each student to develop personal knowledge, skills, and competence to maximum capacity, and to learn behavior patterns which will make each a responsible member of society. In terms of their individual ability, all students should achieve:

(1) Intellectual Discipline
  (A) Competence in the traditionally accepted fundamentals of reading, writing, and arithmetic in the early elementary grades, accompanied by studies in higher mathematics, science, history, free enterprise system, English and other languages, as they progress through the upper grades. These should be accompanied by a wide variety of optional courses.
  (B) Skill in the logical processes of search, analysis, evaluation, and problem solving.
  (C) Competence and motivation for continuing self-evaluation, self-instruction, and adaptation to changing environment.
  (D) Competence in reading, communication, and other language arts skills according to grade level and individual ability.

(2) Economic and Occupational Competence
  (A) Knowledge of the fundamental economic structure and processes of the American system, of the contributions of free enterprise, and of opportunities for individual participation and success in the system.
  (B) Occupational skills prerequisite to enter and advance in the economic system and/or academic preparation for acquisition of technical or professional skills through post-high school training.
  (C) Competence in the application of economic knowledge to practical economic functions such as planning and budgeting for the investment of personal income, calculating tax obligations, financing major purchases, and obtaining desirable employment.

(3) Citizenship and Political Understanding and Competence.
  (A) Knowledge about the United States and Texas systems of government and their political subdivisions.
  (B) Competence in judging the merits of comparative political systems and ideologies with emphasis on democratic institutions, the American heritage, the responsibilities and privileges of citizenship, and the comparative merits of candidates for political position.
  (C) Skills for communicating with public officials at different levels of government.
  (D) Skills for participating in the processes of public and private political organizations and for influencing decisions made by such organizations.

(4) Physical and Environmental Health, Ecological Balance, and Safety
  (A) Knowledge about the requirements of personal hygiene, nutritional consumption, and physical exercise essential to the maintenance of personal health. Knowledge about the dangers to health from addiction to harmful practices or consumption of harmful materials.

Example:

1. State the Goal from list above—(3) Citizenship and Political Understanding and Competence. (B) Competence in judging the merits of political systems and ideologies with emphasis on democratic institutions, the American heritage, the responsibilities and privileges of citizenship, and the comparative merits of candidates for political position.

2. State the Content Area Responsible—The general content areas of the social studies claim responsibility for assisting individuals in developing qualities of good citizenship, especially the use of rational decision-making as a means of approaching the election of a political candidate.

3. State the Course or Grade Level Responsible—One of the objectives of high school civics or government classes is to help students recognize bias and emotional reasoning in materials produced by candidates for political office.

4. State the Instructional Objective—When given a copy of campaign materials developed by local candidates, the student will underline statements of fact and circle generalizations not supported by facts.

Figure 6.3 Reducing goals to instructional objectives. (*Source:* Texas State Board of Education. [1979]. *Goals for public education in Texas.* Texas Education Agency, GEO 402 05. Austin: TEA Publications Office.)

cess that requires knowledge not only about the goals but also about the subject matter and learner. Figure 6.3 shows the goal reduction process using a general goal statement from the "Goals for Public Education in Texas" (Texas State Board of Education, 1979).

The first decision a teacher makes in reducing goals to instructional objectives concerns what students will be expected to learn each day of each unit during the school year. The fundamental question that the teacher must answer is, "What do I want the students to know or be able to do following instruction?" To make this decision, the teacher needs to decide on the scope and sequence for the course by determining the essential concepts and skills to be learned every six weeks. By writing instructional objectives, the teacher articulates, in great detail, the specific behaviors the students will be expected to exhibit or demonstrate. Then the teacher can develop an appropriate sequence, or order, for the objectives.

According to Mager (1962), instructional objectives describe observable or measurable behaviors that are to be demonstrated by each learner. In addition to behaviors that are measurable, instructional objectives include a condition under which the behavior will occur, such as on an exam or in the lab. A third criterion to include when writing instructional objectives is a minimal level of performance, which is often expressed as "correctly" or as a percentage correct (for instance, 80 percent correct). Using the Magerian technique of listing precise measurable or observable behavior, the condition under which the behavior will take place, and a level of acceptable performance ensures that the teacher has a clear understanding of what the student is expected to do and what the teacher will need to do to accomplish the objective.

Once instructional objectives are written, they can be classified according to specific levels and domains of learning. The classification system, or taxonomy, provides a way to categorize or evaluate instructional objectives. The learning outcomes can be classified into three domains of learning: cognitive, affective, and psychomotor.

Objectives written in the *cognitive domain* involve intellectual skills that range from remembering or reproducing material that has been learned, to higher-order thinking skills such as reasoning, problem solving, and synthesizing and evaluating ideas and materials. According to the *Taxonomy of Educational Objectives. Handbook I: Cognitive Domain* (Bloom et al., 1956), cognitive objectives can be assessed by moving from simple behaviors to more complex behaviors using the following levels:

1. knowledge—recalling previously learned material or factual information
2. comprehension—translating information from one form to another without fully understanding implications
3. application—using information or abstractions (rules, laws, principles, theories) in new or concrete situations
4. analysis—dissecting or breaking down information or material into smaller component parts so that structure and relationships can be seen
5. synthesis—putting elements or components together to form or create a new entity (such as a book, speech, painting, musical score)
6. evaluation—judging material or information according to external criteria provided or internal criteria that the individual derives

The *affective domain* emphasizes values, feelings, and attitudes; relevant behavior ranges from simply paying attention, to personal actions that are consistent with a set of values. According to Krathwohl and others (1964), the affective domain can be assessed using the following hierarchy:

1. receiving—is sensitive to external stimuli and pays attention to the stimuli
2. responding—is involved with, and reacts or responds to, the stimuli
3. valuing—appreciates or values a particular object, phenomenon, or behavior
4. organizing—internalizes values and develops a value system that helps guide or shape behavior
5. characterizes by a value—consistently operates or behaves according to a value system

The *psychomotor domain* stresses muscular or motor skill that requires neuromuscular coordination. Bloom, Krathwohl, and their associates developed an early version of the levels of this domain, but Harrow (1972) has revised the earlier work and developed the following levels:

1. reflex movements—involuntary movements that begin at birth and continue to maturation and include such behaviors as flinching or ducking when an object is thrown
2. fundamental movements—inherent movement patterns,

such as crawling or swaying, which become a part of more specialized and complex movements

3. perceptual abilities—integration of physical and mental abilities, such as the neuromuscular response of catching a ball
4. physical abilities—behaviors such as strength, endurance, and agility, which, as they develop, can provide a sound, efficient body to conduct skilled movements
5. skilled movements—movements, such as dance steps or sports skills, that are complex and require learning through practice
6. nondiscursive communication—behaviors that range from facial expressions to dance choreographies and incorporate all previously learned behaviors to communicate

These domains of learning and the levels within each domain give supervisors and teachers a framework for examining instructional objectives. For Smith (1975), each unit or topic should have objectives in each of the three domains, and these objectives should be written for different levels of the domains. Instructional supervisors can assist teachers in planning instruction by helping them see the need to incorporate within the curriculum multiple levels of the different domains of learning.

TASK ANALYSIS

Once the instructional objectives have been developed and analyzed according to domain and level, the next step in the curriculum planning process is for the supervisor and teacher to conduct a task analysis, or task detailing, for each objective. A *task analysis* involves examining the prescribed student behavior indicated in the objective and identifying prerequisite skills. This procedure helps teachers decide on the appropriate learning activities, the necessary teaching behaviors, and the best evaluation procedures, including test material.

Supervisors can help teachers conduct a task analysis. The question is, "How can supervisors help teachers get from stating an objective to teaching the material appropriate to that objective?" Suppose, for instance, that, as an instructional supervisor, you have detected some difficulty in the science curriculum and the teacher has asked you for assistance in the preparation of a lesson on reptiles. What would you do to help this teacher develop the lesson? Figure

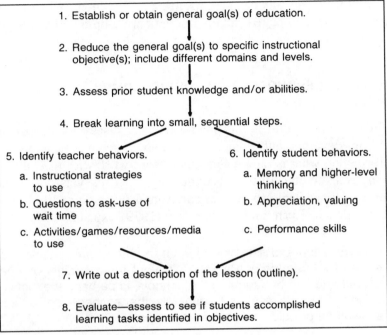

Figure 6.4 The task analysis process.

6.4 illustrates the task analysis process and the steps that supervisors can use in working with teachers in the development and implementation of curriculum content.

You might begin the task analysis by having the teacher state the objectives for the lesson and then reviewing those objectives with the teacher to make sure that different cognitive levels are included as well as other domains and levels. Next, focus on each objective and have the teacher identify any prior knowledge, experience, or skills that would be needed in order for the objective to be accomplished. Have the teacher establish a starting point for teaching the lesson—what should be done first, second, and so on. Ask the teacher to specify what materials and activities will be used to teach the concept or information. Now have the teacher write out what would be included in the lesson presentation. If a narrative description of the lesson is too cumbersome, have the teacher prepare an outline of the lesson that contains the major steps and activities. Finally, help the teacher think through a process for determining if the students have accomplished the objective(s) for the lesson. Perhaps the teacher could (1) have the students summarize the main points of the lesson by writing a single paragraph, (2) play a game in which students, either individually or in teams, are asked to identify key material from the lesson, or (3) call on students at random and ask questions related to the lesson for the day.

ADDITIONAL RESOURCES FOR CURRICULUM PLANNING

The focus of the chapter to this point has been a discussion of various curriculum development models that employ a systematic approach in determining what is taught. As supervisors work with teachers in reducing goals to objectives and conducting a task analysis, additional resources are available to help in curriculum planning and development. As Beach, Ryan, and Funkhouser (1979) explain:

> Consideration and selection of what to teach from . . . the vast store of knowledge available . . . [given] the restraints of what should and can be taught in the schools, is perhaps the highest calling of the . . . teacher. Fortunately, the teacher is not without assistance or guidance in this endeavor. (p. 37)

As indicated earlier in the chapter, one of the first decisions teachers make in the curriculum development process is the determination of scope and sequence. According to Saylor and Alexander (1954):

> By scope is meant the breadth, variety and types of educational experiences that are to be provided pupils as they progress through the school program. Scope . . . may be thought of as the "what" of the curriculum. . . . By sequence is meant the order in which educational experiences are developed with pupils. Sequence refers to the "when" in curriculum planning. (pp. 248–249)

Scope and sequence charts are often available from the district, the state department of education, or from the textbook publisher. Figure 6.5 is an example of a scope and sequence chart developed by a publisher to show the treatment of science concepts through the elementary grades. Such charts vary in degree of specificity but do provide some direction that can be useful in curriculum development and planning. Supervisors can assist teachers by helping them develop a scope and sequence outline that is divided into the units that are included in every six-week reporting period.

DISTRIBUTION OF ENVIRONMENTAL SCIENCE TOPICS AMONG LEVELS K–SIX
OF THE SILVER BURDETT ELEMENTARY SCIENCE PROGRAM

Environmental Science Topics	Levels						
	K	One	Two	Three	Four	Five	Six
The Biological Sciences							
The living world		X		X	X		X
Plants	X	X		X	X	X	
Animals	X	X	X	X	X	X	X
Human growth and development		X	X		X	X	X
The Earth Sciences							
The earth and its resources	X	X		X		X	
Atom	X		X		X		X
Water and oceanography			X		X		X
Weather	X		X		X	X	X
The universe and space science	X	X		X		X	X
The Physical Sciences							
Matter and energy		X		X		X	X
Sound	X	X		X		X	
Machines and work	X	X		X	X	X	
Heat and light	X		X		X		X
Magnetism and electricity	X		X		X		X

(NOTE: Because of the interdisciplinary nature of science, no attempt has been made to categorize these topics rigidly. The chart merely indicates the level at which major emphasis is placed on the basic topics.)

Figure 6.5 A representative scope and sequence chart. (*Source:* Mallinson, G. B., et al. [1975]. *Science: Understanding your environment* [Teacher's ed.], p. 26. Morristown, N.J.: Silver Burdett. Used with permission.)

Curriculum guides are another helpful tool in the curriculum development process. A *curriculum guide,* sometimes called a *course syllabus,* is a document that describes in detail the material to be covered for specific content areas for a specific grade level or subject area. Curriculum guides may also include the objectives that are to be mastered within each area and grade level. Figure 6.6 is a typical example of a district curriculum guide for elementary mathematics, showing a continuum of skills at two levels—1 and 16. Often the curriculum guides are written by the local school district or by the state department of education to assist teachers in planning for instruction.

Finally, another planning aid that supervisors have available to

Elementary School

Continuum of Math Concepts and Skills

Level 1

1. Identifies sets concretely and semiconcretely
2. Compares sets in terms of properties of the elements, such as color, size, and shape
3. Uses the term *elements* to refer to the members of a set
4. Identifies equivalent and nonequivalent sets by matching elements in one-to-one correspondence
5. Uses the terms *more than* and *fewer than* to express the relationship between nonequivalent sets
6. Constructs sets having one more element or one fewer element than a given set
7. Recognizes that sets which can be matched one-to-one have the same number property
8. Matches sets and numbers 0 through 10
9. Recognizes the set with no elements as the empty set
10. Uses the terms *greater than* and *less than* when comparing the number property of sets
11. Completes number sentences expressing inequalities by writing the symbols $>$ and $<$ with numbers to 10
12. Matches sets and points on a number line so that the cardinality of set and the coordinate of the point are equal
13. Writes the numerals in order from 0 to 10

Level 16

1. Visualizes and identifies space figures, such as a cube, triangular prism, rectangular prism, and pyramid, all of which are formed by the union of four or more planes
2. Finds the volume of a cube and a rectangular prism
3. Computes the surface area of a cube or a rectangular prism
4. Multiplies a whole number by a fractional number
5. Multiplies a fractional number by a fractional number
6. Multiplies a mixed number by a whole number
7. Multiplies a fractional number by a mixed number
8. Multiplies a mixed number by a mixed number
9. Uses the commutative and associative properties with multiplication of fractions
10. Finds the reciprocal of any nonzero fractional number
11. Divides with fractional numbers by multiplying by the divisor's reciprocal
12. Develops an intuitive understanding of what a decimal fraction is
13. Reads and writes decimal numerals through hundredths
14. Uses the $>$ and $<$ symbols for comparison of decimal fractions
15. Adds and subtracts decimal fractions through hundredths
16. Multiplies decimal fractions using tenths, hundredths, and whole numbers
17. Develops a concept of probability intuitively with frequent reference to objects, such as flipping coins, choosing cards, etc.
18. Compares the number of ways one could make the choice desires with the total set of choices by writing a fraction
19. Uses 1 to indicate that something is a certainty
20. Uses 0 to indicate that something cannot happen

Figure 6.6 A representative curriculum guide. (*Source:* Adapted from Fort Worth Independent School District. [1970]. *Mathematics continuum of concepts and skills: Elementary school and middle school.* Curriculum Bulletin No. 240, pp. 3, 18.)

them as they work with teachers is the resource unit. The *resource unit* is a collection of suggested materials, activities, procedures, and, sometimes, objectives that teachers can use in planning to teach a given unit or topic. This collection of ideas may be developed locally at the district level by supervisors and teachers, but, most often, it takes the form of the teacher's edition of the textbook. Figure 6.7 is an example of the type of information that is often provided in a

Chapter 25 Oceans as a Resource

Concepts: The oceans can supply water for human use if salt is removed from the water. The oceans contain a supply of dissolved minerals from the earth's crust.

Instructional Objectives
The student will be able—

- To classify ocean water as a mixture rather than as a compound.
- To classify the processes of salt removal as physical changes, not as chemical changes.
- To analyze the processes involved in desalting in terms of changes in the state of water and to describe the involvement of heat energy in these changes.

Lesson Materials
Step 3: See list in text, p. 305.
**Extension: Clear glass bowl; 2 shallow dishes or pans, one with a diameter larger than that of the bowl, the other with a diameter smaller than that of the bowl; salt water.

Lesson Capsule
(p. 302–top p. 307)
Time Allotment: Three periods
1. The picture on this page shows one of the ways in which humans use water. Ask students to tell about fountains or pools of water they have seen.
   The caption states that this water is being used for beautification. Ask if this is an important use of water. Beauty is an important factor in human life. Have the class discuss the difference between essential uses of water and important uses of water.

Figure 6.7 A representative resource unit. (*Source:* Mallinson, G. B., et al. [1975]. *Science: Understanding your environment* [Teacher's ed.], p. 26. Morristown, N.J.: Silver Burdett. Used with permission.)

teacher's edition of a textbook. As indicated in Figure 6.7, many textbook publishers provide a wealth of information and suggestions for teaching different units or topics.

The role of the instructional supervisor is critical in the curriculum development and planning stages that occur prior to classroom instruction. By helping teachers incorporate in their repertoire the suggestions presented here, the supervisor can promote a systematic approach to curriculum development. Supervisors, using the different models and resources identified in this chapter, can be more effective in promoting comprehensive planning prior to instruction. For some teachers, this is a significant step in their professional development.

SUMMARY

Curriculum development is a dynamic and complex process that is subject to many variables. The chapter begins by offering several definitions of *curriculum,* including the definition that views knowledge and content as the foundations for effective learning. Effective instruction requires comprehensive and detailed planning. Three models of curriculum development are discussed. The Taba model advocates the use of an eight-step guide to unit development. The

Ohio State Department of Education model is a more recent approach to curriculum planning. The Tyler rationale deals with classroom curriculum development in a highly systematic way. In this chapter, the Tyler model is presented as a means of helping teachers answer the question "Where does curriculum come from?" Curriculum decisions are often made at the classroom level, so there is a need for teachers to understand what curriculum is, where it comes from, and how it affects instruction. The Tyler model provides a schema for making decisions about the purposes of education and translating the purposes into curriculum goals and instructional objectives that ultimately guide daily instruction.

As a planning model, the Tyler rationale considers the origin and purpose of what is taught and the philosophical and psychological questions regarding the learner and the nature of the content. It provides a vehicle for identifying and writing precise instructional objectives. This model encourages the instructional supervisor to examine the relationship that exists between curriculum development, the process of planning for instruction, and teaching—that is, the implementation of the plans.

The values of society regarding what to teach and how to teach it provides the first data source. Two other data sources, students' needs and recommendations from subject matter specialists, also help determine what is taught in school and how it is taught. Students themselves serve as a valuable source of information and subject matter specialists also influence the curriculum development process. All three sources have a profound effect on determining the general goals of a school system.

The philosophies of education and a psychology of learning serve as screens that supervisors and teachers can use in filtering the goals of education and interpreting them for the classroom. Educational philosophies help to guide the selection of the goals that seem most viable and of the implementation process to attain those goals. Supervisors and teachers must be aware that a philosophical view ultimately determines what happens instructionally in the classroom. A psychology of learning also provides a framework for developing goals and practices. The use of a range of learning theories, from a behavioristic approach to a cognitive-field psychology, guides teacher instructional and managerial behavior.

Supervisors can assist teachers in the curriculum planning process by conducting a task analysis once the instructional objectives have been written. Other materials that can be used in the curriculum development process include scope and sequence charts, curriculum guides, and resource units or guides. These materials can be valuable tools for the supervisor to use with teachers who are having difficulty in articulating learner behaviors and planning appropriate activities to accomplish the objectives.

YOUR TURN

6.1. You are working with a new teacher who is assigned to four government classes. One of the goals of schools has been to foster the development of good citizenship. The school district is trying to emphasize character education in light of the many news stories, court cases, and investigations involving insider trading on Wall Street, lying by public servants to cover up damaging information or activities, and abuses of power that have occurred in business and government. The goal of "good citizenship," when incorporated into the school curriculum, is to strengthen a student's sense of civic responsibility. The novice teacher does not have any notion of how to incorporate the goal into the curriculum and is in fact nervous about the potentially controversial nature of the topic. What steps could you, as an instructional supervisor, take to assist this teacher in incorporating this goal into his or her government curriculum? First, suggest that the teacher go through the steps of goal reduction to determine appropriate objectives for this particular topic and goal. As you go through the process outlined in *a, b,* and *c* here, write out each response as if you were helping the teacher develop the information.

   a. To assist the teacher in taking this goal and reducing it to observable or measurable objectives, you prepare an example that lists several subgoals related to fostering good citizenship. After the subgoals are identified, you "reduce" them to objectives that suggest specific tasks or behaviors to be performed by students. These tasks are designed to show that the subgoals have been achieved by the students.

   b. In order to define the responsibilities of both the teacher and students, compile a list that you could share with the teacher that identifies the conditions under which the tasks or behaviors will be performed.

   c. To complete the model, suggest to the teacher two objectives at different levels of the cognitive domain and one objective each for the affective and the psychomotor domains.

6.2. Refer to the Tyler rationale for curriculum development (Figure 6.1). You are working with a teacher who is excellent, but who views the curriculum as only what is defined in the district's curriculum guide and included in the textbook. You have asked this teacher to develop additional curriculum for his or her subject area but the teacher does not feel comfortable and is reluctant to participate. You ask the teacher to use the Tyler rationale as a beginning point. To ensure that the teacher understands how the rationale works, you prepare an example using the topic of health education. Write out your example as you would present it to the teacher as a sample to use in the curriculum development process.

6.3. According to the author J. Abner Pediwell (*Saber-Tooth Curriculum,* McGraw-Hill, 1939), the first school was established in Paleolithic times to teach fish-grabbing, tiger-scaring, and horse-clubbing. Paleolithic society believed that

> the essence of true education is timelessness. It is something that endures through changing conditions like a solid rock standing squarely and firmly in the middle of a raging torrent. You must know there are some *Eternal Verities,* and the Saber-Tooth Curriculum is one of them. (pp. 43–44)

  a. Do you believe that there are eternal truths in education? Why or why not? If you believe that there are, what do you consider them to be?
  b. What philosophy of education does your response to question *a* support?

6.4. You are the elementary/secondary consultant in mathematics and you have been appointed to the districtwide curriculum committee. The charge to the committee is to write a mathematics curriculum guide for primary grades (K–3 if elementary) or grades 7 and 8 (if secondary). Before you begin this task, you examine several other guides (certainly at least one in detail) to be sure that your new guide will include all the essential elements of a mathematics curriculum, especially a manipulative approach to mathematics instruction. Your task is to become an expert in evaluating curriculum guides so that you will be more proficient at writing one for your own district. As you go through the review process, here are some questions to answer:

  a. Can you ascertain the educational philosophy that permeates the objectives and activities? If so, what is it?
  b. Was the guide written for the appropriate student population or grade level? Give reasons for your response.
  c. What political, social, economic, and local community forces (if any) seem to have influenced the scope and sequence of the curriculum guide?
  d. Are objectives included? If so are they clearly stated? Are the objectives appropriate and comprehensive for the math curriculum? Give reasons for your response.
  e. Are teaching/learning strategies or activities listed? Does the curric-

ulum guide emphasize direct experiences and purposeful learning activities? Explain your answer.

  f. Are evaluation procedures listed to help assess student learning and progress toward accomplishment of objectives?

6.5. Based on the following descriptions of three school programs, determine what the dominant philosophy operating in each school is and write a brief rationale for your choice.

  a. At the Strawberry Hill School, we view each student as "a lamp to be lighted, not a vessel to be filled." We realize that each student is an individual. Therefore, the primary objective at Strawberry Hill is self-development, self-fulfillment, and self-realization.

  b. At the University Academy, we stress the great ideas from literature and history. We have few frills here in the way of competitive sports or vocational programs. We take great pride in the ability of our students, their motivation, their ability to articulate thoughts both in spoken language and in written work, and their admission to the finest universities.

  c. At Rosemont School, we stress the practical nature of an education to equip students to solve problems, particularly social problems. Therefore, we emphasize the scientific method and those areas of the curriculum that encourage students to analyze situations and find solutions to problems.

REFERENCES

Beach, D., Ryan, G. T., and Funkhouser, C. W. (1979). *Applications of the learning process: A laboratory approach.* Dubuque, Iowa: Kendall/Hunt.

Bigge, M. L. (1982). *Learning theories for teachers.* New York: Harper & Row.

Bloom, B. S., et al. (1956). *Taxonomy of educational objectives. Handbook I: Cognitive domain.* New York: McKay.

Dewey, J. (1902). *The child and the curriculum.* Chicago: University of Chicago Press.

Dewey, J. (1906). *Democracy and education.* New York: Macmillan.

Funkhouser, C. W., et al. (1981). *Classroom applications of the curriculum: A systems approach.* Dubuque, Iowa: Kendall/Hunt.

Harrow, A. J. (1972). *Taxonomy of the psychomotor domain: A guide for developing behavioral objectives.* New York: Mckay.

Ikenberry, O. S. (1974). *American education foundations: An introduction.* Columbus, Ohio: Charles E. Merrill.

Krathwohl, D. R., et al. (1964). *Taxonomy of educational objectives. Handbook II: Affective domain.* New York: McKay.

Mager, R. F. (1962). *Preparing instructional objectives.* Palo Alto, Calif.: Feron Publishers.

Neill, A. S. (1960). *Summerhill.* New York: Hart.

Ohio State Department of Education Model (1980). Columbus: State Department of Education.

Ornstein, A. C., and Levine, D. U. (1984). *An introduction to the foundations of education* (2nd ed.). Boston: Houghton Mifflin.

Ornstein, A. C., and Levine, D. U. (1987). *An introduction to the foundations of education* (3rd ed.). Boston: Houghton Mifflin.

Pfeiffer, I. L., and Dunlap, J. B. (1982). *Supervision of teachers: A guide to improving instruction.* Phoenix: Oryx Press.

Popham, W. J., and Baker, E. L. (1970). *Establishing instructional goals.* Englewood Cliffs, N.J.: Prentice-Hall.

Reinhartz, J. (1980). Stemming the tide: A case against spontaneous curriculum generation. *Kappan, 10,* 2, 6–8.

Rosen, B. (1968). *Philosophic systems and education.* Columbus, Ohio: Charles E. Merrill.

Saylor, J. G., and Alexander, W. M. (1954). *Curriculum planning for better teaching and learning.* New York: Holt, Rinehart and Winston.

Sergiovanni, T. J., and Starratt, R. J. (1983). *Supervision: Human perspectives* (3rd ed.). New York: McGraw-Hill.

Smith, M. D. (1975). *Educational psychology and its classroom applications.* Boston: Allyn and Bacon.

Taba, H. (1962). *Curriculum development: Theory and practice.* New York: Harcourt, Brace and World.

Tanner, D., and Tanner, L. (1980). *Curriculum development: Theory into practice.* New York: Macmillan.

Tanner, D., and Tanner, L. (1987). *Supervision in education: Problems and practices.* New York: Macmillan.

Texas State Board of Education (1979). *Goals for public education in Texas.* Austin: Texas Education Agency.

Tyler, R. (1949). *Basic principles of curriculum and instruction.* Chicago: University of Chicago Press.

Wilds, E. H., and Lottich, K. V. (1970). *The foundations of modern education* (4th ed.). New York: Holt, Rinehart and Winston.

Wiles, J., and Bondi, J. C. (1984). *Curriculum development: A guide to practice* (2nd ed.). Columbus, Ohio: Charles E. Merrill.

chapter 7

Teaching: Lesson Implementation

As described in the previous chapter, the hallmark of good teaching is planning, and lesson planning involves a series of systematic decisions made by the teacher prior to delivering instruction. As supervisors work with teachers in establishing priorities for instruction, a continuous series of decisions are made about the learners, the objectives to be accomplished, the learning task, the method of instruction, time allocations, and the content to be taught.

After planning for instruction comes the implementation of what has been planned. Lesson implementation is more commonly known as *teaching*. Teaching puts into action the collective information generated from over two decades of research studies. There are many definitions of *teaching*. Hunter (1984) defines teaching

> as the constant stream of professional decisions that affects the probability of learning: decisions that are made and implemented before, during, and after interaction with the students. (p. 169)

In addition, Hunter goes on to say, "Teaching is an applied science derived from research in human behavior: an applied science that utilizes the findings from psychology, neurology, sociology, and anthropology" (p. 170).

For others (Eisner, 1983; Dawe 1984; Rubin, 1985), teaching is an artistic endeavor. Rubin (1985) provides a comprehensive view of teaching that involves "skill, originality, flair, dexterity, ingenuity, . . . which, together, engender exceptional performance" (p. 15). Whether we consider teaching a science, an art, or both, it is a complex, complicated, and multidimensional enterprise that takes many forms.

Teaching may be all or some of the following: telling, explaining, defining, providing examples and nonexamples, stressing critical attributes, modeling and, demonstrating. Using their knowledge of curriculum development and of the delivery of instruction, supervisors will be in a better position to diagnose instructional problems in the classroom.

This chapter will first examine five common teaching areas in which problems are likely to occur as supervisors help teachers become more effective. Next, the chapter will list and describe the teacher behaviors that research has found to be linked with student achievement. This chapter will also provide a structure, or framework, for developing efficient teaching behaviors. One such framework that instructional supervisors can offer teachers is the General Model of Instruction, which focuses on four components of teaching: the selection of specific instructional objectives, the assessment of the learner's present understanding, the choice of suitable teaching method, and the evaluation of students' progress. A more extensive framework is contained in the General Cycle of Teaching, which encompasses nine steps: establishing set, communicating objectives, input, modeling, checking for understanding, guided practice, independent practice, evaluation, and closure. Despite their best efforts, teachers may find that, based on assessment, students have not learned the material and reteaching will be needed. The chapter discusses strategies for modifying instruction for learners. The chapter concludes with an examination of some of the issues involved in providing instruction for students with special needs, including gifted students and students with handicaps.

COMMON INSTRUCTIONAL PROBLEMS

In addition to their own knowledge and experience related to instruction, supervisors should be aware of the five most common instructional problems that teachers experience (Davis, Alexander, and

Yelon, 1974). These problem areas are (1) direction, (2) evaluation, (3) content and sequence, (4) method, and (5) constraints. The first of these problems can arise during a lesson if the teacher fails to provide direction—a "map" as to what will happen instructionally. Students will be at a disadvantage if the teacher fails to communicate the goals, objectives, and expectations for the day, the week, or even the semester.

The second problem area is evaluation. Feedback about results is a prime motivator, and students need feedback concerning their progress. Teachers should build in procedures that provide both oral and written feedback to students so they can monitor their own progress. The evaluation procedures for daily, weekly, or unit progress are vital to successful instruction. Without direction or focus, knowledge of performance expectations, and awareness of results, students often become disinterested and uncaring about learning.

The third instructional problem that supervisors face as they work with teachers is the lack of content in the lesson or the lack of organization in the presentation of the material. In editing some material and feeling the pressure to cover "everything in the book," teachers often present information that lacks sufficient depth, or that lacks a logical or well-organized sequence. Teachers may try to cover a breadth of information and, in doing so, fail to provide the necessary depth to promote effective instruction.

Tied closely to content and organization are problems dealing with methodology. The methods used in presenting the material will determine the degree to which the students are motivated. Teachers should have in their instructional repertoire a "cafeteria of alternatives" (Joyce and Weil, 1980) available from which to choose. Reinhartz and Beach (1983) suggest that supervisors view teaching methods as occurring along a continuum as in Figure 7.1. As Figure 7.1 indicates, teachers have options available to them as they match content with the appropriate method. When only one method or

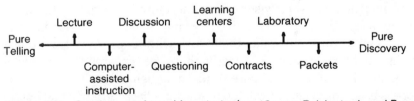

Figure 7.1 Continuum of teaching strategies. (*Source:* Reinhartz, J., and Beach, D. M. [1983]. *Improving middle school instruction: A research-based self-assessment system,* p. 26. Washington, D.C.: National Education Association. Used with permission.)

strategy is used, students may become passive and unmotivated as the lesson progresses.

The last instructional problem, constraints, becomes a factor when the teacher fails to consider resources (environmental, institutional, human) in the implementation of the lesson. Teachers who try to teach a lesson using laboratory equipment in a space that is not designed appropriately, for example, will probably experience difficulty with the lesson. The presence or absence of resources can enhance or detract from the teaching–learning process. *Constraints* are those resources that, when absent or insufficient, negatively impact on learning.

Figure 7.2 provides a summary of the five common instructional problems, with a description of each problem, possible symptoms, and the instructional consequences.

The instructional problems identified here may begin in the planning phase of instruction, but normally the consequences are most evident when the lessons are taught. As indicated in Figure 7.2, if direction, evaluation, content and sequence, method, and constraints are not consciously considered, problems may occur when the lessons are implemented.

EFFECTIVE TEACHING BEHAVIORS

In addition to the previously identified problems, teaching is affected by variables such as the overall school environment and climate. Yet educators and noneducators alike may try to simplify teaching as if it could be reduced to a recipe with a few basic ingredients to be used by all teachers. Good teaching results when there is a match between strategies, content, students, and teacher. For good teaching to occur, teachers must not only draw upon what is known about the teaching–learning process from research, but they must also orchestrate all the variables within the classroom to produce maximum learning for all students.

Instructional supervisors must therefore be aware of the complexities associated with effective teaching. What information is available to guide supervisors as they work with teachers in their quest for instructional excellence? Clearly, there are research studies which have identified a technical core of teaching behaviors. This technical core is based on research related to teacher characteristics that correlate positively with student learning outcomes or achievement gains

Type of Problem	Description of the Problem	Some Consequences
The direction of the lesson	Goals or objectives are not stated, and the students are confused about what they are going to study and what they are expected to do.	Students try to predict what the lesson objectives are. Questions such as, "What are we learning?" "Why are we learning this?" are frequently voiced during the lesson.
The evaluation procedures to assess student progress	Students do not know how they will be evaluated and what skills or knowledge will be assessed.	The evaluation instruments (tests, projects, demonstration of skills) are not predetermined and communicated to the students, which may result in unfair testing and grading practices; students may become dissatisfied.
The organization and sequencing of the content	The key concepts, skills, facts, and generalizations are not included. The content is not organized in a sequential manner to reflect logical development of information	Course content is perceived as disorganized and confusing. Questions such as "What is the teacher doing?" "How come I don't understand what is going on?" are heard.
The methods and instructional strategies	The students are not motivated or interested in what is being taught. Strategies that do not actually involve the students results in boredom.	Student attitudes are affected. Students feel that what they are learning is irrelevant; as a result, students may cut class and perform poorly on tests.
The constraints that are context-related and/or self-imposed	Available resources (human, institutional, and environmental) are not being used to enhance the learning process.	The type of instruction provided is limited by the lack of resources, and more demands are made on students.

Figure 7.2 Types of instructional problems. (*Source:* Adapted from Davis, R. H., Alexander, L. T., and Yelon, S. L. [1974]. *Learning system design: An approach to the improvement of instruction,* p. 4. New York: McGraw-Hill. Used with permission.)

(Ryan, 1960; Rosenshine and Furst, 1971; Walberg, Schiller, and Haertel, 1979; Manatt, 1981a, 1981b; Rosenshine, 1983; Greenblatt, Cooper, and Muth, 1984; Manatt, 1987).

One state, Texas, has embraced this technical core of teaching behaviors and defined effective teaching as

observable and job-related behaviors . . . an intentional act which has as its goal student growth. Teaching includes, but is not limited to planning, delivering, evaluating, and reporting student learning. (Texas Teacher Appraisal System, 1986–1987, pp. 3, 5)

This definition of effective teaching includes the following domains and criteria directly related to the technical core of classroom teaching behaviors.

Domain I. Instructional Strategies
  Criterion 1. Provides opportunities for students to participate actively and successfully
  Criterion 2. Evaluates and provides feedback on student progress during instruction
Domain II. Classroom management and organization
  Criterion 3. Organizes materials and students
  Criterion 4. Maximizes amount of time available for instruction
  Criterion 5. Manages student behavior
Domain III. Presentation of subject matter
  Criterion 6. Teaches for cognitive, affective, and/or psychomotor learning
  Criterion 7. Uses effective communication skills
Domain IV. Learning environment
  Criterion 8. Uses strategies to motivate students for learning
  Criterion 9. Maintains supportive environment

Supervisors, knowledgeable about teaching and effective teaching behaviors that are supported by research, can establish an instructional mind set, or frame of reference, as they help teachers increase their ability to reach more students by providing a rich and diverse environment (Joyce and Showers, 1982). As indicated previously, research has identified numerous teacher characteristics associated with greater student learning and more desirable student affective behaviors (Berliner, 1984; Gage and Berliner, 1984; Greenblatt, Cooper, and Muth, 1984; Manatt, 1987). Our purpose here is to provide instructional supervisors with an overview of some of the teacher behaviors commonly described in the research as the technical core of effective teaching practice. Figure 7.3 presents a list of commonly used teacher behaviors and a definition of the behavior.

A word of caution, however, should be sounded against overgeneralizing about these behaviors, because the research studies are often situation-, subject-, and student-specific (Griffin, 1985). Nevertheless, there are representative correlational studies, from state-of-the-art data, that have consistently identified the same qualitative skills that effective practitioners use to increase student achievement.

Behavior	Definition
1. Task orientation	The extent to which the classroom is businesslike, the students spend their time on academic subjects, and the teacher presents clear goals to the students
2. Opportunity to learn criterion material	The extent to which criterion material is covered in class
3. Variability	The amount of flexibility or adaptability of teaching methods; the amount of extra materials, displays, or resource materials in the classroom
4. Enthusiasm and interest	The amount of the teacher's vigor, power, and involvement
5. Feedback	The extent to which the teacher provides the student with positive and negative feedback
6. Structuring	The extent to which the teacher directs instruction
7. Questioning	The extent to which the teacher asks questions at different levels and adjusts them appropriately in the classroom
8. Management	The extent to which the teacher is able to conduct the class without instruction being interrupted
9. Direct instruction	The extent to which the teacher sets and articulates the learning goals, actively assesses student progress, and frequently makes class presentations illustrating how to do assigned work
10. Instructional time	The allocation of a period of time for a lesson adequate to cover the material yet flexible enough to allow for the unexpected
11. Pacing	The extent to which the level of difficulty and the pace of the lesson is appropriate for the student's ability and interest

Figure 7.3 Effective teaching behaviors. (*Source:* Greenblatt, R. B., Cooper, B. S., and Muth, R. [1984]. Managing for effective teaching. *Educational Leadership, 41,* 5, 58. Used with permission of the Association for Supervision and Curriculum Development. Copyright © by ASCD. All rights reserved.)

In Figure 7.4, eleven effective teaching behaviors are presented. In the listing below, these behaviors are described and pertinent research studies are cited.

1. *Daily review of previous day's work.* Teacher provides an appropriate review and relates that prior content to new

learning (Medley, 1977; Good and Grouws, 1979; Rosenshine, 1983).

2. *Direct instruction.* Teacher presents information clearly and stresses important points and dimensions of the content (Rosenshine and Furst, 1971; Kennedy et al, 1978; Good and Grouws, 1979; Peterson, 1979; Rosenshine, 1979; Walberg, Schiller, and Haertel, 1979; Evertson, Emmer, and Brophy, 1980).

3. *Actively engaged in learning.* Teacher maximizes amount of time available for instruction and keeps students engaged in learning activities—bell-to-bell instruction (Good and Grouws, 1977; Emmer, Evertson, and Anderson, 1980; Ellett, Capie, and Johnson, 1981).

4. *Corrective feedback.* Teacher monitors students' performances and provides corrective feedback, clarifies, or reteaches (Stallings and Kaskowitz, 1974; Stallings, 1978; Anderson, Evertson, and Brophy, 1979; Reid, 1980; Rosenshine, 1983).

5. *Guided and independent practice.* Teacher presents information in an appropriate sequence—guided practice precedes independent practice and practice activities follow explanation, demonstration, or modeling (Stallings and Kaskowitz, 1974; Good and Grouws, 1979; Coker, Lorentz, and Coker, 1980; Evertson et al., 1980; Fisher et al., 1980; Sharan, 1980; Slavin, 1980; Hunter and Russell, 1981; Rosenshine, 1983).

6. *Instructional clarity.* Teacher clearly states objectives and tasks, and presentation is well organized (Rosenshine and Furst, 1971; Walberg, Schiller, and Haertel, 1979; Rosenshine, 1983; Hines, Cruickshank, and Kennedy, 1985).

EFFECTIVE TEACHING BEHAVIORS

1. Daily review of previous day's work
2. Direct instruction
3. Actively engaged in learning
4. Corrective feedback
5. Guided and independent practice
6. Instructional clarity
7. Time on task
8. Questioning
9. States expectations
10. Classroom management and organization
11. Varies instruction

Figure 7.4 Teacher behaviors that contribute to effective performance.

7. *Time on task* (academic learning time). Teacher keeps students engaged during instruction (Rosenshine and Furst, 1971; Fisher, Marliave, and Filby, 1979; Walberg, Schiller, and Haertel, 1979; Capie, Tobin, and Bowell, 1980; Caldwell, Huitt, and Graeber 1982; Emmer, 1982).

8. *Questioning.* Teacher asks questions that produce high success rates as well as questions that promote higher-order thinking (Rosenshine and Furst, 1971; Rowe, 1974; Barnes, 1981; Barell, 1985).

9. *States expectations.* Teacher communicates to students what they are to accomplish (objectives) based on the lesson (Brophy, 1981; Manatt, 1981a, 1981b; Purkey and Smith, 1983; Good and Brophy, 1984; Good, 1987).

10. *Classroom management and organization.* Teacher specifies expectations for class behavior and uses techniques to prevent, redirect, or stop inappropriate behavior (Sanford and Evertson, 1980; Emmer, 1982; Evertson and Emmer, 1982; Doyle, 1985).

11. *Varies instruction.* Teacher uses learning opportunities other than listening (Rosenshine and Furst, 1971; Joyce and Weil, 1986).

These behaviors identified by research are concrete images of what successful teachers do and should be considered within the overall context of the classroom (such as age of students, content area, and background of students).

GENERAL MODEL OF INSTRUCTION

As supervisors work with teachers in the instructional setting, it is helpful to view the characteristics within a framework or model of instruction. The General Model of Instruction (Kibler et al., 1974) can be a useful tool for supervisors when they are working with teachers who need basic information about the complex process called teaching. Funkhouser and others (1981) note that the main purpose of the General Model of Instruction is to "(1) guide instruction design and implementation; [and] (2) . . . provide structure for viewing and studying instruction" (p. 7).

As shown in Figure 7.5, the General Model of Instruction has four components related to instruction and begins where the Tyler curriculum development model ends (see Figure 6.1). The first step in the instructional process involves the selection, classification, analysis, and identification of specific instructional objectives, which are

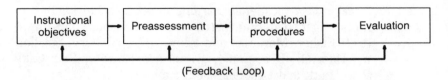

(Feedback Loop)

Figure 7.5 General model of instruction. (*Source:* Kibler, R. J., Cegela, D. J., Barker, L. L., and Miles, D. T. [1974]. *Objectives for instruction and evaluation,* p. 28. Boston: Allyn and Bacon. Used with permission.)

communicated to the students. These objectives focus and clarify the direction of the lesson. The second step is an assessment of the learner's present understanding. The teacher can review previous material to measure students' abilities and prerequisite knowledge and skills. In addition, the teacher can develop individual learning prescriptions to ensure student success.

The third step of the General Model involves instructional procedures or methods. At this point, the teacher couples the content with appropriate learning activities designed to keep the students motivated and engaged in the learning process. Decisions are made about the type of strategies that are being used throughout the lesson to motivate students, materials needed to enhance instruction (those available and those to prepare), and the scope and sequence of the actual presentation. These decisions occur twice—once in the initial preparation of the lesson and then as the lesson is being taught. By using a variety of instructional procedures to involve the learners actively in ways other than listening, the teacher can increase the amount of time the students are engaged in the learning process.

The last step in the model is evaluation. The teacher assesses the progress made by the students in accomplishing the objective(s) and evaluates the overall effectiveness of the lesson. When teachers evaluate informally, students are given feedback on their progress and misunderstandings are clarified. Depending on the number of questions asked by both the teacher and the students and the general level of student comprehension or lack thereof, the teacher becomes aware of which concepts have been mastered and which ones need to be retaught. If reteaching is needed, the content and activities in the lesson must be modified to meet the different levels and abilities of the students. Modification entails altering or adjusting what was taught by using different examples, activities, and explanations. Specific suggestions for modifying lessons will be provided later in the chapter. In formal evaluation such as testing, the students as well as the teacher receive feedback about the level of content mastery.

Based on such feedback, some of the concepts may need to be retaught, especially if the knowledge and skills will be needed for future learning.

GENERAL CYCLE OF TEACHING

There are other instructional models that, by design, have incorporated many of the characteristics of effective teachers along with the components of the General Model of Instruction. Many of the later instructional models are based on the work done by Hunter (1981; with Russell, 1984). Some of these models have five steps, others seven; they are generally referred to as *lesson cycles.* For the purposes of this text, the General Cycle of Teaching is presented in Figure 7.6; it is a synthesis of several models and incorporates many of the elements advocated by Hunter and others. The General Cycle of Teaching is helpful to supervisors in that it attempts to link what is known about the total instructional process with effective teaching behaviors.

The General Cycle of Teaching is structured in such a way as to ensure that curriculum requirements are implemented and that current research regarding effective teaching is incorporated. Teaching involves making decisions; some decisions occur before instruction, during the planning and task analysis stages, while other decisions are made during the actual teaching act. It is important, then, that the General Cycle of Teaching acknowledges that prior instructional decisions have been made and planned but actually begins with the teaching act. The General Cycle of Teaching includes nine steps: (1) establishing set, (2) communicating objectives and purposes, (3) input, (4) modeling, (5) checking for understanding, (6) guided practice, (7) independent practice, (8) evaluation, and (9) closure. These steps, although listed sequentially, may occur simultaneously as well. A description of each step is provided to assist instructional supervisors in their understanding of the teaching cycle.

1. *Establishing set.* One of the essential steps in the General Cycle of Teaching is to establish the focus of the lesson and give direction to the teaching–learning process. This is sometimes referred to as *anticipatory set,* which implies that the students are ready for learning; something is going to happen in the learning process. Establishing set initiates the communication between the teacher and the students and sets the stage for learning. In this first step, the

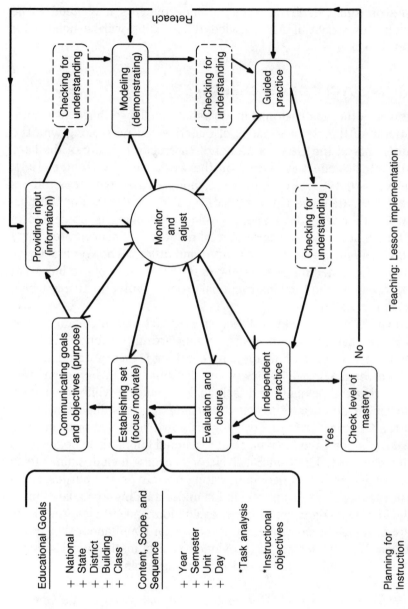

Figure 7.6 General cycle of teaching.

focus should be varied through the use of different types of stimuli to involve students quickly in the lesson. This part of the instructional sequence should motivate and prepare the students for what is to come in the remaining parts of the lesson. Some of the various ways to introduce the topic under study are to (a) use advance organizers to outline the flow of concepts and information, (b) review the previous day's work with questions, (c) begin the lesson with a provocative question, (d) provide visuals (pictures) and discuss similarities and differences, and (e) within an inductive lesson, involve other stimuli that cause the students to use their senses.

2. *Communicating objectives and purposes.* This step in the instructional sequence helps students understand what they should know or be able to do following instruction. It provides the necessary clue for students as to what is important and expected in terms of learning and helps to eliminate guessing. In this step, the teacher is communicating more than the activity, and the objectives may be stated throughout the lesson as the teacher moves from one concept or skill to the next. Two examples of this teaching behavior are such statements as: "Today we will learn an important geography skill by finding places on the globe using latitude and longitude readings" or "When you finish this lab, you should be able to name four common acids and bases and give the properties of each."

3. *Input.* This step in the teaching cycle refers to the actual teacher-directed, or "teaching," portion of the lesson. It includes the introduction, the content and the order of presentation (sequence), the instructional strategies or methods used, and the kinds of activities the students are engaged in. The overall purpose of this instructional step is to identify, define, and describe the critical attributes of concepts, skills, and attitudes included in the lesson. As the critical attributes are identified, examples as well as nonexamples should be used as illustrations. The instructional methods should be varied to stimulate thinking and retention, to transfer previous learning to current topics under study, and to involve and challenge the students. Although there are a variety of instructional methods that teachers can use, as identified earlier in Figure 7.1, two basic strategies are most helpful in implementing the various methods. These two teaching strategies are inductive and deductive. The *inductive* strategy views teaching–learning from a part-to-whole perspective. For example, components or aspects of a principle are provided and students are expected to construct the general rule or principle from these elements. The part-to-whole approach requires students to synthe-

size and create a whole from apparently unrelated pieces of data given. The opposite strategy, teaching *deductively,* begins with a definition of the principle. Students analyze the principle or rule and provide examples to illustrate it. Once these two basic strategies are understood, the teacher has a multitude of methods (lecture, role play, learning packets, and so on) and resources that can be used to enhance instruction.

4. *Modeling.* This step in the instructional cycle allows students to view a process or to observe calculations or operations. Later, students can imitate the process or procedure during practice. Modeling—or demonstrating a concept, process, skill, procedure, technique, or attitude—can be done by the teacher, through the use of media (films, audio and video tapes, and so forth), or by expert resource personnel in the school or community. Modeling aids the student in remembering what was taught. It is a critical part of the teaching segment, for it provides the basis for the student to replicate the essential behaviors or skills at the appropriate time in the lesson. For instance, math teachers provide examples and model, or illustrate, the process of solving math problems (such as derivation of the quadratic equation). Students can then practice the skill.

5. *Checking for understanding.* This step involves an informal assessment (by means of individual or choral responses, or thumbs up/down signals) to determine if the students comprehend what has been taught, modeled, or practiced. Checking for understanding often relies heavily on questioning techniques. The teacher may ask students simple, factual recall questions. To verify the depth of comprehension, however, the teacher should ask students to explain in their own words, provide examples and nonexamples, elaborate on critical attributes, or add to other responses. Although there are a variety of other ways (such as games and worksheets) to determine the level of understanding, simplicity is the rule for this informal assessment procedure. Aside from classroom questions that students respond to individually or as a class, the teacher might ask the students at the end of the lesson or period to write on a sheet of paper the five or six main points covered. Students then turn in the responses with or without their names, and the teacher has some indication of class comprehension. More important, the activity provides the teacher with the opportunity to clarify and correct and to give students feedback on their level of proficiency.

6. *Guided practice.* During this part of instruction, students have the chance to practice skills or tasks presented during earlier parts

of the lesson. Students are not left alone but are carefully monitored by the teacher to ensure that the task is completed accurately and correctly. An important part of this lesson component is "feedback with guidance" (Goodlad, 1984); knowledge of results provides students with information about their progress. Generally, the purpose of practice is to help students gain command of a concept or a skill. Practice gives meaning to the concept or skill by directly involving the learner in some task or operation. Before moving to independent practice, it is critical that the learner has success at least once; and the more success the learner has, the greater the level of mastery. When different kinds of guided practice are designed, the following variables should be considered: the amount of material covered, the amount of time available, the schedule (mass or distributive practice), and degree or level of overlearning.

7. *Independent practice.* This step should come only after the student has had an opportunity to demonstrate mastery of the skill or concept under the controlled environment of guided practice. In this part of the teaching cycle, students are given the chance to demonstrate the skills or concepts with little or no teacher supervision or encouragement. The independent practice may take the form of surveys and science fair projects in the elementary school and projects or papers in high school. Usually homework or creative assignments require students to work more independently and apply what they have learned. The goal of independent practice is to provide an opportunity for students to demonstrate mastery by completing an assignment on their own. A common concern, however, is that teachers often use independent practice as a punishment or have it precede instruction. For example, teachers may assign a chapter in a textbook and have students answer the questions before any of the previous six steps in the General Cycle of Teaching have occurred. When this happens, the teacher is less effective.

8. *Evaluation.* This step may occur continuously throughout the lesson as the teacher monitors and adjusts instruction based on students' responses to questions, students' involvement in learning activities, and students' performance during guided practice. Evaluation can be either formative or summative. In the classroom, *formative* evaluation includes an examination of the ongoing process of the teaching cycle. The teacher asks himself or herself, "How am I doing and how are the students doing?" Within the classroom, *summative* evaluation involves making a judgment about the effectiveness of instruction (formative and summative evaluation relative to teacher

performance are discussed in Detail in Chapter 10). At this point, the teacher decides either to continue on to a new topic, concept, or unit or to reteach the lesson. The evaluation tools that teachers can use range from formal daily tests or unit tests to informal summary statements or projects. At the conclusion of the evaluation step, the teacher makes a judgment about the level of student mastery and determines what further learning is needed. One of the questions that continue to plague teachers is, "When is it appropriate to move on to the next concept, skill, or unit of instruction?" There is no simple answer to this question because there are too many variables associated with the teaching cycle. But the instructional supervisor can provide valuable guidance in helping teachers answer this question based on the specific situation and class. Clearly, at some point, the teacher must decide to move on. Teachers may want to use the 70-70 rule; that is, when 70 percent of the students have mastered 70 percent of the objectives.

9. *Closure.* This step brings the lesson or a part of the lesson to a logical conclusion. Closure may take many forms that include such things as a summary by the teacher of the main points covered in the lesson or a review of what has been discussed in the lesson. Often teachers will combine this step with checking for understanding by asking the students to identify the main points and listing them on the board.

Taken together, the nine steps in the General Cycle of Teaching form a script that teachers can use during the lesson. It is important to remember that these steps are associated with effective teaching behaviors that foster student achievement and are supported in the research literature.

MODIFYING INSTRUCTION FOR LEARNERS

From the results teachers obtain after they check for understanding, monitor guided and independent practice activities, and conduct informal and formal evaluations, it will become apparent that some of the material will need to be retaught. Reteaching individual concepts may be necessary if students do not understand them or have misconceptions about them. This means that the material must be modified or altered before it can be assimilated. The supervisor may suggest some or all of the following six ways to modify instruction to help meet the needs of individual students.

1. *Establish learning stations or centers.* These stations or centers should contain resources, experiments, activities, games, and manipulatives for students to use individually or in small groups. Instructions for the stations or centers should be clearly written to minimize student dependence on the teacher for completing the activity.

2. *Reduce the amount of in-class work and outside-class assignments to be done.* Careful editing of reading assignments, of questions or problems to answer, and of experiments to be performed will help the student identify the major focus of the instructional task. The basics, or essentials, of the lesson content should remain, however.

3. *Provide material in a format other than reading.* Teachers can tape material from the textbook, questions to be answered, problems to be solved, or any other material so that students can listen as they read along in their text.

4. *Provide an outline or brief summary.* An outline helps students follow the major points in the lesson by listing content in sequential order. A summary provides an overview of major points and helps students focus on important information.

5. *Use visuals (charts/posters) to illustrate concepts.* When introducing new concepts or information, teachers can use pictures, posters, or charts to illustrate the important aspects. The charts and posters can be used in combination with learning station or learning center activities or any of the other ways to modify the lesson.

6. *Simplify lengthy passages, technical descriptions, or complex problems.* The lesson presentation, activities, examples, and discussions provided by the teacher can make the instructional material more understandable to students. Thus teachers can edit long written passages from the textbook, focus on technical vocabulary, and/or reduce complex procedures to the simplest steps.

These six ways of modifying a lesson can help teachers reach those students who have not mastered the content at an appropriate level. In addition to these six ways that teachers can use to modify instruction for special learners, many, if not most, school districts have programs that provide opportunities for students to leave the regular classroom for part of the day to receive specialized instruction.

Developing curriculum programs to meet the special needs of students and to accommodate individual differences is a time-consuming and challenging task for the teacher and the instructional supervisor. There are many legal classifications and definitions used in categorizing students. Some of these categories are *gifted, talented, learning-disabled, disadvantaged,* and *culturally and linguistically different.* An array of decisions must be made by those who deal with special learners. According to Wiles and Bond (1986), these decisions revolve around the following issues.

1. *Testing* provides the means of assessing skills, abilities, talents, and language proficiency. While a variety of intelligence tests are available, the Stanford-Binet, the Wechsler (WISC), and the Otis-Lennon are commonly used to identify the "intelligence" level of students. Achievement test scores from the Iowa Test of Basic Skills and the California Achievement Test (CAT) are also used in assessing student abilities. In addition, several states have developed their own achievement tests for pupil assessment. Clearly, caution is called for in the use of tests to prevent labeling students and lowering expectations of student performance. Tests can be helpful, but they should be used with discretion to guard against an overreliance on the results. Tests alone should not determine the type of educational program for special students. Test results should be only a part of the data used in tailoring a curricular program for special learners.

2. *Grouping* is an educational practice that is used to organize students for the purpose of instruction. Groups can be based on the abilities or interests of students, or students can be randomly assigned to groups for a specific activity. Often, ability groups become static, and students are forced to remain in the same group regardless of academic progress. The issue of homogeneous and heterogeneous groups is still controversial, but the practice of grouping is found in 80 percent of the schools today (Wiles and Bondi, 1986). By taking students' cognitive, emotional, physical, and affective abilities into consideration and continuously monitoring growth in these abilities, the supervisor can help teachers use grouping as an effective tool to assist students who have special learning needs.

3. *Special programs* are scheduled within the school day and are superimposed over the regular educational program. Pull-out programs, such as those for talented and gifted students, resource, reading improvement, and English as a second language, allow students to remain in the regular classroom for much of the school day and to spend the remaining time with specialists who help them with their individual learning needs. Instructional supervisors, along with teachers, are involved in making recommendations about which students qualify for these special pull-out programs.

4. *Mainstreaming* came into the educator's vocabulary with the

implementation of P.L. 94-142. Instructional supervisors and teachers are a part of the team that develops Individualized Educational Plans (IEP) for students requiring modified instructional programs. The team of supervisors and/or administrators, teachers, and other specialists must ensure that a quality education is provided for students with handicaps in their district and building. The placement of students in what the law calls the "least restrictive environment" is intended to assign students with handicaps to a normal classroom setting as much as possible. Mainstreaming addresses a number of handicapping conditions and has given new direction and emphasis to the designing of educational programs for special learners.

5. *Gifted and talented programs* are designed to provide opportunities for students who have abilities, skills, and talents that have not been sufficiently developed or cultivated within the regular classroom. Students are selected for these programs based on such factors as I.Q. test scores, achievement test scores, classroom performance, teacher recommendations, and personal interviews. In the elementary school, such programs are generally geared to specific grade levels; at the secondary level, these programs are often given different names such as *independent study* or *advanced placement*. As gifted and talented programs have mushroomed around the country in the last few years, questions have been raised about whether the general educational program is sufficiently challenging for *all* students in grades K–12. Instructional supervisors serve as valuable resources for teachers in these programs by assisting with the development of curriculum and sometimes securing necessary funding. Helping teachers select special curriculum materials or obtain books with ideas for curriculum development, keeps the instructional supervisor busy.

From a positive perspective, special programs of all types attempt to meet the individual needs of learners. Negatively viewed, these programs can siphon off critical funds and human resources from the regular educational program. This dichotomy will continue to confront instructional supervisors as their roles extend to helping teachers who are responsible for improving the educational experiences of all learners.

SUMMARY

Effective lesson implementation requires planning, and inherent in the planning process is decision making. Chapter 6 dealt with the pre-teaching activities that lead to effective planning and instruction.

This chapter focuses on the instructional phase—specifically, the teaching act itself. According to Hunter (1984), teaching, like planning, requires the teacher to make a "constant stream" of decisions related to the teaching–learning process.

Davis, Alexander, and Yelon (1974) recognize the importance of decisions and their impact on instruction by identifying five common instructional areas that may cause problems: (1) direction (communicating the focus of the lesson), (2) evaluation (providing feedback to students), (3) content and sequence (organizing the presentation of concepts and skills), (4) methods (providing activities to engage the students in the lesson), and (5) constraints (being aware of limitations of materials and resources). To help teachers avoid pitfalls in these areas, supervisors can use different models of instruction coupled with effective teaching behaviors identified by research to ensure instructional effectiveness.

According to numerous correlational studies on teaching, teachers who are described as effective or successful, based on increased student learning, exhibit the following behaviors: (1) they conduct daily reviews, (2) they teach clearly, (3) they actively engage students, (4) they give corrective feedback, (5) they provide guided and independent practice, (6) they state objectives and tasks and are well organized, (7) they keep students on task, (8) they ask questions to stimulate higher-order thinking, (9) they communicate expectations about students' ability to perform, (10) they use appropriate classroom management techniques, and (11) they vary their instructional strategies.

The General Model of Instruction is a four-step procedure that provides teachers with a framework for viewing their tasks. The components are the selection of objectives, the assessment of students' present understanding, the presentation of the content by means of appropriate learning activities, and the evaluation of students' progress.

The General Cycle of Teaching provides a structure for incorporating effective teaching practices, along with the essential lesson components, that can also contribute to successful teaching. These components include (1) establishing set, (2) communicating objectives and purposes, (3) input, (4) modeling, (5) checking for understanding, (6) guided practice, (7) independent practice, (8) evaluation, and (9) closure.

An important area of instructional supervision involves the modification of instruction for learners. After assessing student abilities, teachers may find that the material needs to be adjusted. Six ways for modifying instruction are (1) establishing learning stations, (2) reducing in-class work or homework assignments, (3) providing material in a format other than reading, (4) providing an outline or summary, (5) using visuals, and (6) simplifying lengthy or complex material. Finally, supervisors can assist teachers in making decisions about students with special needs. The instructional areas involved include testing (ability assessment); grouping; special programs, such as pull-out programs, for those who need instruction from specialists; mainstreaming of students with handicaps; and gifted or talented programs.

Supervisors have the responsibility of helping teachers to link theory, or what is known about good teaching gained from the research litetature, with effective instructional practice. The information presented in this chapter is an attempt to help supervisors as they work with teachers to make that linkage.

YOUR TURN

7.1. Read the following class descriptions and indicate if the teaching strategy is inductive or deductive and explain why.

a. The teacher writes the word *osmosis* on the board and says, "Today we are going to examine the meaning of this word. It pertains to a particular biological process which involves diffusion through a special membrane. First, you will look up some definitions of the word and find examples of where the process occurs." The students begin looking up definitions of the word while the teacher passes out a worksheet illustrating *osmosis* that the students are to label. The students spend the remainder of the period on this assignment.

b. As the students enter the room, a record is playing and two slides of famous paintings are projected on two sides of the room. Students are directed to be seated, listen to the record, and look carefully at projected paintings. After a few minutes, the teacher calls the students together and asks them to share their observations. The teacher asks, "What did you see in the paintings?" "What did you hear on the record?" "Are the record and paintings related?" The teacher helps the students recall their observations and experiences and begins to group these responses into examples and then makes a generalization about what the students have seen and heard.

c. Each day as students enter their math class the teacher reviews their homework with them. Sometimes the teacher works the problems on the board; at other times the teacher asks for student volunteers to do so. After questions regarding the homework have been answered, the teacher proceeds by putting a new theorem or math principle on the board, works some sample problems for the students to illustrate the principle, assigns 30 problems for homework, and allows students to spend the remainder of the period working quietly in class while the teacher moves about the room helping individual students.

7.2. Using the four steps in the General Model of Instruction provided below, decide where each item that follows would fit in the model.

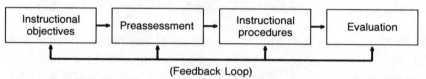

(Feedback Loop)

(*Source:* Kibler, R. J., Cegala, D. J., Barker, L. L., and Miles, D. T. [1974], p. 28. *Objectives for instruction and evaluation.* Boston: Allyn and Bacon. Used with permission.)

- *a.* movie *Gone With the Wind*
- *b.* stated learner behaviors
- *c.* reading inventory
- *d.* research conducted by students in library or museum
- *e.* field trip
- *f.* final exam
- *g.* task analysis
- *h.* state or district requirements for student learning

7.3. Some educators perceive teaching as an art, practiced by individuals who are born with intuitive awareness; others perceive teaching as a science, practiced in a scientific manner. Still others view teaching as both an art and a science. Using the ideas presented in this chapter and combining those with your own personal experience, develop your view of teaching. How would you explain your position to someone else?

7.4. Read each of the following statements. Then, using one of the five choices provided, identify the type of classroom instructional problem represented by each statement.

Direction	Evaluation
Constraints	Method
Content and Sequence	

A. STUDENT: What am I supposed to be studying?

B. TEACHER: How can I teach this course without the necessary lab equipment?

C. STUDENT: I can't follow the teacher's presentation. There's too much skipping around.

D. TEACHER: My students thought the exam was unfair and that it did not reflect what they had learned.

E. STUDENT: It's hard to pay attention in class when we don't know what we're supposed to be learning.

F. STUDENT: We never have any lab activities in our biology class this year.

7.5. Analyze the following written lesson plan and answer the questions that follow.

Lesson Plan

Objective: When shown a film that depicts the flow of blood through the heart and body *(Hemo the Magnificent),* the student will be able to identify at least two differences and two similarities between veins and arteries.

A. Explain the task to the students. Tell them to view the film and take notes about veins and arteries, recording similarities and differences.

B. Show the film.

C. Have each pupil use notes to list two similarities and two differences.

D. Discuss the similarities and differences as a class. Ask students how they felt as they watched certain parts of the film— for example, the heart pumping.

a. What is the cognitive level of the objective?

b. Does the teacher provide for individual differences? Explain your answer.

c. Does the teacher provide an opportunity for active student participation? Explain your answer.

REFERENCES

Anderson, L. M., Evertson, C. M., and Brophy, J. E. (1979). An experimental study of effective teaching in first grade reading groups. *The Elementary School Journal, 79,* 4, 193–223.

Barell, J. (1985). You ask the wrong questions. *Educational Leadership, 42,* 18–23.

Barnes, S. (1981). *Synthesis of selected research on teaching findings.* Austin: Research and Development Center for Teacher Education, University of Texas at Austin.

Berliner, D. (1984). The half-full glass: A review of research on teaching. In P. L. Hosford (Ed.), *Using what we know about teaching.* Alexandria, Va.: Association for Supervision and Curriculum Development.

Brophy, J. E. (1981). Teacher praise: A functional analysis. *Review of Education Research, 51,* 5–32.

Caldwell, J. H., Huitt, W. G., and Graeber, A. O. (1982). Time spent in learning: Implications from research. *Elementary School Journal, 82,* 5, 471–479.

Capie, W., Tobin, K. G., and Bowell, M. (1980). Using student achievement to validate ratings of student teacher competencies. Paper presented at the annual meeting of the American Educational Research Association, Boston.

Coker, H., Lorentz, C. W., and Coker, J. (1980). Teacher behavior and student outcomes in Georgia study. Paper presented at the annual meeting of the American Educational Research Association, Boston.

Davis, R. H., Alexander, L. T., and Yelon, S. L. (1974). *Learning system design: An approach to the improvement of instruction.* New York: McGraw-Hill.

Dawe, H. A. (1984). Teaching: A performing art. *Phi Delta Kappan, 65,* 548–552.

Doyle, W. (1985). Classroom organization and management. In M. C. Wittrock (Ed.), *Handbook of research on teaching* (3rd ed.). American Educational Research Association. New York: Macmillan.

Eisner, E. (1983). The art and craft of teaching. *Educational Leadership, 40,* 4, 4–14.

Ellett, C. D., Capie, W., and Johnson, C. E. (1981). *Further studies of the criterion-related validity of the Teacher Performance Assessment Instruments.* Athens, Ga: Teacher Performance Assessment Project.

Emmer, E. T. (1982). *Management strategies in elementary school classrooms.* Report No. 6052. Austin: Research and Development Center for Teacher Education, University of Texas at Austin.

Emmer, E. T., Evertson, C. M., and Anderson, L. M. (1980). Effective classroom management at the beginning of the school year. *Elementary School Journal, 80,* 219–231.

Evertson, C. M., and Emmer, E. T. (1982). Effective management at the beginning of the school year in junior high classes. *Journal of Educational Psychology, 74,* 4, 485–498.

Evertson, C. M., Emmer, E., and Brophy, J. E. (1980). Predictors of effective teaching in junior high mathematics class. *Journal of Research in Mathematics Education, 11,* 167–178.

Evertson, C. M., et al. (1980). Relationship between classroom behaviors and student outcomes in junior high mathematics and English classes. *American Educational Research Journal, 17,* 43–60.

Fisher, C., Marliave, R., and Filby, N. (1979). Improving instruction by increasing academic learning time. *Educational Leadership, 37,* 1, 52–54.

Fisher, C. W., et al. (1980). Teaching behaviors, academic learning time, and student achievement: An overview. In C. Denham and A. Lieberman (Eds.), *Time to learn*. Washington, D.C.: Department of Education.

Funkhouser, C. W., et al. (1981). *Classroom applications of the curriculum: A systems approach*. Dubuque, Iowa: Kendall/Hunt.

Gage, N. L., and Berliner, D. (1984). *Educational psychology* (3rd ed.). Boston: Houghton Mifflin.

Good, T. L. (1987). Two decades of research on teacher expectations: Findings and future directions. *Journal of Teacher Education, 38,* 4, 32–47.

Good, T. L., and Brophy, J. E. (1984) *Looking in classrooms* (3rd ed.). New York: Harper & Row.

Good, T. L., and Grouws, D. A. (1977). Teacher's manual: Missouri Mathematics Effectiveness Project. Columbia: Center for Research in Social Behavior, University of Missouri.

Good, T. L., and Grouws, D. A. (1979). The Missouri Mathematics Effectiveness Project. *Journal of Educational Psychology, 71,* 355–362.

Goodlad, J. I. (1984). *A place called school*. New York: McGraw-Hill.

Greenblatt, R. B., Cooper, B. S., and Muth R. (1984). Managing for effective teaching. *Educational Leadership, 41,* 5, 57–59.

Griffin, G. (1985). Teacher induction: Research issues. *Journal of Teacher Education, 36,* 42–46.

Hines, C. V., Cruickshank, D. R., and Kennedy, J. J. (1985). Teacher clarity and its relationship to student achievement and satisfaction. *American Educational Research Journal, 22,* 1, 87–99.

Hunter, M. (1984). Knowing, teaching and supervising. In P. L. Hosford (Ed.), *Using what we know about teaching*. Alexandria, Va.: Association for Supervision and Curriculum Development.

Hunter, M., and Russell, D. (1981). Planning for effective instruction: Lesson design. In *Increasing your teaching effectiveness*. Palo Alto, Calif.: Learning Institute.

Joyce, B., and Showers, B. (1982). The coaching of teaching. *Educational Leadership, 40,* 1, 4–10.

Joyce, B., and Weil, M. (1980). *Models of teaching*. Englewood Cliffs, N.J.: Prentice-Hall.

Joyce, B., and Weil, M. (1986). *Models of teaching,* (2nd ed.). Englewood Cliffs, N.J.: Prentice-Hall.

Kennedy, J. J., et al. (1978). Additional investigations into the nature of teacher clarity. Paper presented at the annual meeting of the American Educational Research Association, Toronto.

Kibler, R. J., et al. (1974). *Objectives for instruction and evaluation*. Boston: Allyn and Bacon.

Manatt, R. P. (1981a). Evaluating teacher performance. Alexandria, Va.: Association for Supervision and Curriculum Development. [Video-tape.]

Manatt, R. P. (1981b). Manatt's exercise in selecting teacher performance evaluation criteria based on effective teaching research. Albuquerque, N.M.: National Symposium for Professionals in Evaluation and Research. [Mimeograph.]

Manatt, R. P. (1987). Lessons from a comprehensive performance appraisal project. *Educational Leadership, 44,* 7, 8–14.

Medley, D. (1977). *Teacher competence and teacher effectiveness: A review of process-product research.* Washington, D.C.: American Association of Colleges for Teacher Education.

Peterson, P. (1979). Direct instruction: Effective for what and for whom? *Educational Leadership, 37,* 1, 46–48.

Purkey, S., and Smith, M. (1983). Effective schools: A review. *The Elementary School Journal, 83,* 4, 427–452.

Reid, E. R. (1980). *The Reader Newsletter.* Salt Lake City, Utah: Exemplary Center for Reading Instruction.

Reinhartz, J., and Beach, D. M. (1983). *Improving middle school instruction: A research-based self-assessment system.* Washington, D.C.: National Education Association.

Rosenshine, B. (1979). Content, time, and direct instruction. In P. L. Peterson and H. J. Walberg (Eds.), *Research on teaching: Concepts, findings and implications.* Berkeley, Calif.: McCutchan.

Rosenshine, B. (1983). Teaching functions in instructional programs. *Elementary School Journal, 83,* 335–352.

Rosenshine, B., and Furst, N. (1971). Research in teacher performance criteria. In B. O. Smith (Ed.), *Research in teacher education.* Englewood Cliffs, N.J.: Prentice-Hall.

Rowe, M. B. (1974). Wait-time and rewards as instructional variables, their influence on language, logic, and fate control. Part 1: Wait-time. *Journal of Research in Science Teaching, 11,* 81–94.

Rubin, L. (1985). *Artistry in teaching.* New York: Random House.

Ryan, D. G. (1960). *Characteristics of teachers.* Columbus, Ohio: Charles E. Merrill.

Sanford, J. P., and Evertson, C. M. (1980). *Beginning the school year at a low SES junior high: Three case studies.* Austin: Research and Development Center for Teacher Education. University of Texas at Austin. [ERIC Document Reproduction Service No. ED 195-547.]

Sharan, S. (1980). Cooperative learning in small groups. *Review of Educational Research, 50,* 241–271.

Slavin, R. F. (1980). Cooperative learning. *Review of Educational Research, 50,* 317–343.

Stallings, J. A. (1978). *Teaching basic reading skills in secondary schools.* Toronto: American Educational Research Association. [ERIC Document Reproduction Service No. ED 166 634.]

Stallings, J. A., and Kaskowitz, D. (1974). *Follow through classroom observa-*

tion evaluation, 1972–1973. Menlo Park, Calif.: Stanford Research Institute.

Texas Teacher Appraisal System, Teacher orientation manual. (1986–1987). Austin: Texas Education Agency.

Walberg, H. J., Schiller, D., and Haertel, G. D. (1979). The quiet revolution in educational research. *Phi Delta Kappan, 61,* 3, 179–183.

Wiles, J., & Bondi, J. (1986). *Supervision: A guide to practice* (2nd ed.). Columbus, Ohio: Charles E. Merrill.

DEPARTMENT OF EDUCATIONAL LEADERSHIP
COLLEGE OF EDUCATION
FLORIDA ATLANTIC UNIVERSITY
BOCA RATON, FLORIDA 33431

three

MODELS AND
MECHANICS OF
SUPERVISION

chapter 8

Models of Supervision

In the process of improving teacher instructional competence, many educators have come to realize that the quality of instruction depends not only on teachers but on the supervisory staff as well. Supervisors and other mid-management personnel are crucial; they have the responsibility for assisting teachers in making decisions regarding the quality of their instructional performance. What an awesome responsibility! Yet supervisors have often lacked the necessary skills to provide teachers with the help they need to develop instructionally. Sometimes diagnosing and assessing instructional competence have been more a matter of personal style, based on past experiences and interpretation, rather than the utilization of clearly defined models of supervision.

The challenge for instructional supervisors is to integrate what is known about supervision into a model that helps remove obstacles to teachers' professional growth and promotes teaching excellence. The supervisor must ultimately reshape the "work environment of teachers into one that is conducive to reflective and collective dialogue among staff members" (Glickman, 1984–1985, p. 40). Mastering a repertoire of supervisory skills is necessary to help improve the school environment and encourage dialogue.

For Alfonso, Firth, and Neville (1984), the theoretical base for

153

instructional supervisors is thin. Further, the skills are acquired on the job rather than from a well-defined knowledge base and an agreed-upon set of supervisory practices. We believe that sufficient theory and knowledge have been generated to assist instructional supervisors in developing a variety of skills to function effectively. Organizational research and the development of models of supervision, particularly clinical and developmental, provide a framework for utilizing and implementing specific skills when supervisors work with people in a school setting.

There is a growing body of knowledge on school effectiveness to assist supervisors in facilitating improved instruction as they work with faculty members (Brookover et al., 1979; Edmonds, 1979; Goodlad, 1984). What do the research findings on effective schools have to say to supervisors? The findings as summarized by Glickman (1985), suggest a need for the following:

1. a collective organization with an agreed-upon purpose (Glickman, 1985)
2. a climate of expectation (Edmonds, 1979)
3. teachers to establish expectations for their students (Brookover et al., 1979)
4. a professional dialogue among teachers (Rosenholtz and Kyle, 1984)
5. participation in and agreement about goals (Goodlad, 1984).

Supervisors, as they work with teachers, should keep in mind the climate of the school, the need for collective dialogue among teachers, and the teachers' involvement in determining the goals and type of supervision they would like to receive.

These findings suggest factors that the supervisor can use when working with teachers to improve classroom instruction. In fact, quality instruction may depend on the supervisor's ability to translate knowledge of effective school research into supervisory practices. It is the supervisory practices used that shape the school organization into a productive unit (Glickman, 1985). It is therefore the supervisor's job to link the needs of the faculty members with the collective goals of the school and determine a plan of action for individual teachers. School improvement begins with supervisors using the prerequisite skills in human relations, organizational behavior, instructional behavior, and management as they talk openly with teachers about problem areas or what Lightfoot (1983) has referred to as dealing consciously with imperfections.

In order for supervisors to be successful in their role of promoting instructional effectiveness and thereby increasing achievement, supervisory models are needed. Such models should encourage interaction between the supervisor and teacher when they establish a supervisory contract (the supervisory contract will be discussed in the section "Clinical Supervision"). The models should also recognize that each teacher is an individual with unique levels of cognitive and professional development and with specific degrees of commitment to his or her position and teaching. Different supervisory contracts, therefore, as well as supervisory styles, are required. Within the context of professional growth, the supervisors should take into consideration what is known about teacher development as they select supervisory practices and procedures. Clinical supervision, for example, is a model that promotes dialogue in establishing a supervisory contract, whereas the developmental supervision model integrates the salient attributes of adult cognitive development with supervisory styles.

Because supervisors have the responsibility of helping teachers achieve their instructional best, the practice of dealing with all teachers in the same way must be abandoned. Just as teachers must employ a variety of methods to reach all their students, supervisors must develop and utilize a repertoire of supervisory strategies to work effectively with different types of teachers. The literature is clear; teachers have different backgrounds and experiences, different abilities in abstract thinking, and different levels of concern for others (Harvey, Hunt, and Schroder, 1961; Santmire, 1979; Bents and Harvey, 1981; Glickman, 1981, 1985; Wilsey and Killion, 1982). Models of supervision can help supervisors create an individualized instructional development plan for teachers.

The primary objective for supervisors is to examine and analyze classroom teaching behaviors so that recommendations can be made regarding which course of action teachers should take instructionally. The chapter examines clinical supervision and developmental supervision, two widely used supervisory models that involve the teacher in improving the quality of instruction. The chapter then discusses the self-assessment model of supervision, a more recently developed approach. Each model has distinct qualities that proponents believe contribute to the improvement of instruction.

CLINICAL SUPERVISION

Clinical supervision is a long-term, field-based process that has been called "supervision up-close" (Reavis, 1976) because it brings clarity to the classroom and seeks to upgrade the quality of instruction. The use of clinical supervision encourages supervisors and teachers to study and practice the craft of teaching. Clinical supervision is based on models developed by Goldhammer (1969) and Cogan (1973).

Goldhammer (1969) was one of the early advocates of clinical supervision. For him, clinical supervision is

> that phase of instructional supervision which draws its data from first-hand observation of actual teaching events, and involves face-to-face . . . interaction between the supervisor and the teacher in the analysis of teaching behaviors and activities for instructional improvement. (pp. 19–20)

Cogan (1973) was also a proponent of clinical supervision, but he viewed it as a professional "colleagueship" that takes place between supervisor and teacher (Tanner and Tanner, 1987).

Goldhammer's Five-Step Process

As clinical supervision is often practiced, it falls short of its potential because the skills required are underdeveloped or undeveloped in both supervisors and teachers. To better develop skills in both teachers and supervisors, the Goldhammer clinical supervision process can be used. Goldhammer's five-step clinical supervision process includes preobservation conference, observation, analysis and strategy, supervision conference, and postconference analysis. In the following section, each step of the five-step process is discussed in more detail.

1. *Preobservation conference.* The purpose of this step is to establish the guidelines for the supervisory sequence that will follow. It provides the mental framework for classroom observation. The supervisor and the teacher discuss the procedures for collecting classroom data and agree on the teaching behaviors that will be examined during the observation period. It is during the preobservation conference that a supervisory "contract" is written; both parties, supervisor and teacher, explicitly agree on the reasons for the observation, the behaviors to be observed, and the kinds of data to be

collected. Throughout the entire conference, the supervisor and the teacher strive for open and honest communication.

2. *Observation.* During this step, the supervisor observes and collects data about the teaching episode. The supervisor acts as another pair of eyes, which can increase the amount of information gathered. Observation puts the supervisor in close proximity to the teacher and students in a specific instructional setting. Information collected about the teaching act is codified by the supervisor in a systematic way in order to make decisions about the teacher's performance level. Because observational data can be used to resolve problematic issues, it is essential for the supervisor to make careful and detailed notes while observing. Manatt (1981) emphasizes the need for accurate notes when he says that a particular behavior or incident did not happen if the supervisor did not write it down, and if the supervisor did not write it down, the supervisor did not see it. Other data collection procedures, such as audiotaping or videotaping, may be helpful but are not essential to the process. The classroom observation step is designed to capture as accurately as possible the teacher's and students' behaviors during a given lesson.

3. *Analysis and strategy.* The purpose of this step is to make sense out of the data collected and to put the information in some format that can be easily interpreted and understood by the teacher. The teacher, using tallies that the supervisor has converted to percentages or behaviors represented on charts, graphs, or diagrams, can then draw his or her own conclusions. Analysis is the heart of clinical supervision; it assists the supervisor and ultimately the teacher in making objective, accurate judgments. The analysis step moves the results of the observation from what could be an arbitrary and, in some cases, punitive view to a more objective interpretation. After the data have been analyzed, a plan of action (strategy) is developed to determine future sequences of instruction and observations by the supervisor. The analysis of the observational data and the subsequent development of strategies provide for continuity in supervision and result in productive decisions about what comes next.

4. *Supervision conference.* "All roads lead to the conference" (Goldhammer, 1969, p. 67). During the conference, the supervisor presents the information to the teacher for analysis and recommendations. The supervisor and the teacher meet to review the behaviors that were agreed upon initially, to assess progress toward mastering teacher competencies, to define "treatable" issues of the instructional performance, to provide reinforcement/rewards for a job well done, to discuss future observation times, and/or to redefine the

supervisory contract. Another benefit of the supervision conference is that it gives the supervisor the opportunity to offer guidance to the teacher and to assist the teacher in developing techniques of self-supervision. In the most ideal situations, the teacher and the supervisor work collaboratively to resolve problem areas and to stimulate interest in long-term professional growth and development. The "critical moment . . . comes when the teacher acknowledges that the procedure has yielded an accurate assessment of existing . . . professional attributes" (Beach and Reinhartz, 1982, p. 9).

5. *Postconference analysis.* During the "postmortem" stage, supervisory techniques, assumptions, emotional variables, and goals are discussed and analyzed. When the teacher acknowledges that the data collected are accurate, then the supervisor, working cooperatively with the teacher, formulates recommendations for change in classroom instructional behaviors. It is at this time that the supervisor verbally assesses his or her own supervisory behavior. The postconference analysis helps the supervisor answer the question "How effective was I?" Figure 8.1 provides an overview of the steps in the clinical supervision process.

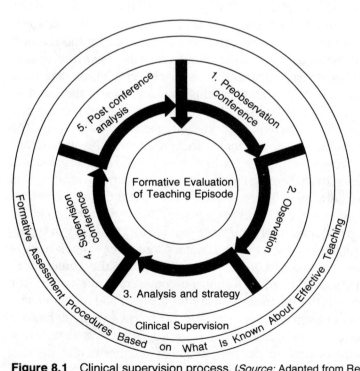

Figure 8.1 Clinical supervision process. (*Source:* Adapted from Reinhartz, J., and Beach, D. M. [1984]. What is good teaching? Using criteria of effective teaching to judge teacher performance. *NASSP Bulletin, 68,* 475, 35. Used with permission.)

Guidelines for Use of Clinical Supervision

Renewed interest in clinical supervision has resulted in several new perspectives that provide additional guidelines for the use of the model. Goldhammer, Anderson, and Krajewski (1980) have conceptualized clinical supervision as a technology to improve instruction. Glatthorn (1984), while cautioning against the use of "reliable generalizations," does offer tentative research findings about the effectiveness of clinical supervision. Supervisors may find the following guidelines helpful:

1. Teachers tend to favor a supervisor who is close and supportive (Gordon, 1976).
2. Most teachers and administrators agree with the basic assumptions of clinical supervision (Eaker, 1972).
3. Teachers seem to prefer clinical supervision to traditional supervision and believe that the techniques of clinical supervision are worthwhile (Shinn, 1976; Reavis, 1977).
4. Clinical supervision can change a teacher's behavior in the direction desired (Garman, 1971; Shuma, 1973; Kerr, 1976; Krajewski, 1976).
5. Supervisors using a clinical supervision approach seem more open and accepting in postobservation conferences than those using a traditional approach (Reavis, 1977).
6. Teachers differ in the type of supervisory interactions they prefer; there is some evidence that experienced teachers prefer nondirective supervision, while beginning teachers seem to prefer a more direct style (Copeland, 1980).

Supervisors, as they employ the clinical supervision model, should be aware of the perceptions of teachers:

1. Teachers favor individualized, close, and supportive supervision.
2. They agree on the basic assumptions and worthwhileness of the model.
3. They are willing to accept recommendations.
4. They believe that change in classroom behavior is possible.

Clinical supervision is not a panacea for supervisors. For Tanner and Tanner (1987), clinical supervision focuses "on actual class practices . . . which . . . ensures that the process is of practical significance to the teacher" (p. 183). It is a way of promoting teacher growth in self-direction and self-confidence by encouraging teachers to make instructional decisions. The supervisor recognizes that the teacher is the decision maker and asks him or her to consider options based on a knowledge of sound instructional practices and the feedback from observational data. The supervisor "can pinpoint inappropriate teaching decisions and behaviors, then offer productive alternatives" (Hunter, 1985, p. 58). Clinical supervision places much of the responsibility for identifying and solving instructional problems on the teacher (Pellicer, 1982).

Clinical supervision is more than a teacher inspection model (Snyder, 1981); it is a model for observing and conferencing with teachers. Goldsberry (1984) identified five characteristics often associated with clinical supervision:

1. a relationship to teacher's goals
2. a cyclical nature
3. a data-based foundation
4. joint (collaborative) interpretation
5. hypothesis generation and testing

Clinical supervision equips the supervisor and the teacher with the knowledge and skills to improve instructional performance.

The Instructional Supervision Training Program

An expanded version of clinical supervision has been developed by Boyan and Copeland (1978). The Instructional Supervision Training Program (ISTP) is an eight-step sequential model that the supervisor and the teacher can use as they focus on classroom instructional practices. The four stages and eight steps of the ISTP model are identified in Figure 8.2 and are outlined below.

> Stage I. Preobservation Conference Between Supervisor and Teacher
>> Step 1. *Behaviorally define the problem.* This step focuses on defining, in behavioral terms, the area of instructional concern.
>> Step 2. *Establish base rate or criterion.* During the second step, a base rate of frequency of the behavior is established.
>> Step 3. *Select observation instrument.* This step involves the selection or creation of an observation instrument for the supervisor to use in collecting data.

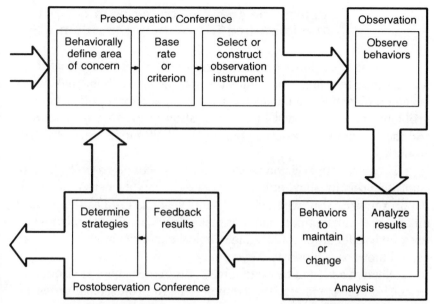

Figure 8.2   Instructional Supervision Training Program (ISTP). (*Source:* Boyan, N. J., and Copeland, W. D. [1978]. *Instructional Supervision Training Program,* p. 5. Columbus, Ohio: Charles E. Merrill. Used with permission.)

Stage II. *Supervisor Observes Teacher's Class*
  Step 4. *Classroom observation.* The collection of data using the observation instrument takes place during this step.

Stage III. Analysis and Strategy Development
  Step 5. *Analyze the data.* In this step, the supervisor analyzes the data and puts them in a visual form that the teacher can easily understand.
  Step 6. *Determine behaviors to maintain or change.* In this step, the supervisor determines which teaching behaviors should be maintained and which ones should be modified.

Stage IV. Postobservation Conference Between Supervisor and Teacher
  Step 7. *Provide feedback to teacher.* The supervisor provides the teacher with the results of the observation presented in a visual form.
  Step 8. *Determine strategies.* The supervisor and the teacher work cooperatively to

determine specific strategies to correct
the identified instructional problem(s).

The basic assumption underlying the ISTP model is that if the teacher initiates, alters, or eliminates specific instructional behaviors, based on objective data collected by the supervisor, the instructional problem will be solved. Close cooperation between the supervisor and the teacher is a basic function of the ISTP model if it is to work smoothly.

If clinical supervision is to operate effectively, a collegial, collaborative relationship between supervisors and teachers is an essential prerequisite. But when clinical supervision is used as the primary means of evaluating personnel, it makes such a collegial relationship extremely difficult or impossible. Clinical supervision should be perceived more as a supportive system, with the supervisor focusing on the collective action of those involved within the school environment. In such an environment, the commitment to professional growth is strengthened.

Clinical supervision links the growth phase of professional development with everyday classroom events and provides supervisors and teachers with the philosophical and methodological framework to improve student performance. "Clinical supervision may be characterized as a partnership in leadership squarely targeted on discovering and refining ways to enhance learning" (Goldsberry, 1984, p. 14). If such a partnership is nurtured, supervision by inspection gives way to supervision as problem solving.

This partnership view of clinical supervision has led to the development of a strategy called *peer coaching* (Joyce and Showers, 1982; Showers, 1984; Joyce, 1987). *Peer coaching* involves groups of teachers across grades and subjects who provide daily support and encouragement in the absence of a supervisor. The coaching approach, when coupled with clinical supervision, emphasizes action by staff members. As they participate in small group sessions, teachers focus on asking questions to clarify their own perceptions about schooling and learning. Through analysis and feedback during clinical supervision, supervisors find out the reasons for a teacher's decision and coach the teacher on the job by translating research on effective instruction into practice.

When supervisors and teachers become proficient in the use of clinical supervision, either in its original form or a modified or expanded version, they are better at diagnosing instructional skills and offering suggestions for improvement. The supervisor serves as the catalyst who cements all the steps of clinical supervision into a comprehensive model. In order to reach a reliable or accurate decision concerning classroom instructional performance, supervisors should utilize data about effective teaching as they work with teachers. The clinical supervision model involves identifying, collecting, and interpreting information germane to the school's, the teacher's, and the supervisor's goals.

DEVELOPMENTAL SUPERVISION

A second model of supervision is called *developmental supervision* (Glickman, 1981, 1985). This model recognizes teachers as individuals who are at various stages of growth and development. According to Glickman (1985), supervisors must foster thinking skills in teachers to help them diagnose classroom instruction and become aware of the many options for change. Typically, all teachers in a district receive the same inservice sessions, have the same types of observations, and are a part of the same evaluation system. Although effective instruction demands autonomous and flexible-thinking teachers, most school systems in fact do not foster autonomy or provide ways to improve teachers' thinking (Glickman, 1985). For many teachers, the only option is to simplify and deaden the classroom environment by disregarding student differences and establishing and maintaining routines that results in a sterility of sameness.

In such a bleak environment, teachers strive just to get through the day. Studies (Thies-Sprinthall, 1980; Sprinthall and Thies-Sprinthall, 1982; Oja, 1981) suggest that, in a supportive and stimulating environment, teachers can think at higher abstract levels. According to Glickman (1985):

> Abstract thought is the ability to determine relationships, to make comparisons and contrasts between information and experience to be used to generate multiple possibilities in formulating a decision. (p. 57)

Teachers, like other learners, can be taught to think in more abstract terms. Developmental supervision is based on the platform that "human development is the aim of education" (Glickman, 1985, p. 85). As supervisors work with teachers in an educational setting, they "should match their assistance to teachers' conceptual levels, but with the ultimate goal of teachers taking charge of their own improvement" (Glickman and Gordon, 1987, p. 64). In addition, supervisors must be knowledgeable about and responsive to the developmental stages and the adult life transitions of teachers. Adult development will be discussed more fully in Chapter 11.

Developmental supervision identifies three primary styles of supervision: directive, collaborative, and nondirective. The *directive* style includes the following kinds of supervisory behaviors: clarifying, presenting, demonstrating, directing, standardizing, and reinforcing. The *collaborative* style includes the following behaviors: listening, presenting, problem solving, and negotiating. A *nondirective* supervisory style assumes that teachers are capable of analyzing and solving their own instructional problems. Behaviors associated with the nondirective approach include listening, clarifying, encouraging, and presenting (Glickman, 1981).

Developmental supervision is also described in terms of two teacher variables that change over time and are related to instruction. These teacher variables include teacher commitment and levels of abstract thinking. The term commitment refers, developmentally, to the willingness of teachers to expend time and energy. It appears that, over time, teachers move from a concern for self, to a concern for their students, and, finally, to a concern for other students and other teachers. This concern is expressed in the teachers' willingness to devote time and energy to help others. One aspect of teacher development, the level of commitment, can be viewed as occurring along a continuum.

As seen in Figure 8.3, at one end of the continuum are teachers who are low in commitment. These teachers tend to show concern for their own success and/or survival and seldom demonstrate any concern for students and others. Supervisors, in working with these

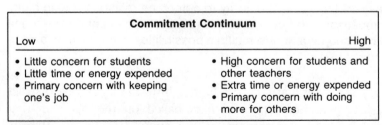

Commitment Continuum

Low	High
• Little concern for students	• High concern for students and
• Little time or energy expended	other teachers
• Primary concern with keeping	• Extra time or energy expended
one's job	• Primary concern with doing
	more for others

Figure 8.3 Teacher variable—commitment. (*Source:* Glickman, C. D. [1981]. *Developmental supervision: Alternative practices for helping teachers improve instruction,* p. 43. Alexandria, Va.: Association for Supervision and Curriculum Development. Used with permission of the Association for Supervision and Curriculum Development. Copyright © by ASCD. All rights reserved.)

teachers, will need to employ a directive style to achieve some movement in a positive direction along the continuum. At the opposite end of the continuum are teachers who have a high level of commitment which is shown in their concern not only for their students but for other students and teachers as well. These teachers are willing to expend extra time, energy, and effort to help others. Supervisors would most likely use a nondirective style in working with these teachers. In the mid-range of the continuum are teachers at various stages of development; because of a wide variance in levels of commitment in this area, supervisors would frequently use a collaborative style in working with teachers.

It is also helpful to view the teachers' level of abstract thinking along a continuum. As seen in Figure 8.4, at one end of the continuum are those teachers with high abstract thinking ability. Teachers at this end of the continuum have the ability to conceptualize a problem from many perspectives, can formulate several alternative plans, and can then select a plan and follow through with each step. In working with teachers who think abstractly, the supervisor encourages and reassures them as they experiment with new ideas and teaching methods and secures appropriate resources for successful lesson implementation. Teachers who are comfortable with the supervisory style that matches their developmental stage and is appropriate to their needs—the nondirective approach—tend to be less rigid, more independent, and adapt more easily to problem-solving situations.

Teachers who are capable of a moderate level of abstract thinking and can define the problem are limited generally in their ability to formulate a plan and follow through. The supervisor would most

| **Continuum of Abstract Thinking** | | |
Low	Moderate	High
• Confused about the problem • Doesn't know what can be done • "Show me" • Has one or two habitual responses to problems	• Can define the problem • Can think of one or two possible responses to the problem • Has trouble thinking through a comprehensive plan	• Can think of the problem from many perspectives • Can generate many alternative plans • Can choose a plan and think through each step

Figure 8.4 Teacher variable—level of abstract thinking. (*Source:* Glickman, C. D. [1981]. *Developmental supervision: Alternative practices for helping teachers improve instruction,* p. 46. Alexandria, Va.: Association for Supervision and Curriculum Development. Used with permission of the Association for Supervision and Curriculum Development. Copyright © by ASCD. All rights reserved.)

likely use a collaborative style of supervision in working with these teachers.

Teachers who function at low levels of abstract thinking are unclear about the problem and therefore cannot conceptualize what should be done. In working with teachers who have a limited ability to think abstractly, the supervisor uses a directive approach and provides the following types of help:

1. Simple, clear statements and explanations
2. Opportunities to practice often what is discussed
3. Assistance in developing a sequence of instructional skills
4. Concrete guidance during frequent conferences
5. Consistent and frequent support and reinforcement
6. Several advance organizers
7. Continuous supervision to ensure that items discussed are implemented

Within the developmental model, the role of the supervisor is to return more responsibility for instructional improvement to the teachers, and a cooperative, problem-solving approach is employed. Supervisors make decisions collectively with teachers. Motivation for continued instructional improvement comes from the supervisor as well as from the teacher. In such an environment, teachers take greater control of their own professional development.

The Clinical and Developmental Models Working Together

The clinical and developmental models give teachers and supervisors choices about how classroom instruction is supervised and analyzed. Clinical supervision can provide the steps to follow in working with teachers. Developmental supervision can provide the supervisor with clues to the level of the teacher's professional development, which can suggest a supervisory style. The two approaches, while unique in their views of the supervision process, are not mutually exclusive and often can be employed together. A supervisor, for example, might use a directive style, which has its roots in developmental supervision, when telling a marginally effective teacher exactly what must be done to improve his or her instructional performance. In the preobservation conference, the supervisor would request that the teacher submit the following information prior to classroom observation: a seating chart, a list of rules for classroom conduct, a list of instructional objectives, lesson plans, and a list of resources used in the preparation of the lesson. In giving the teacher precise instructions, the supervisor uses a directive style. The preobservation conference and data collection take place within the context of clinical supervision. In this example, the characteristics of clinical supervision are not violated even though modifications have been made and a directive supervisory style used. In fact, the clinical and developmental models of supervision can complement each other and can enhance the supervisor's effectiveness.

SELF-ASSESSMENT SUPERVISION

Another model of supervision involves teachers in self-evaluation and is called *self-assessment* supervision. To improve instructionally, teachers must learn to analyze their own classroom behavior. Although supervisors become involved as objective observers to collect data, assessment of classroom performance begins with teachers who are developmentally ready. Teachers, therefore, need to have the self-analysis skills for examining all aspects of their instructional delivery system. Such skills assist teachers in making appropriate decisions about their teaching (Reinhartz and Beach, 1983).

> As defined by Bailey (1981), self-assessment is: the process of self-examination in which the teacher utilizes a series of sequential feedback strategies for the purpose of instructional improvement. . . . the purposes of teacher self-assessment are to enable the teacher to become aware of personal classroom instructional behaviors [and to] become self-directed in improvement activities. (p. 9)

During self-assessment, teachers are called upon to evaluate their own performance so that they will be more aware of strengths and weaknesses associated with their classroom instruction. One way to begin self-assessment is to focus on the characteristics of effective instruction. Figure 8.5 shows the sequence of steps in the self-assessment process.

The first step in self-assessment supervision is to have the teachers analyze and reflect on their teaching performances. Self-diagnosis and self-awareness are the keys to the model. As they

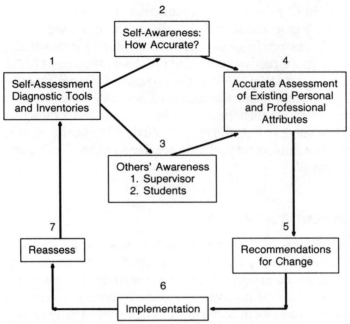

Figure 8.5   Self-assessment system. (*Source:* Adapted from Reinhartz, J., and Beach, D. M. [1983]. *Improving middle school instruction: A research-based self-assessment system,* p. 33. Washington, D.C.: National Education Association. Used with permission.)

reflect on their performances, teachers can use carefully developed inventories that are based on behaviors associated with effective instruction (Rosenshine and Furst, 1971; Walberg, Schiller, and Haertel, 1979; Manatt, 1981a, 1981b, 1987; Greenblatt, Cooper, and Muth, 1984). The inventories should be specific enough to encourage teachers to make critical decisions regarding their instructional efficacy. Figure 8.6 provides an example that a teacher can use in making a diagnostic assessment. The results generated from this first step give teachers a beginning data base for developing an instructional profile. In the second step of the self-assessment system, the teacher uses the information generated from the completed inventory when answering the question, "How objective have I been in assessing my own performance?"

The third step in self-assessment involves feedback from other sources. Figures 8.7 and 8.8 provide examples of inventories similar to the teacher's self-assessment. These can be used to obtain information from supervisors and students. The inventories provided here are designed to gather information about the teacher's instructional behavior that relates to variables associated with effective instruction (Rosenshine, 1983). As they work together, supervisors and teachers

As I conduct instruction in the classroom, am I or do I do the following?

1.

1	2	3	4	5

Even-tempered, friendly — Moody, often cross

2.

1	2	3	4	5

Perceive students as capable of accomplishing — See limited, narrowly defined success for students

3.

1	2	3	4	5

Open to student feedback — Do not allow students to express likes and dislikes

4.

1	2	3	4	5

Present materials in appropriate ways for student understanding — Do not plan instruction relative to student needs and abilities

5.

1	2	3	4	5

Follow up instruction with reasonable and interesting assignments — Rarely give assignments; if given, they are worksheets or terms and questions from textbook

6.

1	2	3	4	5

Give individual help when students do not understand material — Avoid individual help and rely on students to understand material

7.

1	2	3	4	5

Knowledgeable of concepts taught — Lack adequate preparation for presentation of concepts

8.

1	2	3	4	5

Regularly state expectations for classroom conduct — Rarely discuss rules of conduct and expectations for class behavior

9.

1	2	3	4	5

Enforce expectations strictly, but fairly — Inconsistent in applying and enforcing rules of conduct

10.

1	2	3	4	5

Monitor classroom behavior closely through movement and nonverbal behavior to manage class — Unaware of many behaviors in classroom and seldom move or use nonverbal behavior in class management

11.

1	2	3	4	5

Have an ability to get things done; complete tasks — Seldom finish a task during an assigned period and seldom get things done on schedule

12.

1	2	3	4	5

Help students accomplish objectives and produce achievement in students — Seldom have students accomplish objectives and provide little evidence of student achievement

Figure 8.6 Assessment of teacher instrument: The teacher. (*Source:* Adapted from Beach, D. M., and Reinhartz, J. [1982]. Improving instructional effectiveness: A self-assessment procedure. *Illinois School Research and Development Journal, 19,* 1, 9–10. Used with permission.)

As the teacher conducts instruction in the classroom, does he or she do the following:

1.
```
   1          2          3          4          5
   |----------|----------|----------|----------|
```
Even-tempered, friendly   Moody, often cross

2.
```
   1          2          3          4          5
   |----------|----------|----------|----------|
```
Perceive students as capable of   See limited, narrowly defined
accomplishing   success for students

3.
```
   1          2          3          4          5
   |----------|----------|----------|----------|
```
Open to student feedback   Does not allow students to express
                                             likes and dislikes

4.
```
   1          2          3          4          5
   |----------|----------|----------|----------|
```
Present materials in appropriate ways for   Does not plan instruction relative to
student understanding,   student needs and abilities
needs, and abilities

5.
```
   1          2          3          4          5
   |----------|----------|----------|----------|
```
Follow up instruction with reasonable and   Rarely give assignments; if given,
interesting assignments   they are worksheets or terms and
                                             questions from textbook

6.
```
   1          2          3          4          5
   |----------|----------|----------|----------|
```
Give individual help when students do   Avoid individual help and rely on
not understand material   students to understand material

7.
```
   1          2          3          4          5
   |----------|----------|----------|----------|
```
Knowledgeable of concepts taught   Lack adequate preparation for
                                             presentation of concepts

8.
```
   1          2          3          4          5
   |----------|----------|----------|----------|
```
Regularly state expectations for   Rarely discuss rules of conduct
classroom conduct   and expectations for
                                             classroom behavior

9.
```
   1          2          3          4          5
   |----------|----------|----------|----------|
```
Enforce expectations strictly, but fairly   Inconsistent in applying and
                                             enforcing rules of conduct

10.
```
   1          2          3          4          5
   |----------|----------|----------|----------|
```
Monitor classroom behavior closely   Unaware of many behaviors in
through movement and nonverbal   classroom and seldom move
behavior to manage class   or use nonverbal behavior
                                             in class management

11.
```
   1          2          3          4          5
   |----------|----------|----------|----------|
```
Have an ability to get things done;   Seldom finish a task during an
completes tasks   assigned period and seldom get
                                             things done on schedule

12.
```
   1          2          3          4          5
   |----------|----------|----------|----------|
```
Help students accomplish objectives   Seldom have students accomplish
and produces achievement in students   objectives and provide little
                                             evidence of student
                                             achievement

Figure 8.7 Assessment of teacher instrument: The supervisor. (*Source:* Adapted from Beach, D. M., and Reinhartz, J. [1982]. Improving instructional effectiveness: A self-assessment procedure. *Illinois School Research and Development Journal, 19,* 1, 9–10. Used with permission.)

As the teacher conducts instruction in the classroom, does he or she do the following:

1. 1 — 2 — 3 — 4 — 5

    Even-tempered, friendly   Moody, often cross

2. 1 — 2 — 3 — 4 — 5

    Perceive students as capable of   See limited, narrowly defined
    accomplishing   success for students

3. 1 — 2 — 3 — 4 — 5

    Open to student feedback   Does not allow students to express
                                                            likes and dislikes

4. 1 — 2 — 3 — 4 — 5

    Present materials in appropriate ways for   Does not plan instruction relative to
    student understanding,   student needs and abilities
    needs, and abilities

5. 1 — 2 — 3 — 4 — 5

    Follow up instruction with reasonable and   Rarely give assignments; if given,
    interesting assignments   they are worksheets or terms and
                                                            questions from textbook

6. 1 — 2 — 3 — 4 — 5

    Give individual help when students do   Avoid individual help and rely on
    not understand material   students to understand material

7. 1 — 2 — 3 — 4 — 5

    Knowledgeable of concepts taught   Lack adequate preparation for
                                                            presentation of concepts

8. 1 — 2 — 3 — 4 — 5

    Regularly state expectations for   Rarely discuss rules of conduct
    classroom conduct   and expectations for
                                                            classroom behavior

9. 1 — 2 — 3 — 4 — 5

    Enforce expectations strictly, but fairly   Inconsistent in applying and
                                                            enforcing rules of conduct

10. 1 — 2 — 3 — 4 — 5

    Monitor classroom behavior closely   Unaware of many behaviors in
    through movement and nonverbal   classroom and seldom move
    behavior to manage class   or use nonverbal behavior
                                                            in class management

11. 1 — 2 — 3 — 4 — 5

    Have an ability to get things done;   Seldom finish a task during an
    complete tasks   assigned period and seldom get
                                                            things done on schedule

12. 1 — 2 — 3 — 4 — 5

    Help students accomplish objectives   Seldom have students accomplish
    and produce achievement in students   objectives and provide little
                                                            evidence of student
                                                            achievement

Figure 8.8 Assessment of teacher instrument: The student. (*Source:* Adapted from Beach, D. M., and Reinhartz, J. [1982]. Improving instructional effectiveness: A self-assessment procedure. *Illinois School Research and Development Journal, 19,* 1, 9–10. Used with permission.)

can modify these inventories or develop similar assessment tools that more closely parallel the objectives of their own school district.

In addition to inventories, videotaping or audiotaping can be useful tools for the teacher in building a teaching profile. These techniques provide a more objective data base for analyzing teacher performance and give teachers the opportunity to see how they look and/or sound. Teachers can view or listen to these tapes in private, which is less threatening. Teachers may ask supervisors to observe a lesson and complete an inventory.

The fourth step in self-assessment supervision is most important in determining the accuracy of the information from other sources. As indicated in Figure 8.5, self-assessment can be considered a success when the teacher verifies that the perceptions of others (steps 2 and 4) have yielded an accurate picture of existing personal and professional attributes. A common reaction a teacher needs to guard against is the rationalizing or explaining away of ineffective classroom behaviors. At this point a teacher may believe that the perceptions of others are inaccurate and feel that no one knows him or her well enough to provide pertinent data. For the process of self-assessment supervision to be effective, teachers should make an honest commitment to analyzing and changing their classroom behaviors. Additionally, teachers must have confidence in the process and in themselves. If these two factors are objectively addressed, the original goal of the model, that of self-improvement, can be achieved.

If the data collected on the inventories or the feedback from others are inconsistent with the teacher's own rating, then there is a misconception concerning classroom effectiveness. In such cases, it is necessary to work toward reconciling the teacher's self-perception with the results of the other measures. For example, the teacher may perceive himself or herself as fair, student-oriented, and committed to the school's philosophy; students, supervisors, or others may view the teacher as inflexible, demanding, and too content-oriented. For the self-assessment model to work successfully, the teacher must be prepared to compare objectively the responses from all sources. The goal of self-assessment is not necessarily to have responses match those of the teacher with those of others. It is essential, however, for the supervisor to help the teacher recognize different perceptions and then work with the teacher to try to do something about them.

A discrepancy may be the result of a teacher's unwillingness to be totally honest and candid when completing the self-assessment inventory. Or the teacher may be unaware of the perception of the class during instruction. Or the teacher may sincerely believe that everything concerning classroom performance is progressing satisfactorily. Whatever the case, in step four, teachers who are genuinely interested in self-improvement will want to deal constructively with the different perceptions as presented by the inventory results. The teacher will need to consider changes in behavior to help bridge the gap between self-perception and the perceptions of others.

The fifth step involves developing recommendations for initiating change in classroom behavior. With the focus on self-assessment, the teachers should develop several recommendations for instructional changes that they would be willing to implement in their classrooms. The supervisor may be asked to provide input regarding the recommendations and may be asked to make some suggestions as well. The next step in self-assessment comes when teachers implement the agreed-upon changes in their own instructional classrooms. As teachers act on recommendations and make changes in their instructional behavior, they begin to think about the teaching act and consequently behave differently. Self-assessment comes to a close when the teacher reassesses the effectiveness of the change or changes and decides if additional changes are needed.

As noted by Joyce and Showers (1980), instructional improvement relies on five components: theory, demonstrations, practice, feedback, and classroom application. The five components necessitate change in teacher behavior, but the magnitude of change may depend on the teacher's willingness and ability to accept feedback.

Supervisors can help increase the teachers' acceptance of feedback by establishing nonthreatening environment in the school. Teachers can work in small teams or groups to demonstrate and practice teaching skills in front of others—peers and/or supervisor(s). Team members assist individual teachers to diagnose the content presented and the effectiveness of the teaching method selected. After experiencing the process of self-assessment and receiving support from others, teachers are more willing and more likely to transfer to their classrooms the skills that they have practiced in the small group.

As mentioned earlier in the chapter, the concept of peer coaching can be a useful strategy for improving instruction, reconciling perceptions, and sharing mutual feelings or problems with other educators (Joyce and Showers, 1982). Coaching, when linked with self-assessment, provides the needed support system for teachers attempting to make changes in their instructional performance. Additionally, it contributes an element of companionship that encourages teachers to share their successes and frustrations and to work out problems that may have surfaced during small group sessions. By adding the coaching dimension to self-assessment, teachers can seek assistance from experienced peers in an acceptable and nonthreatening manner.

The steps outlined for self-assessment in Figure 8.5, should be conducted several times during the school year as a part of staff development procedures. The key to successful self-assessment supervision on a districtwide basis is to identify criteria of effective teaching and link that information with the self-assessment and the formative data provided by supervisor(s). The undergirding philosophy of self-assessment supervision becomes one of formulating an objective perception and analysis of the instructional self based on what is known about effective instruction.

The ambiguities and uncertainties often associated with current and past supervisory practices must give way to more clearly defined roles and responsibilities based on the recognition of individual differences in both supervisors and teachers. It is through the repeated use of a model of supervision that incorporates self-analysis that teachers can identify their own effective teaching.

To be effective in their roles, supervisors must begin to utilize various models of supervision that provide a consistent pattern of interaction with teachers. The currently employed practice of a supervisor making one or two visits a year and calling this supervision is totally unacceptable and ineffective. Second, the current approach, in which a supervisor observes a class, completes an evaluation, and discusses the evaluation, should be modified. How many supervisors, when they were teachers, found this series of events helpful? Most will admit that such an approach was not (Shanker, 1985). Yet many supervisors continue to conduct classroom observations in this manner.

Thus supervisors must become committed to a long-term process of initiating and sustaining instructional growth and change for teachers. Supervisors can help teachers reach their highest potential as classroom instructors by implementing the most appropriate supervisory model which assists the supervisor and teacher in formulating strategies for improved classroom performance.

SUMMARY

Improving instruction is a complex yet challenging task for both teachers and supervisors. This chapter highlights three specific models of supervision: clinical, with the Instructional Supervision Training Program (ISTP) presented as a version; developmental; and self-assessment. These models were discussed in light of fostering professional development among teachers. The intent was not to put the models in competition with each other but rather to encourage supervisors and teachers to use the one(s) that will be most effective in a specific setting. The supervisory model selected depends on a number of variables that the supervisor considers before employing one or a combination.

The five-step clinical supervision model includes preobservation conference, observation, analysis and strategy, supervision conference, and postconference analysis. Although research documenting the effectiveness of clinical supervision is limited, there are tentative findings that can guide supervisors. Supervisors, as they employ the clinical supervision model, should be aware that teachers favor individualized, close, and supportive supervision; agree on the basic assumptions and worthwhileness of the model; are willing to accept recommendations; and believe that change in classroom behavior is possible.

The Instructional Supervision Training Program (ISTP) model, an expanded model of clinical supervision, is an eight-step sequential approach in which the supervisor assists the teacher in resolving instructional problems. The basic premise of the model is the belief that an observer in the classroom can objectively collect data to help the teacher "see" the behavior problems and determine a course of action to correct the situation.

Supervisors who employ the developmental model of supervision treat teachers as individuals who are at various stages of growth and development. The model is based on the premise that teacher development is human development. There are three primary supervisory styles (directive, collaborative, and nondirective), and supervisors select a style that is the most compatible with two developmental characteristics related to teacher effectiveness (level of commitment and level of abstract thinking).

The self-assessment model of supervision helps teachers become aware of their own instructional performance. This model asks the teacher to compare data collected from self-assessment inventories with input from other sources. The primary aim of self-assessment supervision is to involve the teacher in self-diagnosis and the development of an instructional profile. This model of supervision offers teachers a positive, nonthreatening approach to self-improvement. Competency in self-assessment comes with practice and requires a willingness on the part of the teacher to engage in systematic analysis on a regular basis in order that continuing instructional improvement and change may occur.

The models of supervision presented in this chapter emphasize comprehensive plans for helping teachers improve their instructional effectiveness and thereby increase student achievement. The models of supervision give supervisors and teachers choices about how classroom instruction is supervised and analyzed. Time invested in teacher instructional improvement is time well spent. As supervisors and teachers participate in the models of supervision, supervisors become educational managers who help teachers make decisions about their teaching.

YOUR TURN

8.1 Read the following case study of Mr. Doe,* a middle school teacher, and then complete the task as instructed.

> As students enter the classroom, Mr. Doe usually greets them at the door, identifying each one by name. He begins each life science class with a lecture which includes a general overview of the concepts to be presented that day, listing on the chalkboard the major vocabulary words that will be encountered during the lesson. In each lesson, he stresses content. Mr. Doe plans activities that students can do during the lesson, particularly laboratory activities. He has a minimum of one lab activity a week, but usually at least two.
>
> During the lesson, Mr. Doe stops periodically to ask if students have any questions before he moves on to the next topic or concept. Students seldom respond to opportunities to elaborate on the material and rarely volunteer information or ask questions. Mr. Doe communicates clearly to the class what he expects in the way of classroom conduct. He often discusses proper classroom

Source: Reinhartz, J., and Beach, D. M. (1983). *Improving middle school instruction: A research-based self-assessment system,* pp. 36–37. Washington, D.C.: National Education Association. Used with permission.

conduct and consistently enforces class rules. The class atmosphere can be described as orderly and cooperative. Misbehavior is minimal.

As he begins a lesson, Mr. Doe usually stands behind the laboratory demonstration table. During his overview and lecture, he seldom moves more than a few feet from the demonstration table to the chalkboard. Not only does he remain in the one area during the lesson, but his students also seldom move about the room. Students move about only when laboratory activities are planned, at which time their movement is restricted to getting equipment and supplies.

Because of the nature of his subject, Mr. Doe feels that there is not enough student–teacher interaction. After his brief lecture, he would like his students to discuss the concepts presented. He is frustrated when they do not respond to his invitation to clarify the content when he asks, "Are there any questions?" He is not convinced that he has an adequate understanding of how well students know the information until he gives them a test. By that time, it is too late.

Student reluctance to participate in discussion, volunteer answers, or initiate questions is creating a problem for Mr. Doe. Consequently, he is beginning to question his effectiveness as a middle school teacher. While several students seem to do well in his classes, he concludes that most students could be doing much better. If he could get them to open up and talk about what they are studying, he thinks he would have a better indication of what they know. He is very concerned that his students do not appear to be motivated, are not responsive, and take a passive role in classroom activities. Mr. Doe would like his students to demonstrate some excitement about what they are studying.

The task: Determined to do something about the situation, Mr. Doe decides to seek help from his supervisor (select a specific supervisory position). After a brief discussion after school one day, the supervisor suggests that Mr. Doe use the self-assessment model to analyze his instructional performance. As the supervisor, what overall plan would you develop to assist Mr. Doe? How would you initiate the self-assessment model of supervision with him? Identify the actions or steps you would take to complete the seven steps in self-assessment. Do you think there are elementary and secondary teachers who have perceptions like Mr. Doe? If so, what are the perceptions? If not, why not?

8.2. Read each of the following situations and answer the questions that follow:

   a. You are a consultant and have observed a fourth grade teacher who ignored many of her students. She did not establish the purpose of the lesson and continued to use the workbook as the single most important resource in her classroom. What supervisory techniques/ models would you use as you work with this teacher during the school year?

b. You are a principal of a junior high school, and the teachers, at your request, turn in lesson plans at the end of each week. How would you evaluate each plan in an effort to assist each teacher achieve his or her instructional best?

c. You are given a new responsibility that includes evaluating teachers' classroom performance. Up to this time, you have been serving in a helping role, and now the role has been expanded to that of evaluator. You are aware that effective schools have teachers who engage in professional dialogue on a regular basis. You want teachers to talk to each other in your school. How could you encourage teachers to talk about their expectations, teaching strategies, curriculum resources, use of time, and so on? What steps would you take to increase teacher talk so that the effective instructional practices of master teachers reach the less effective teachers?

d. You are working with a secondary teacher who refuses to "write" a supervisory contract during the preobservation conference. Yet this teacher on the whole is fairly effective with his students. What do you do as his supervisor? Where do you turn for help? You are caught between your desire to show him who is in charge and the need for implementing the aspects of successful supervisory practices. Which supervisory model(s) would help you resolve this dilemma? How? In what ways?

e. You have completed your observation of a ten-year veteran elementary teacher, but you do not have anything positive to offer during the supervision conference. She constantly yells at students; she rarely moves from sitting at her desk; she ignores student questions; students are seldom on-task and their assignments appear to be more busy work than constructive activities. What action would you take with this teacher? How could the models of supervision help you be honest yet caring with this teacher, especially if she becomes defensive or belligerent? How could you show concern for her professional growth and still inform her of areas that may need to be modified?

8.3. Sometimes supervisors who espouse a preference for self-assessment supervision do not use that approach when working with teachers. Read the following brief exchange between a teacher and a supervisor.

TEACHER: I really felt that the questions were coming easier today. After many weeks of struggling, the task of formulating

questions became natural for me. Even the students responded enthusiastically. They hadn't been this active
before. Rather than responding with short yes-or-no answers, the students seemed to be ready to discuss each
comment offered.

SUPERVISOR: So you thought the questioning part of the lesson was
greatly improved today in comparison to previous days?

TEACHER: *(eagerly responds)* Yes!

SUPERVISOR: *(after a long pause)* Umhm.

Rewrite the dialogue in such a way to indicate that the supervisor
supports self-assessment supervision for teachers.

8.4. Under what circumstances would you suggest that teachers use student
and parent questionnaires in building a professional profile for teacher
evaluation?

REFERENCES

Alfonso, R. J., Firth, G., and Neville, R. (1984). The supervisory skill mix.
Educational Leadership, 41, 7, 16–18.

Bailey, G. D. (1981). *Teacher self-assessment: A means for improving classroom instruction* Washington, D.C.: National Education Association.

Beach, D. M., and Reinhartz, J. (1982). Improving instructional effectiveness: A self-assessment procedure. *Illinois School Research and Development Journal, 19,* 1, 5–12.

Bents, R. H., and Harvey, K. R. (1981). Staff development: Change in the
individual. In B. Dillon-Peterson (Ed.), *Staff development/organization
development.* Alexandria, Va.: Association for Supervision and Curriculum Development.

Boyan, N. J., and Copeland, W. D. (1978). *Instructional Supervision Training
Program.* Columbus, Ohio: Charles E. Merrill.

Brookover, W., et al. (1979). *School social systems and student achievement:
Schools can make a difference.* New York: Praeger.

Cogan, M. L. (1973). *Clinical supervision.* Boston: Houghton Mifflin.

Copeland, W. D. (1980). Affective disposition of teachers in training toward
examples of supervisory behavior. *Journal of Educational Research,
74,* 37–42.

Eaker, R. E. (1972). An analysis of the clinical supervision process as perceived by selected teachers and administrators (doctoral dissertation,
University of Tennessee). *Dissertation Abstracts International.*

Edmonds, R. (1979). Effective schools for the urban poor. *Educational
Leadership, 37,* 2, 15–27.

Garman, N. B. (1971). A study of clinical supervision as a resource of college teachers of English (doctoral dissertation, University of Pittsburgh). *Dissertation Abstracts International.*

Glatthorn, A. A. (1984). *Differentiated supervision.* Alexandria, Va.: Association for Supervision and Curriculum Development.

Glickman, C. D. (1981). *Developmental supervision: Alternative practices for helping teachers improve instruction.* Alexandria, Va.: Association for Supervision and Curriculum Development.

Glickman, C. (1984–1985). The supervisor's challenge: Changing the teacher's work environment. *Educational Leadership, 42,* 4, 38–40.

Glickman, C. (1985). *Supervision of Instruction: A developmental approach.* Boston, Mass.: Allyn and Bacon.

Glickman, C. D., and Gordon, S. P. (1987). Clarifying developmental supervision. *Educational Leadership, 44,* 8, 64–68.

Goldhammer, R. (1969). *Clinical supervision.* New York: Holt, Rinehart and Winston.

Goldhammer, R., Anderson, R. H., and Krajewski, R. J. (1980). *Clinical supervision: Special methods for the supervision of teachers* (2nd ed.). New York: Holt, Rinehart and Winston.

Goldsberry, L. F. (1984). The realities of clinical supervision. *Educational Leadership, 41,* 7, 12–15.

Goodlad, J. I. (1984). *A place called school.* New York: McGraw-Hill.

Gordon, B. (1976). Teachers evaluate supervisory behavior in the individual conference. *Clearing House, 49,* 231–238.

Greenblatt, R. B., Cooper, B. S., and Muth, R. (1984). Managing for effective teaching. *Educational Leadership, 41,* 5, 57–59.

Harvey, O. J., Hunt, D., and Schroder, H. M. (1961). *Conceptual systems and personality organization.* New York: Wiley.

Hunter, M. (1985). What's wrong with Madeline Hunter? *Educational Leadership, 42,* 5, 57–60.

Joyce, B. (1987). On teachers coaching teachers: A conversation with Bruce Joyce. *Educational Leadership, 44,* 5, 12–17. [Interview with Ron Brandt, editor of *Educational Leadership*].

Joyce, B., and Showers, B. (1980). Improving inservice training: The messages of research. *Educational Leadership, 37,* 5, 379–384.

Joyce, B., and Showers, B. (1982). The coaching of teaching. *Educational Leadership, 40,* 1, 4–10.

Kerr, B. J. (1976). An investigation of the process of using feedback data within the clinical supervision cycle to facilitate teachers' individualization of instruction (doctoral dissertation, University of Pittsburgh). *Dissertation Abstracts International.*

Krajewski, R. J. (1976). Clinical supervision to facilitate teacher self-improvement. *Journal of Research and Development, 9,* 58–66.

Lightfoot, S. (1983). *Good high schools: Portraits of character and culture.* New York: Basic Books.

Manatt, R. P. (1981a). Evaluating teacher performance. Alexandria, Va.:

Association for Supervision and Curriculum Development. [Video-tape.]

Manatt, R. P. (November 1981b). Manatt's exercise in selecting teacher performance evaluation criteria based on effective teaching research Albuquerque, N.M. National Symposium for Professionals in Evaluation and Research. [Mimeograph.]

Manatt, R. P. (1987). Lessons from a comprehensive performance appraisal project. *Educational Leadership, 44,* 7, 8–14.

Oja, S. N. (April 1981). Deriving teacher educational objectives from cognitive-developmental theories and applying them to the practice of teacher education. Paper presented at the annual meeting of the American Educational Research Association, Los Angeles.

Pellicer, L. O. (1982). Providing instructional leadership—a principal challenge. *NASSP Bulletin, 66,* 456, 27–31.

Reavis, C. A. (1976). Clinical supervision: A timely approach. *Educational Leadership, 33,* 5, 360–363.

Reavis, C. A. (1977). A test of the clinical supervision model. *Journal of Educational Research, 70,* 311–315.

Reinhartz, J., and Beach, D. M. (1983). *Improving middle school instruction: A research-based self-assessment system.* Washington, D.C.: National Education Association.

Rosenholtz, S. J., and Kyle, S. J. (1984). Teacher isolation: Barrier to professionalism. *American Educator, 8,* 10–15.

Rosenshine, B. (1983). Teaching functions in instructional programs. *Elementary School Journal, 83,* 335–352.

Rosenshine, B., and Furst, N. (1971). Research in teacher performance criteria. In B. O. Smith (Ed.), *Research in teacher education.* Englewood Cliffs, N.J.: Prentice-Hall.

Santmire, T. E. (1979). *Developmental differences in adult learners: Implications for staff development.* Lincoln: University of Nebraska. [Mimeograph.]

Shanker, A. (1985). The revolution that's overdue. *Phi Delta Kappan, 66,* 5, 311–315.

Shinn, J. L. (1976). Teacher perception of ideal and actual supervisory training programs sponsored by the Association of California School Administrators (doctoral dissertation, University of Oregon). *Dissertation Abstracts International.*

Showers, B. (1984). *Peer coaching: A strategy for facilitating transfer of training.* Eugene, Ore.: Center for Educational Policy and Management.

Shuma, K. Y. (1973). Changes effectuated by a clinical supervisory relationship which emphasizes a helping relationship and a conference format made congruent with the establishment and maintenance of this helping relationship (doctoral dissertation, University of Pittsburgh). *Dissertation Abstracts International.*

Snyder, K. (1981). Clinical supervision in the 1980's. *Educational Leadership, 38,* 7, 521–525.

Sprinthall, N. A., and Thies-Sprinthall, L. (1982). Career development of teachers: A cognitive developmental perspective. In H. Mitzel, *Encyclopedia of educational research* (5th ed.). New York: Free Press.

Tanner, D., and Tanner, L. (1987). *Supervision in education: Problems and practices.* New York: Macmillan.

Thies-Sprinthall, L. (1980). Promoting the conceptual and principled thinking level of the supervising teacher (doctoral dissertation, St. Cloud State University). *Dissertation Abstracts International.*

Walberg, H. J., Schiller, D., and Haertel, G. D. (1979). The quiet revolution in educational research. *Phi Delta Kappan, 61,* 3, 179–183.

Wilsey, C., and Killion, J. (1982). Making staff development programs work. *Educational Leadership, 40,* 2, 36–43.

chapter 9

Mechanics of Supervision

The mechanics of supervision involve specific procedures and techniques that supervisors use when working with teachers and observing in classrooms. These procedures and techniques are essential to supervisors in the observation and documentation of teaching–learning behaviors and contribute to the overall effectiveness of the instructional supervision process. This chapter will describe the mechanics that supervisors can use on a day-to-day basis as they employ a model or models of supervision.

In the monograph *Clinical Supervision* Hunter notes that "clouds of mysticism have shrouded the process of instruction obscuring cause–effect relationships" (p. 13). The "clouds of mysticism" associated with effective instruction begin to dissipate when supervisors use classroom observation techniques that objectively record teacher–pupil classroom behavior. This chapter, then, will seek to dissipate the mysticism by (1) identifying some observation pitfalls to avoid, (2) describing some general principles of classroom observation, (3) outlining data collection and data analysis procedures, and (4) discussing postobservation conference procedures. By examining some of the fundamental mechanics of the supervisory process, especially those areas concerned with classroom observation and data collection, supervisors can be more effective in recording and analyzing teacher–pupil interactions and presenting the data to teachers.

OBSERVATION PITFALLS

To be effective as observers, supervisors should be aware of several factors that can hinder the observation process and limit objective, accurate data collection. Observing, or "seeing in classrooms," as described by Good and Brophy (1984), is a complex process that is often influenced by our past experiences, attitudes, and prejudices. It is exceedingly difficult to function as an impartial observer—that is, to observe without adding one's personal interpretations. Supervisors who serve as observers should confine their activities to collecting and coding descriptive information when viewing classroom interactions. Only *after* classroom behaviors have been observed and recorded is it appropriate for the supervisor to formulate hypotheses. And, at that time, supervisors should be cautioned to let the data suggest the hypotheses rather than letting their own interpretations influence the formulation of the hypotheses.

To avoid misinterpretation of classroom behavior, supervisors need to be aware of their "perceptual blinders" (Good and Brophy, 1984). For some supervisors, for instance, highly verbal teachers are perceived as effective, while more soft-spoken teachers, who listen a great deal to their students, may be perceived as less effective. Such conclusions, based on a general perception of teacher style, can be inaccurate and unfair. Such "perceptual blinders" prevent supervisors from "seeing" in classrooms. Therefore, as they gather classroom data, supervisors should guard against personal biases that can influence what they see.

A second element of bias that supervisors should guard against is having a list of personal likes and dislikes that they apply universally to all teaching situations. These personal interpretations may lead to erroneous analyses, hypotheses, and recommendations.

Another aspect that can influence classroom observations is teacher anxiety. Teachers who feel threatened or are insecure while being observed will behave differently in this situation, and their lack of ease will influence the behavior of their students. Teacher anxiety, then, can distort classroom events and supervisors should be cognizant of this distortion (Coates and Thoresen, 1976). Teachers who are uncomfortable during in-class observations often have a more difficult time in assessing and assisting students. As a result, the quality of a teacher's instructional competency may be masked. It becomes the supervisor's responsibility to help this type of teacher develop the necessary self-confidence to demonstrate the technical skills required of effective teachers.

GENERAL PRINCIPLES OF OBSERVATION

The following general principles are related to the observation process. Although classrooms will vary, as will the teachers, these principles can serve as general guidelines for supervisors to follow as they conduct in-class observations and follow-up sessions.

The first principle of observation is to concentrate on student behavior. Although some supervisors may want to focus the observation on the actions of the teacher, Good and Brophy (1984) disagree; they believe that "the key to looking in classrooms is student behavior" (p. 60). For them, as long as students are engaged, it does not matter what the teacher is doing. By looking at the effect of teacher behavior on student behavior, supervisors are less tempted to view what is observed through a preconceived personal bias. Focusing on how students respond to their teacher can contribute to a more objective observation. This is not to say that the supervisor should ignore teacher behavior. The important point to remember, however, is that the focus should be on the students.

A second principle of observation is to focus on a small number of specific classroom dimensions. Classroom dimensions that may prove helpful to examine are on-task/off-task behaviors, transitions, pacing, general class climate, the attitudes of the students toward class assignments, and aspects of student–teacher interactions. Whatever the specific focus of the observation, however, the number of dimensions should be limited.

The third principle—not to disrupt the natural setting of the classroom—may seem obvious but should be stated. Any supervisor entering a classroom can upset the delicate balance that exists. To maintain this balance, supervisors should be as unobtrusive as possible, by avoiding eye contact with the students and the teacher, by refraining from talking to or helping students at their desks, and by finding a quiet place in the room to sit and take notes. By blending in, supervisors convey a message to teachers that they are to carry on as usual. Supervisors soon discover that this is difficult to do even under the best observation conditions.

Fourth, supervisors should take complete, clear, and accurate notes during classroom observations. Notetaking is a skill that supervisors need to develop to minimize interpolation of what is viewed and to maximize reliability as an observer. Supervisors should take notes and not try to remember what happened. To make notetaking easier, they can use a form of shorthand. Symbols can be used to represent common words, student responses to teacher, and transitions. Two commonly used systems are Hunter's script taping (1983) and the Flanders Interaction Analysis Categories System (1967). The Flanders System will be described in greater detail later in the chapter.

Following the observation, the fifth general principle is for the supervisor to perform a detailed analysis of the data recorded during the observation. The supervisor should first systematically review all notes and then look for patterns, correlations, and/or contradictions. Careful analysis of the data may help the supervisor answer such questions as: "Are there identifiable hypotheses relating to teacher–student interaction?" "Is there a recurring pattern of behaviors?" "What additional information is needed?" Taking time to comb through the notes and organizing the data can help prevent the tendency to jump to unwarranted conclusions. The analysis process can also add more credibility to the information when it is presented to the teacher.

The sixth and last general principle of observation is to provide feedback to the teacher. Reporting results of the observation to the teacher during the postobservation conference requires the supervisor to be organized and present the data in a visual form (with graphs, charts, or other materials) that the teacher can easily understand and readily acknowledge. If the situation warrants, the supervisor can offer suggestions for instructional improvement.

These general principles, if followed, can help the supervisor be more effective in conducting classroom observations and reporting results to teachers. It should be emphasized that the observation process is designed to yield the most accurate and objective information possible.

DATA COLLECTION PROCEDURES

By using a variety of data collection techniques, supervisors can focus on specific student behaviors during a classroom observation. Acheson and Gall (1987) suggest several data collection procedures such as verbatim and selective verbatim records, observations based on seating charts (that is, on-task behavior, verbal flow, and movement), and anecdotal records. These data collection techniques become the starting point for breaking down the complex nature of the instructional process. Although data collection procedures do not guarantee total objectivity, they can provide a basis for a nonjudgmental record of student–teacher interactions. The following techniques, which are discussed in detail in the section that follows, may prove helpful as supervisors observe in classrooms: coding on-task and off-task behavior, coding and recording transitions and lesson pacing, recording behaviors associated with classroom management, and coding verbal interactions.

Coding on-task and off-task behavior. When supervisors observe teachers, a check of on-task and off-task student behavior may be helpful or necessary. Supervisors can use a checklist to mark at 5-minute intervals; the checklist should include student behavior as well as the time it is occurring (Glickman, 1985). Figure 9.1 is an example of an on-task/off-task behavior checklist. If, for example, at 1:15 p.m. a student is listening, is doing his or her assigned work, or is engaged in the discussion, the supervisor records a check in the "Attentive to Task" column for this time period. If, on the other hand, a student at 1:30 p.m. is staring into space or sitting with his or her head on the desk, that student is considered to be passively off-task, and a check is placed in the "Inattentive/Passive" column. Another type of off-task behavior is labeled "Inattentive/Active" and a check is placed in this column when a student is out of his or her seat, wandering around the room, or talking to others about noninstructional matters. This technique, developed by Glickman, allows the

RECORD OF STUDENT ON-TASK/ OFF-TASK BEHAVIOR

Class Time	Attentive to Task	Inattentive/ Passive	Inattentive/ Active

Figure 9.1 Data collecting—student attentiveness levels. (*Source:* Reprinted from Glickman, C. D. [1981]. *Developmental supervision: Alternative practices for helping teachers improve instruction,* p. 19. Alexandria, Va.: Association for Supervision and Curriculum Development. Used with permission of the Association for Supervision and Curriculum Development. Copyright © by ASCD. All rights reserved.)

observer to record individual student behaviors during nine 5-minute intervals in a 45- or 50-minute class period.

The observer may focus on up to 5 or 6 specific students, or randomly select 5 or 6 students to observe based on the preobservation contract with the teacher. After the observation, the results are analyzed and then presented to the teacher and discussed.

Coding and recording transitions and lesson pacing. Techniques that can be used to gather information about lesson transitions and pacing during in-class observations are more open-ended in nature. If the supervisor is monitoring lesson transitions and pacing, the instrument identified in Figure 9.2 may be more appropriate. The supervisor records the type and nature of each transition that takes place during a single class period. With each transition entry, it is important to record the time, type, and nature of the transition. The patterns (what the teacher says or does and /or what the students say or do) recorded provide information not only about the nature of the transition but also about the pacing of the lesson; both aspects can be charted and analyzed.

The written lesson plan analysis checklist (Figure 9.3) can be used when reviewing lesson plans. For example, after reviewing a teacher's written plans, the supervisor may have found transitions from one topic or concept to the next. However, during an in-class observation, the supervisor notes that the teacher does not overtly

RECORD OF LESSON TRANSITIONS AND PACING

Topic of lesson: _____

Type of lesson: _____

Date and time of observation: _____

Class size: _____

Directions: Record the time and the nature of each transition in the lesson
as the teacher moves from one topic to another or from one
activity to another.

Time	Nature of transition

Figure 9.2   Data collecting—record of lesson transitions and pacing.

WRITTEN LESSON PLAN ANALYSIS CHECKLIST

Name of teacher: _____

Name of person analyzing plans: _____

Use the following scale to rate the lesson plans:

5 = clearly outstanding
4 = exceeds expectations
3 = meets expectations
2 = falls below expectations
1 = needs improvement/inadequate

Include written comments in the spaces provided. Be sure comments are related to specific indicators and give examples if possible. Offer suggestions for improving the lesson plans.

	Rating	Comments
I. The teacher's plan included:		
1. a transition from previous learning		
2. an introduction to the lesson		
3. a motivational activity		
4. a large number of questions		
5. probing type questions to elicit higher-order responses		
6. a variety of verbal reinforcers of student responses		
7. suggestions for refocusing to emphasize a point (verbal and nonverbal)		
8. several activities (i.e., games, boardwork, role-play)		
9. modeling or presentation of several examples		
10. practice activities		
11. provisions to close or end the lesson		
II. General category		
1. Overall, the lesson was well organized.		
2. Transitions were included and noted.		
3. Formative evaluation questions were included.		
4. Summative evaluation is included (i.e., test, checklist, written summary).		
III. Specific suggestions for improvement:		

Figure 9.3 Data collecting—lesson plan checklist.

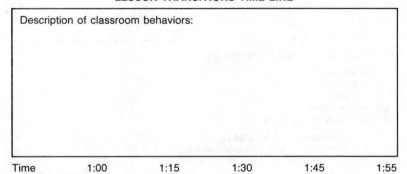

LESSON TRANSITIONS TIME LINE

Description of classroom behaviors:

Time 1:00 1:15 1:30 1:45 1:55

√ = transition made or can also be used to indicate a change in methodology or strategy.

0 = transition needed but not present

Figure 9.4 Data collecting—time line of lesson transitions.

make the needed transitions. If a teacher fails to make an adequate transition to new information as indicated in the written plan, the supervisor provides specific written documentation. Such documentation will help the teacher practice ways of "shifting gears" when moving from one topic or content area to the next.

Another way to present the teacher with helpful information about lesson transitions is through the use of a time line as shown in Figure 9.4. In addition to a brief description of teacher/student behavior, a check is placed on the time line when transitions are made and a zero (0) when a transition is needed but not presented. A time line also can be used to examine methodology. A check would indicate when the teacher changes from one strategy to another with a brief comment about the strategy.

Coding classroom management behaviors. If, on the other hand, the supervisor is monitoring classroom management skills, the data collection forms identified in Figures 9.5 and 9.6 might be helpful. Using Figure 9.5, the supervisor jots down pertinent information regarding what steps the teacher is or is not taking to prevent or address management problems. Figure 9.6 is an abbreviated form that identifies specific student and teacher behaviors. The supervisor places a check in the appropriate box and records the time.

Figure 9.5 enables the observer to record a variety of behaviors. For example, a teacher's lack of movement in the classroom can contribute to management problems. If, during a classroom presentation, some students are off-task and talking but the teacher remains "glued to the same spot," the supervisor can make a sketch of the

CLASSROOM MANAGEMENT DATA

Topic of lesson: _____

Lesson content and organization: _____
_____

Date: _____   Class size: _____

A. Time intervals   B. Arrangement of class

C. Preparation and implementation (presenting information, responding to
   questions, distributing materials, beginning and ending the lesson,
   clarity of instruction, mobility, etc.):

D. Behaviors that could contribute to classroom management
   problems (distracting mannerisms, inappropriate voice quality,
   lack of preparedness, negative student-teacher interaction,
   lack of mobility, etc.):

E. Recommendations

Figure 9.5 Data collecting—evaluation of teacher's handling of classroom
management.

classroom arrangement by using **X**'s to mark students' desks. The
supervisor circles the **X** of each student who is disruptive. Then the
supervisor takes notes and diagrams the location of the teacher at
5-minute intervals (Fifer, 1980). This sketch can be shared with the
teacher and conclusions drawn about the teacher's consistently remaining in one spot, rather than moving closer to those students who
were disruptive. The supervisor might pose questions to encourage
the teacher to think about his or her instructional behavior. For
example, the supervisor might ask the following questions:

1. Where did you stand at the beginning, middle, and end of the
   lesson?
2. Where in the room did student problems develop?

CLASSROOM MANAGEMENT DATA

Teacher: _____   Date: _____

Supervisor: _____   School: _____

Class/Grade and Subject: _____   Number of students: _____

Time	Behaviors to observe	Teacher On-Task	Teacher Off-Task	Student On-Task	Student Off-Task
	Giving directions				
	Asking questions				
	Answering questions				
	Making statements				
	Yelling				
	Moving around room				
	Listening				
	Following rules				
	Giving rules				
	Accepting answers				
	Praising				
	Criticizing				

Comments:

Figure 9.6 Data collecting—record of teacher management of student behavior. (*Source:* Adapted from Kilgore, A. M., Coffey, M., and Nordell, G. [1985]. Developing and implementing a teacher assessment system. Presented at the Association for Supervision and Curriculum Development annual meeting, March, Chicago. Used with permission.

3. How will proximity to students influence their behavior?
4. What changes might you make tomorrow?

Coding verbal interactions (Flanders Interaction Analysis Categories System). There are several other tools that can be used to collect data about specific dimensions of classroom life.* One commonly used tool, developed by Flanders (1967), is an observation called the Flanders Interaction Analysis Category System, or FIAC. Dunkin and Biddle (1974) attribute many of the developments as-

*For additional observation tools to use, consult Acheson and Gall's book *Techniques in the clinical supervision of teachers: Preservice and inservice applications* (1987).

sociated with describing classroom climate to the work of Flanders. For them, "Flanders' contribution to research in classrooms has been important and pervasive," and they go on to say that he was responsible for developing the "single most-often-used instrument for observing classroom behaviors" (p. 100). Flanders's contribution to classroom observation lies in his conceptualization of "the continuum along which teacher behavior is hypothesized to vary" (p. 101) and his introduction of the terms "direct" and "indirect" teacher influence (Dunkin and Biddle, 1974).

The Flanders System is helpful because it describes and codes common verbal patterns that teachers and students follow in the classroom. Not only does it contain the seven categories for coding teachers' verbal behavior, but, unlike Withall's system (1949), it includes two additional categories. One category is for student verbal behavior (either "response" or "initiation"); the other category is for "silence or confusion."

Flanders identifies the general classifications "teacher talk," "student talk," and "periods of silence or confusion." Teacher talk is divided into two major headings: indirect influence and direct influence. According to Flanders (1967), "Indirect influence consists of soliciting the opinions or ideas of the pupils, applying or enlarging on those opinions or ideas, praising or encouraging the participation of pupils, or clarifying and accepting their feelings" (p. 109). Within the indirect influence heading there are four categories: accepts feelings, praises or encourages, accepts or uses ideas of students, and asks questions. Teacher talk using indirect influence indicates that the teacher's behavior is such that students are encouraged to respond more freely.

As Flanders (1967) noted, "Direct influence consists of stating the teacher's own opinion or ideas, directing the pupil's action, criticizing his behavior, or justifying the teacher's authority or use of that authority" (p. 109). Teacher direct influence contains three categories: lectures, gives directions, and criticizes or justifies authority. Direct influence by the teacher refers to teacher statements that restrict or limit student responses.

Student talk includes two categories: student talk response and student talk initiation. The first category involves students responding to the teacher (that is, answering a question). The second category involves talk by students that they initiate. The last category consists of periods of silence or confusion. During this period there is no talking, or the communication, if spoken, cannot be understood by the observer.

Teacher Talk	Indirect Influence	*1. Accepts feeling: Accepts and clarifies the feeling tone of the students in a nonthreatening manner. Feelings may be positive or negative. Predicting or recalling feelings is included.
		*2. Praises or encourages: Praises or encourages student action or behavior. Jokes that release tension, but not at the expense of another individual; nodding head or saying "un huh" or "go on" are included.
		*3. Accepts or uses ideas of students: Clarifying, building, or developing ideas suggested by a student. As a teacher brings more of his [or her] own ideas into play, shift to category 5.
		*4. Asks questions: Asking a question about content or procedure with the intent that a student answer.
	Direct Influence	*5. Lecturing: Giving facts or opinions about content or procedures; expressing his [or her] own ideas, asking rhetorical questions.
		*6. Giving directions: Directions, commands, or orders with which a student is expected to comply.
		*7. Criticizing or justifying authority: Statements intended to change student behavior from nonacceptable to acceptable pattern; bawling someone out; stating why the teacher is doing what he [or she] is doing; extreme self-reference.
Student Talk		*8. Student talk response: Talk by students in response to teacher. Teacher initiates the contact or solicits student statement.
		*9. Student talk initiation by students: Talk by students which they initiate. If "calling on" student is only to indicate who may talk next, observer must decide whether student wanted to talk. If he [or she] did, use this category.
		*10. Silence or confusion: Pauses, short periods of silence, and periods of confusion in which communication cannot be understood by the observer.

*No scale is implied by these numbers. Each number is classificatory; it designates a particular kind of communication event. To write those numbers down during observation is to enumerate, not to judge a position on the scale.

Figure 9.7 Summary of categories for interaction analysis. (*Source:* Flanders, N. A. [1967]. Teacher influence in the classroom. In E. J. Amidon and J. B. Hough (Eds.), *Interaction analysis: Theory, research and application.* Reading, Mass.: Addison-Wesley. Used with permission.)

Taken together, there are ten categories, and each category is assigned a specific number, but the numbers do not imply a particular value on a scale. Figure 9.7 indicates the number assigned to each of the categories. As an examination of Figure 9.7 reveals, teacher statements can stand alone or influence how students respond. For example, in category 1, "accepts feelings," the teacher can communicate the acceptance of positive as well as negative pupil feelings and actions.

When using the FIAC, instructional supervisors will spend considerable time observing various types of classroom settings. For the first 5 to 10 minutes of a class, the supervisor sits and observes without recording any information. This period of time allows the supervisor to get a "feel" for the total classroom environment and diminishes the effect of an outside observer on student–teacher behavior. Before beginning to record numbers or encode data, the supervisor should make a brief description of the class and activity. Once this has been accomplished, the recording process begins.

The supervisor codes teacher and/or student behavior and records the appropriate number of the interaction for every 3 seconds of the behavior or until there is a change in the behavior. The numbers are recorded in a column, and for every minute of observation there will be approximately 20 numbers recorded. At the conclusion of a 15- or 20-minute observation, the supervisor will have recorded several columns of numbers. It is essential for the supervisor to be accurate in coding the behavior and to develop a consistent tempo when recording numbers. When the class activity is no longer teacher-directed and students work in groups, work at their desks individually, or read silently, the supervisor stops recording. A line is drawn under the last number recorded and notes are made concerning the new activity. It is not unusual for supervisors as they code behaviors to make notes that further explain and interpret what they have observed.

Clearly, there will be discrepancies between supervisors regarding classifications of behaviors into one category or another. Some ground rules, therefore, have been established to help eliminate major discrepancies and improve observer reliability (Amidon and Amidon, 1967). These ground rules are useful, and in some cases necessary, in establishing a baseline for coding total class interactions.

> *Rule 1.* If the supervisor is uncertain about which category a statement belongs in, the category furthest from category 5 should be selected (for instance, if the choice is either category 1 or category 3, category 1 would be picked). The exception occurs if one of the two categories in doubt is category 10. When category 10 is one of the choices, it should never be selected if there is another category under consideration.
>
> *Rule 2.* If the tone of the teacher's statements is consistently either direct or indirect, the coding should stay in the same

category unless there is a distinct shift indicated by the teacher. The supervisor is in the best position to make the decision about a teacher's behavior as it relates to restricting the freedom of students in the class.

Rule   3. The supervisor should remain bias-free and not be concerned about the teacher's intent. The question that the supervisor continually asks himself or herself is, "What does this behavior mean to the pupils as far as restricting or expanding their freedom is concerned?" (Amidon and Amidon, 1967, p. 71).

Rule 4. If, during a given 3-second time span, several behaviors are exhibited, then all categories are recorded. If the same behavior occurs during each 3-second interval, the category number should be reported accordingly.

Rule 5. Directions (category 6) occur when statements made by the teacher result in observable pupil behavior. Sometimes teacher statements may sound like directions, but they are not followed by observable student compliance. Often the actual student behavior comes after statements like, "Let's get ready to go to physical education class [category 5, orientation]. Row 6 is ready; get your clothes."

Rule 6. If the teacher identifies a pupil by name, the category is recorded as 4.

Rule 7. If there are at least 3 seconds of silence, laughter, board work, or the like, the observer should record a 10 for every 3 seconds.

Rule 8. If the teacher repeats a correct answer given by a student, it is category 2. By doing this, the teacher communicates to the student that he or she is correct, and the teacher's response therefore functions as a praise statement.

Rule 9. If the teacher repeats a student's idea without changing it (almost verbatim), the idea will be considered accepted. Since the teacher does not judge the idea, category 3 is used.

Rule 10. If two students talk without a comment from the teacher, a 10 is marked between the 9's and 8's to record that there is a change of student.

Rule 11. When the teacher verbally indicates encouragement after a student speaks by saying, "Yes," "All right," or "Okay," a 2 is inserted between two 9's.

Rule 12. If a teacher makes or tells a joke that does not ridicule a student, the statement is coded as category 2. If the joke is at the expense of a student, then a 7 is recorded.

Rule 13. If a teacher uses rhetorical questions, they are coded as category 5 because they are part of the presentation. They are not really questions because the teacher is using them to motivate and no answer is expected.

Rule 14. If a narrow question is asked and the student gives a specific and predictable response, it is coded as category 8. If the response includes a justification or expands on the expected answer, it is coded as a 9.

Rule 15. When the entire class responds to a question or direction in unison in the same way, the behavior is coded as category 8 (a choral response) rather than 10 (confusion).

The coding system developed by Flanders aids the supervisor in recording behaviors quickly and efficiently. As in the case of other data collection procedures cited earlier, the next step for the supervisor is to analyze the data and information that have been recorded.

DATA ANALYSIS PROCEDURES

The data analysis phase requires that the supervisor be as objective as possible. A way to begin, according to Clements and Evertson (1980), is to write a descriptive narrative citing specific observed behaviors and communicating in nonjudgmental language, as discussed in Chapter 5. Typically in this phase, the supervisor prepares the narrative based on the raw data collected during the in-class observation. The advantage of preparing a narrative is that it provides a holistic perspective of what took place. The narrative includes major categories that reflect the focus of the observation—off-task behavior and teacher–student interactions—along with examples. In addition to preparing a narrative, the supervisor may choose to develop visuals that clarify items addressed in the narrative. As the adage goes, a picture—charts, diagrams, graphs—may be worth a thousand words. It is at this point that diagramming the teacher's mobility in the classroom, charting transitions from one topic to the next, or preparing a graph of the time the teacher spent in different types of dialogue with students can be useful to the supervisor.

The narrative, charts, and graphs become the basis for the postobservation conference. The information in the narrative, along with other items such as charts, provides the supervisor with a guide in determining what material to present and discuss with the teacher. During the data analysis phase, the supervisor seeks answers to the following questions:

1. What do the results mean?
2. What patterns seem to emerge?
3. Is the teacher keeping students on-task?
4. Does the teacher recognize off-task behavior?
5. What teacher action was taken, if any?

The information regarding the verbal classroom interaction patterns generated by the Flanders System will be used here as an example of how the supervisor can prepare for the postobservation conference. The interaction patterns can be compiled and reported to the teacher in various formats. Figure 9.8 provides one such format. It shows results obtained during a 55-minute world history class; the data have been compiled and put in a graphic format for the teacher. In analyzing the results, the supervisor plots the percentage of total time for each of the 10 Flanders categories.

Once the data have been put in a graphic form, the interpretation phase begins. An interpretation of Figure 9.8 indicates that the

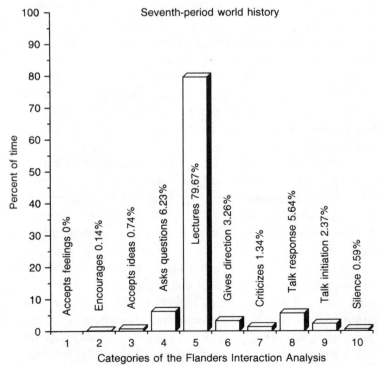

Figure 9.8 Representative compilation of verbal classroom interaction patterns, based on Flanders interaction analysis.

teacher lectured 79.67 percent of the time, or nearly 44 minutes of the period. In addition, the teacher spent 3.26 percent of the time giving directions and 6.23 percent of the time asking questions, leaving only 8 percent of the time for student responses or student talk. With a graphic representation of the data, the teacher should find it difficult to dispute the fact that he or she was responsible for the majority of the verbal interaction during the class period. The supervisor can use the graph as one indicator to show the teacher that student involvement was limited during this lesson.

The FIAC can be a useful tool for supervisors to use with teachers to describe what took place in the classroom while they were teaching. The results generated are indicators of the verbal interaction patterns between teachers and students.

POSTOBSERVATION CONFERENCE PROCEDURES

Once the raw data collected during the classroom observation have been analyzed and translated into a form that is meaningful to the teacher, the supervisor is ready to conduct the postobservation conference. Regardless of the model or models of supervision employed, there are guidelines that supervisors should consider as they prepare for a conference with a teacher. For Griffin (1973), a good conference is like a good lesson; it has to be well planned, well organized, and evaluated.

A good place for the supervisor to begin, as he or she prepares for a meeting with the teacher, is a quick review of the postobservation conference form as seen in Figure 9.9. The questions on this form can assist the supervisor in structuring the conference.

A primary consideration in planning for the postobservation conference is to give teachers accurate, specific data obtained from the classroom observations. Since one of the primary functions of the conference is to provide feedback to the teacher, it is important to focus on actual occurrences that took place. At this point, the narrative and the graphic representations of the data can be used to reference specific classroom dimensions that were observed.

Communication is an important part of the postobservation conference. The communication process is highly variable and complex. When supervisors send a message, they communicate not only facts gathered but feelings, perceptions, and innuendoes. As supervisors participate in the conference, they should be aware that they communicate messages through gestures, physical posture, facial expressions, tone of voice, and by what is said as well as how it is said.

POSTOBSERVATION CONFERENCE FORM

	Yes	No or needs improvement	Comments
1. Did you establish goals for the conference?			
2. Did you begin the conference in a manner that encouraged the teacher to feel comfortable?			
3. Would you describe the type of conference as: cooperative? confrontational? passive?			
4. Did you present information in a format the teacher would understand?			
5. Did you use a format that included a: graph? chart? continuum?			
6. Did you prepare a narrative?			
7. Did the teacher understand what you presented? Did the teacher agree with your interpretation of the data? Did you check for understanding?			
8. Was the general tone of the conference: positive? constructive? negative?			
9. Did you close the conference: with a description of what was observed? with modifiable items? by making plans for another observation?			
10. Were the instruments you used appropriate? List each: a. b. c. d.			

Figure 9.9 Checklist for evaluation of postobservation conference with teachers.

A supervisor's communication style, then, becomes a part of the message; it refers to the total range of verbal and nonverbal behaviors the supervisor displays. In addition, the same message may carry both an intentional and an unintentional meaning. Double meanings can often pose unusual difficulties for both the supervisor and the teacher. As discussed in Chapter 5, supervisors should always be conscious of what they communicate and the manner in which they communicate it.

Another consideration during the postobservation conference is that the supervisor is selective in the words that are used. Words that convey a value of "good and bad" or "appropriate and not appropriate" should be avoided. The extreme would be for the supervisor, showing the teacher the data represented in Figure 9.8, to say to the teacher, "Look at the data. You dominated the classroom interaction and you really did a poor job of involving students in the lesson," or even "You seemed to talk too much during this lesson." The intent is to let the data "speak" in an objective way so that the teacher can recognize areas that need improvement.

It is also important for the supervisor to avoid making assumptions and hasty conclusions from inferences. Supervisors may need to ask questions during the postobservation conference that provide additional information and/or insight into the instructional environment. For example, the supervisor should be cautious about assuming that the teacher talked a great deal during the lesson because the students were not adequately prepared to respond in class. The supervisor should stick to the data and ask the teacher, "Is this a typical pattern for classroom interactions?" or "Were you aware of this pattern during the lesson?" If the supervisor does offer an "outside, objective" interpretation, the teacher should be encouraged to respond to the interpretation or offer an alternative explanation. Even though there is often a temptation to make judgments and offer advice, the supervisor must guard against such temptations, which can emotionally charge the dialogue.

Throughout the postobservation conference, the supervisor not only sends messages but receives them. Listening is a crucial component of the communication process, and supervisors should "really hear" what teachers are saying. Good listening includes the following verbal skills: acknowledging, reflecting, paraphrasing, summarizing, clarifying, and elaborating on what is said (Conoley and Conoley, 1982).

As the conference comes to an end, modifiable behaviors should be summarized. The teacher and supervisor should come to a mutually agreed-upon plan of action. By focusing on and stressing instructional behavior that can be modified, the supervisor offers the teacher a place to begin. The supervisor should strive to create a situation in which he or she is asked questions about the modifiable behaviors discussed. Then, to check for understanding, the supervisor should review the postobservation conference form again. This time, the checklist should help the supervisor evaluate his or her performance during the conference.

A major purpose of the postobservation conference is for supervisors to assist teachers in establishing short-term as well as long-term goals. Setting instructional goals requires teachers to make a commitment to some course of action. It becomes the supervisor's task to distill and clarify the essential elements during the conference. The supervisor should ask questions that encourage the teacher to think about what he or she will do in the future. For example, the supervisor might ask one or more of the following questions: "What will you do tomorrow if the same students are disruptive?" "What preventive measures will you take so these students' behaviors will not occur next week?" "How can you involve reluctant learners in the class discussion?" or "What instructional priorities are you going to set for yourself?" The entire discussion during the postobservation conference should be directed toward guiding teachers to higher-order thinking as they process information about their instructional performance.

SUMMARY

This chapter has described the mechanics that supervisors can use on a daily basis when observing and conferencing with teachers. The specific procedures and techniques identified can be used as supervisors plan their in-class observations and prepare and discuss these findings with teachers. The data collection and analysis procedures, along with the communications techniques, offer options and suggestions to guide supervisors in their role as observers and communicators.

The list of observation pitfalls serves to caution supervisors against biases that often influence an interpretation of what they viewed. The pitfalls that supervisors should strive to avoid include making personal interpretations, not letting the information speak for itself, having perceptual blinders, establishing a set of personal likes and dislikes, and fostering teacher anxiety.

The general principles of observation provide supervisors with additional guidelines as they prepare for, conduct, and report to teachers about the in-class observation. The six principles of observation are (1) focus on student behaviors, (2) concentrate on a few classroom dimensions at a time, (3) blend into the classroom environment when observing, (4) develop good notetaking skills, (5) analyze the data collected, and (6) provide feedback to the teacher.

Four data collection procedures discussed are (1) coding on-task and off-task behaviors, (2) coding and recording transitions and lesson pacing, (3) coding classroom management behaviors, and (4) coding verbal interactions. The Flanders Interaction Categories Analysis System, or FIAC, is an example of the fourth procedure discussed in the chapter. The Flanders System divides the three general events "teacher talk," "student talk," and "silence or confusion" into 10 more specific categories that take place in the classroom as part of the teacher–student interaction. Because interactions are sometimes interpreted differently by users of the Flanders System, ground rules have been established as a guide.

After the raw data have been collected, supervisors must analyze the information objectively and accurately. In preparing for the postobservation conference, the supervisor can present the results of the observation both as a narrative and in graph, chart, or other visual form. The supervisor, in working with the data obtained from the observation, is cautioned to be as nonjudgmental as possible.

At the postobservation conference, the supervisor should convey the findings in a visual, objective format. The supervisor should be careful about the messages that nonverbal gestures such as facial expressions convey.

It is important for the supervisor to avoid making hasty assumptions about conditions in the classroom, or reasons behind the teacher's behavior, based on the data collected. It is better to ask the teacher questions than simply to come to conclusions from the numerical data. The supervisor, by asking the teacher questions, should encourage him or her to think about ways of handling difficult classroom situations if they should occur again. At the end of the conference the supervisor should direct the teacher to higher-order thinking about his or her instruction performance.

Taken together, the cautions as well as the guidelines presented in the chapter provide supervisors with the mechanics or tools for conducting objective observations. The mechanics provide supervisors with the foundation for accurately communicating information to teachers.

YOUR TURN

9.1. You have been working with a secondary art teacher for the past month and you are ready to observe the teacher. The teacher has admitted, and you concur, that he or she has a problem that centers on "coming across" to students. The teacher cannot be more specific in describing this concern. What observational procedures would you select and use? Why have you selected these procedures? What type of data will be generated that can be shared with this teacher?

9.2. You have observed a science class. You developed the following chart of the teacher's behavior as you observed. The **X**'s mark the students' desks and the circles around the **X**'s represent disruptive students. The **T** represents the location of the teacher during various times of the lesson. Look at the diagram below. What teacher mobility and student behavior patterns seem to be present? What recommendations would you make to the teacher based on the data collected during this lesson?

T (leaning on wall)   T (seated at desk)
First 15 minutes   Remainder of period

×   ×   ×   ×   ×   ×   ×   ×   ×

×   ×   ×   ⊗   ×   ×   ×   ×   ⊗

×   ×   ×   ×   ⊗   ⊗   ×   ×   ×

9.3. The following is a verbatim transcript obtained from a classroom observation. After reading the transcript, code it using the numbers of the Flanders Interaction Analysis Categories System. You may assume that each complete printed line of a sentence in a student or teacher statement is three seconds in duration.

[T = Teacher statement   S = Student statement]

T: Who can tell me what a microscope is? What is it used for?
S: It is something scientists use; it gives a picture of something small. I've used it before; it's neat.
T: Now. What else can you say about the microscope?
S: It is heavy.
T: How many of you think so too?
S: Me, and some are really powerful.
T: Good. What does that mean?
S: You can see a lot more.
T: More in terms of number?
S: Yes, but also in terms of size and detail.
T: Good for you. Terry has the right idea—that a microscope is a tool which makes organisms and objects larger. It magnifies them. Ok, why is magnification so important?

    s: Well, makes things big.

    t: But why is making something big so important?

9.4. You are planning to observe a social studies teacher. Before the observation, it was decided that you would focus on the types of questions asked during the period. At the completion of a 55-minute period, you had the following categories of data:

    5 rhetorical questions
    3 probing (analysis/synthesis/evaluation) questions
    10 recall questions
    12 comprehension questions

Before the visit, the teacher convinced you that he or she has a varied repertoire of question types. Now you have to present these results to the teacher. Do the data correspond with your prior assessment? Was this a typical lesson for this teacher? Outline the steps you will take during the conference and describe the way you plan to present this information to the teacher.

9.5. You are ready to begin the postobservation conference with a teacher who, on the whole, is very good. But you want to help this teacher be even better. You conclude, based on the data collected from many in-class observations, that at the beginning of the school year the teacher was exceptionally accommodating to students. This had a positive effect on the classroom climate, but now, with three months of school left, the teacher is getting to be more controlling, disagreeable, unpredictable, and often harsh in interacting with the students. You feel that this teacher will agree with you about the situation and that ways will be identified to correct this more negative spiral, which is having an effect on classroom climate. Your attitude coming into the conference is one of hopeful anticipation.

    However, when you present the results from the observations, the teacher totally rejects the data and what you say and becomes highly defensive. What do you do? What overall strategy will you use? What techniques will you employ? What steps will you take to communicate your findings and help the teacher "hear" what you are saying?

REFERENCES

Acheson, K. A., and Gall, M. D. (1987). *Techniques in the clinical supervision of teachers: Preservice and inservice applications* (2nd ed.). New York: Longman.

Amidon, E. J., and Amidon, P. (1967). *Interaction analysis training kit—Level 1 training tape manual* (rev. ed.). Minneapolis: Association for Productive Teaching.

Clements, B., and Evertson, C. (1980). *Developing an effective research team for classroom observation* (R & D Report N. 6103). Austin: University of Texas, R & D Center for Teacher Education.

Clinical supervision. Prepared by Long Beach Unified School District. Hunter, p. 13.

Conoley, J. C., and Conoley, C. W. (1982). *School consultation: A guide to practice and training.* Pergamon General Psychology Series.

Coates, T., and Thoresen, C. (1976). Teacher anxiety: A review with recommendations. *Review of Educational Research, 46,* 159–184.

Dunkin, M. J., and Biddle, B. J. (1974). *The study of teaching.* New York: University Press of America.

Fifer, F. (1980). Teacher in-class observation form. Dallas: University of Texas at Dallas. [Mimeograph.]

Flanders, N. A. (1967). Teacher influence in the classroom. In E. J. Amidon and J. B. Hough (Eds.), *Interaction analysis: Theory, research and application.* Reading, Mass.: Addison-Wesley.

Glickman, C. D. (1985). *Supervision of instruction.* Boston: Allyn and Bacon.

Good, T. L., and Brophy, J. E. (1984). *Looking in classrooms* (3rd ed.). New York: Harper & Row.

Griffin, F. (1973). *A handbook for the observation of teaching and learning.* Midland, Mich.: Pendell.

Hunter, M. (1983). Script taping: An essential tool. *Educational Leadership, 41, 3,* 43.

Withall, J. (1949). The development of a teaching technique for the measurement of social-emotional climate in classrooms. *Journal of Experimental Education, 17,* 347–361.

four

OTHER DIMENSIONS
OF SUPERVISION

chapter *10*

Evaluating Teaching Performance

One of the most controversial issues confronting instructional supervisors today is their role in the evaluation of teaching. Like it or not, instructional supervisors are becoming a part of the summative as well as the formative evaluation of teachers. During the last few years, news items such as "Incompetent Teacher Remains on the Job" and "Why Teachers Can't Teach," as well as numerous articles on accountability, merit pay, performance criteria, and career ladders, have spurred states and local school districts to put in place teacher evaluation systems. One of the national reform reports, *A Nation at Risk* (1983), recommended that "salary, promotion, tenure and retention decisions . . . be tied to an effective [evaluation] system" (p. 30).

Historically, most supervisors, unless they served in a direct line of authority (that is, as principal), have shunned the role of evaluator because they viewed this function as counterproductive to promoting staff development. According to Pfeiffer and Dunlap (1982), instructional supervisors

> should not evaluate for hiring, firing or promotion, since a helping relationship is difficult to maintain with a person who makes decisions about termination. No teacher wants to seek help from an individual who may use the request as evidence of inability to cope. (p. 162)

Recent events would suggest, however, that instructional supervisors who have generally played a supporting role will be asked to become more directly involved in personnel decisions as well as staff development. Many states and local districts are establishing evaluation systems that require classroom observations by supervisory personnel for the purpose of assessing teacher performance.

The evaluation of teaching is a complicated and complex task, and few teachers, supervisors, and administrators are satisfied with the results. Duke and Stiggins (1986) note that teacher evaluation is like so many of life's ironies in that it can be a most rewarding experience but it also has the potential for being most frustrating. They summarize by saying:

> Done well, teacher evaluation can lead to improved performance, personal growth, and professional esteem. Done poorly, it can produce anxiety or ennui and drive talented teachers from the profession. (p. 9)

Scriven (1981) takes the point of view that "teacher evaluation is a disaster" (p. 244); his view seems to be shared by many.

Much of the dialogue about teacher evaluation ties the process to some form of material reward (such as merit pay, career ladder); in a study conducted by Wise and others (1985), however, monetary rewards and sanctions alone did not necessarily improve instruction. Clearly this research should serve as a caution. It seems to suggest that as supervisors become more involved in all phases of the teacher evaluation process, the evaluation could serve as feedback to provide the teacher with information about classroom performance as well as effective instructional practices (Buttram and Wilson, 1987).

The controversial element of teacher evaluation seem to be in how the evaluation system is implemented; the problem in many cases is the system itself (McGreal, 1983). Difficulties associated with teacher evaluation systems are numerous and well documented in the literature. These problems develop because (1) the criteria used to measure teacher performance are not consistent (Travers, 1981); (2) the techniques used are not reliable (Scriven, 1981); (3) teachers are provided little input in the development of the system (Wise et. al., 1985), and (4) the preparation and training for both teachers and supervisors are inadequate (McGreal, 1983).

Another complicating factor associated with teacher evaluation has been the lack of systems to link or combine what is known about the evaluation process with research on effective teaching practices (Gephart and Ingle, 1983; Duvall, 1983). In addition, many educators, especially supervisors, admit that they lack the prerequisite knowledge and skills to evaluate teaching. According to a report from the Rand Corporation (1985), teacher evaluation is poorly conceptualized and underdeveloped.

This chapter will provide instructional supervisors with a variety of ways to view teacher evaluation, which may prove helpful as they participate in both formative and summative teacher evaluation. To aid the supervisor in focusing on instruction in the evaluation of teaching, the chapter will examine perceptions about teaching and teachers, the purposes and assumptions concerning teacher evaluation, characteristics of effective evaluation systems, and the formative and summative evaluation phases of evaluation. It is hoped that this information will assist the supervisor in linking evaluation with the supervision of instruction. Supervisors' knowledge of evaluation, and their skills in implementing an evaluation system, should bring about a greater degree of professional improvement among teachers.

PERCEPTIONS OF TEACHING AND TEACHERS

This section examines views of teaching and teachers in relation to the evaluation process because how teachers, instructional supervisors, and administrators perceive teaching becomes the cornerstone of an evaluation system. In Chapter 7, the act of teaching was examined in detail. Specifically, characteristics of effective teachers, generated from research, were presented. Brandt (1987) observes that "school systems are systematically incorporating research knowledge into their teacher evaluation programs" (p. 3). Several districts and states have utilized evaluation criteria based on data from research studies (Florida Coalition, 1983; Caldwell, 1986; Delaware Department of Public Instruction, 1986; *Texas Teacher Appraisal System,* 1986–1987).

Regardless of the name, form, or type, an evaluation system revolves around teaching (McGreal, 1983). Findings from process/product studies provide a valid content base for establishing a teacher evaluation system (Peterson and Smith, 1986). Teacher performance indicators are derived from several hundred studies. "If evaluation systems with clear research-based criteria help supervisors make fewer arbitrary judgments and give more informed, constructive feedback, they will aid student learning" (Brandt, 1987, p. 3).

The focus on instruction is a constant reminder that the quality of teaching is necessary to improve teacher classroom skills. The emphasis on teaching is "the single most important aspect of building a successful evaluation/supervision system" (McGreal, 1983, p. 72). If districts do not focus on teaching, then the evaluation system will be impractical and unrealistic in its attempts to help teachers improve.

How administrators and supervisors perceive teachers is also important in the implementation of a successful, effective evaluation system. If teachers "are considered a professional resource rather than the object of bureaucratic scrutiny," the evaluation system gains credibility (Wise and Darling-Hammond, 1984–1985, p. 28). If teachers, on the other hand, are viewed as objects of "bureaucratic scrutiny," the task of evaluation becomes a perfunctory duty that yields limited information and assistance to the teachers involved. In addition, how teachers are perceived will affect which teacher evaluation system is used and how. "Professional evaluation is designed to meet teachers' needs for guidance in addressing specific problems of classroom practice" (Wise and Darling-Hammond, 1984–1985, p. 31). Such an evaluation system is clinically based and developmentally oriented. A professional system, not the bureaucratic teacher evaluation system, is advocated in this text.

OTHER CONSIDERATIONS: PURPOSES AND ASSUMPTIONS

The primary purposes of teacher evaluation are twofold: first, to improve instruction and student performance and, second, to encourage professional growth and development for teachers. For many, "teacher evaluation is a process which determines . . . the worth or value of a teacher in a given situation" (Gephart and Ingle, 1983, p. 1). The purpose should not necessarily be to hire and fire, or separate the effective teachers from the ineffective ones, but these results are often byproducts of the evaluation process. For many states and school districts, however, teacher evaluation serves as a means of

distinguishing among the performance of teachers. In order to do so, the . . . [evaluation] process is designed to collect samples of valid information about teacher classroom behaviors and make reliable decisions about those behaviors. (*Texas Teacher Appraisal System*, 1986–1987, p. 3).

The approach used within the system will vary, depending on the purposes of the evaluation system. For example, a management by objectives approach might be used with an evaluation system that promotes self-assessment and the development of professional goals.

As seen in Figure 10.1, a management by objectives approach does not necessarily require classroom observations and relies heavily on information supplied by the teacher during a conference with the supervisor. A checklist or rating scale might be used with an evaluation system that focuses on the presence or absence of specific classroom teacher behaviors. A checklist or rating scale, as seen in Figure 10.2, requires classroom observations in order to verify the

PROFESSIONAL GOAL-SETTING PLAN

1. Professional goal
2. Resources and support needed
3. Limiting factors
4. Plan of action

| 5. Timetable | 6. I agree to the plan of action.

____ Yes?   ____ No?
Signature of teacher
_____
Signature of supervisor
_____

7. Progress achieved
Date   Evidence
_____
_____
_____

Date of summative conference
_____ |

Figure 10.1 Management by objectives approach to teacher evaluation—professional goal-setting plan.

PROFESSIONAL EVALUATION FORM

Teacher _____   School _____

I. Professional Evaluation Rating

	Successful	Marginal	Unsuccessful	Comments
1. The teacher maintains a continuous effort to achieve professional improvement, attitudes, and conduct. Also, the teacher observes professional ethics; works cooperatively with the entire staff; seeks, shares, and respects ideas of others; refrains from revealing confidential information regarding pupils and their families.	☐	☐	☐	_____ _____ _____
2. The teacher supports established administrative policies and directives, and performs all required school routines and responsibilities on time.	☐	☐	☐	_____ _____
3. The teacher's absences are minimal and do not significantly impede the learning progress of students.	☐	☐	☐	_____ _____
4. The teacher is consistently fair and impartial; praise and criticism are based on fact; all criticism is constructive; individual pupils are not excessively criticized; the teacher avoids criticism which may result in any embarrassment.	☐	☐	☐	_____ _____
5. The teacher sets an example of, and encourages, socially acceptable behavior (e.g., dress, correct usage of speech, and manner), which results in an educational climate free of disruption.	☐	☐	☐	_____
6. The teacher maintains an atmosphere conducive to freedom of thought and creative expression, and shows respect for pupil opinions and suggestions. He or she also fosters a positive self-concept in each pupil.	☐	☐	☐	_____
7. The teacher demonstrates and communicates a vital interest in and understanding of each pupil's social, physical, and intellectual growth.	☐	☐	☐	_____
8. Classroom management is orderly and businesslike and gives evidence of student knowledge of teacher expectations for routines and classroom procedure. The teacher resolves behavior problems with minimal disruptions to the learning climate and creates a teaching environment conducive to learning.	☐	☐	☐	_____ _____ _____
9. The teacher's condition of health enables the teacher to achieve the instructional goals of the District.	☐	☐	☐	_____
10. The teacher establishes and conducts a system of communication wherein the parents are able to interpret the periodic progress reports in terms of course goals, student level of achievement of these goals, reasons for student achievement, and means for continued progress.	☐	☐	☐	_____ _____ _____

II. Instructional Evaluation Rating

A. Appraisal of original or modified goals   ☐ ☐ ☐
(December of a school year)

_____
_____
_____
_____

B. Attainment of original or modified goals   ☐ ☐ ☐
(March 31 of a school year)

_____
_____
_____
_____

Figure 10.2 Checklist or rating scale approach to teacher evaluation—professional evaluation form.

presence or absence of each teacher performance criterion or indicator.

The approach to evaluation in a given district may often be based on assumptions about teaching, and about evaluation, that the district adheres to. Thus, before districts embark on developing an evaluation system, teachers, administrators, and supervisors should examine fundamental assumptions related to teacher evaluation. The *Texas Teacher Appraisal System* (1986–1987) uses the following assumptions to guide the statewide teacher evaluation system:

1. The primary purpose of teaching, which is an intentional act, is to increase student learning (achievement).
2. All teachers, regardless of level and teaching assignment, can improve instructionally.
3. There are common teaching behaviors that are shared by teachers who are effective.
4. The quality of teacher effectiveness will vary depending on the years of experience, the school environment, subject matter presentation, and the student population.
5. The evaluation of teaching should be based on several (at least two) observations by different observers. (p. 3).

As indicated by the assumptions, the primary purpose of teacher evaluation is to further the intellectual, psychomotor, and affective growth of all students. A secondary purpose is to foster the professional growth of teachers. As instructional supervisors guide teachers in their quest for professional growth, they use the evaluation data collected. Only after they have used their findings for growth and development purposes do they use the data to make difficult decisions about retention and dismissal (Brown, 1983; *Texas Teacher Appraisal System,* 1986–1987).

CHARACTERISTICS OF EFFECTIVE TEACHER EVALUATION SYSTEMS

Evaluation systems are available that can be purchased (Manatt, 1976; Iwanicki, 1981; Harris and Hill, 1982), but if local conditions are not taken into account, the evaluation system may fail. Good and Brophy (1987) sound a word of caution when they say that, before school districts consider "innovative personnel practices," districts should have a workable evaluation system in place and fully operational. It seems evident, in turn, that the development of any evaluation system must be based on agreed-upon teacher performance criteria and that supervisors must be trained in implementing the system (McGreal, 1983). These procedural steps are crucial, and, before an evaluation system is selected, the characteristics of effective systems should be reviewed.

Wise and others (1985) have identified characteristics of effective teacher evaluation systems. Using the work of Shannon (1982), Hoyle, English, and Steffy (1985) developed what they call the "cardinal principles of evaluation" (p. 128). Dillon-Peterson (1986), Glatthorn and Holler (1987), and Good and Brophy (1987) have identified similar characteristics in separate projects on effective teacher evaluation systems. The following is a composite list of these traits:

1. The evaluation process and the criteria used are consistent with district goals and objectives. For example, if the goal of the district is to have a standardized model of teaching, the evaluation system should not encourage multiple interpretations of what good teaching is. The evaluation process ties in with district goals and objectives.

2. There is a high level of commitment by administrators, supervisors, and teachers. Commitment to the evaluation process is critical. Without support for teacher evaluation at all levels, the evaluation process will not be taken seriously.

3. The purpose and procedures of the evaluation system are evident and clearly communicated. If the purpose is to help teachers improve instructionally, then steps are taken and financial support provided to assist teachers in their quest to improve their instruction. Evaluation procedures, criteria, and forms are communicated to all involved, and the appeal process is clearly defined and explicated.

4. Consideration is given to cost-effectiveness, legislative support, and usefulness. Essential questions that must be answered in implementing a teacher evaluation system are "Is the process worth the effort and cost?"; "Would another system be more effective?"; "Do teachers feel more satisfied/better about their teaching, and are they rewarded for a job well done?"; and "Do teachers improve instructionally under the system?"

5. There is adequate teacher input and involvement. Teacher involvement in the development of the evaluation process provides psychological and emotional support. Teacher in-

volvement in all phases—planning, implementing, and evaluating—encourages teachers to reflect upon their own teaching and to consider its impact on students (Dillon-Peterson, 1986).

6. The evaluation process is conducted on a regular basis and multiple techniques are used for assessing performance. The evaluation process is conducted on a continuing basis and includes opportunities for formal and informal evaluation. In addition, the system employs several techniques for assessing performance, including multiple observations.

7. The system encourages self-evaluation and improvement. The information gained through the evaluative process is used for planning staff development and inservice activities.

8. Supervisors and evaluators are adequately trained in procedures. All individuals responsible for the implementation of the evaluation system must be trained in the techniques and skills of observation and evaluation.

A different perspective on evaluation systems is provided by McGreal (1983) and Conley (1987). Using their findings as a basis, we have listed the common areas inherent in effective evaluation systems:

1. Participants have a positive attitude toward evaluation and accept the validity of the system.

2. An evaluation model is a district priority and is complementary to the desired purpose.

3. The goal-setting phase of the evaluation system is a major activity involving participants.

4. *Teaching* is defined in narrow terms.

5. All participants know the criteria for evaluation and have a thorough understanding of the mechanics governing the system.

6. Evaluators are trained in system procedures and data collection techniques.

The characteristics that have been identified can help supervisors design and implement more consistent, reliable, and fairer evaluation systems. As one elementary teacher put it, when there is "a well-defined [evaluation] model, there is more trust between teacher and supervisor" (Glatthorn and Holler, 1987, p. 58). These traits, drawn from a variety of sources as noted, provide a conceptual framework for developing an effective teacher evaluation system. Such an evaluation system attempts to assess and foster teacher growth and improvement.

FORMATIVE AND SUMMATIVE EVALUATION PHASES

For us, teacher evaluation involves collecting information about teachers and their instructional interactions with students in the classroom and attaching interpretations or judgments to that data. The teacher evaluation process should occur in two phases that serve two distinctly different purposes and yet are indirectly tied to each other. One phase should be concerned with observing teachers for developmental reasons—to help them improve instructionally. This phase is called *formative evaluation* and is a process that many instructional supervisors have participated in. The second phase involves the use of data in making decisions about hiring or continuing on contract, firing, or granting merit rewards. This is called *summative evaluation.* While many supervisors have not been directly involved in this phase, there is evidence to suggest that instructional supervisors will be involved in *both* phases, "since the two are not intrinsically distinct" and since there is a substantial indirect relevance of formative to summative evaluation (Scriven, 1981, p. 244).

Manatt (1981) suggests a teacher performance evaluation cycle that would include several formative evaluations that would ultimately become a part of the summative phase. In such a cycle, it is important that the formative data, which provide direction for teacher instructional improvement, become a part of the decision-making process concerning the worth and value of teachers and their performance. We agree with Tanner and Tanner (1987) when they say that, in order to bring about continued instructional improvement, there is a "persistent need for formative and summative evaluation" (p. 307). Duke and Stiggins (1986) believe that it is possible to construct an evaluation system that is both highly individualized and personally productive. They identify five keys to effective evaluation that include (1) the teacher, (2) the evaluator(s), (3) performance data, (4) feedback, and (5) context (p. 17). The success of any evaluation system, either formative and/or summative, is based on the interaction of these five key elements.

As supervisors walk the evaluation tightrope and balance their actions by being a helper or a judge, they need to be aware of these key elements and use the core of effective teaching behaviors. The teacher performance criteria used should be sufficiently differentiated

---

EFFECTIVE TEACHING BEHAVIORS

1. Daily review of previous day's work
2. Direct instruction
3. Actively engaged in learning
4. Corrective feedback
5. Guided and independent practice
6. Instructional clarity
7. Time on task
8. Questioning
9. States expectations
10. Classroom management and organization
11. Varies instruction

Figure 10.3   Behaviors that contribute to effective performance.

to deal with individual teachers and situations and should form the focus of the formative phase of teacher evaluation (Glatthorn and Holler, 1987). The list of professional teacher behaviors cited in Chapter 7 is restated in Figure 10.3. We do not view this as an absolute list of teaching behaviors, but rather as a general core of teaching behaviors that appear frequently in the teaching effectiveness literature and that should therefore be considered in the evaluation process.

The list presented in Figure 10.3 can serve as a frame work for helping teachers change and shape their instructional behaviors in the formative, staff development process. Research has shown that it is possible to change teaching practices . . . enough to make an educationally important difference" (Gage, 1984, p. 89). Identifying or selecting the criteria that will be used to appraise effective teaching at the state or local school district levels is an essential step in the development of a good evaluation system. According to Medley (1979), "If teachers know the criteria on which decisions affecting their career are based, they will meet the criteria if it is humanly possible to do so" (p. 25).

To help teachers during the formative phase of teacher evaluation, supervisors use primary sources of data to collect the most accurate and objective information about teacher performance. According to Macdonald (1979), primary sources include self-reports and reports from students, peers, supervisors, and administrators. In addition, there are secondary sources, which include systematic observations of classroom instructional interactions, domain-referenced testing, and a written narrative compiled during observation. To get the most accurate and objective information when relying on secondary sources, Macdonald recommends the use of video and/or audio taping, and Flanders Interaction Analysis Categories System (see Chapter 9). A more recent development is the Florida Performance Measurement System (FPMS). It is designed for "observing and coding the behaviors of teachers and for the subsequent comparative measurement and evaluation of teacher performance in the classroom" (Smith, Peterson, and Micceri, 1987, p. 19). The authors claim that this is one of the first evaluation systems "to break completely with the rating-scale mode of observation and evaluation of teacher performance" (p.19).

Figure 10.4 depicts one of the formative classroom observation instruments used as part of the Florida Performance Measurement System. It focuses on the management of student conduct domain and includes five categories of behaviors that can be observed. Multiple sources and techniques are recommended as a means of obtaining a composite picture of individual teacher performance to better provide feedback to teachers. Establishing criteria and identifying the sources make the process of evaluating teaching possible. Inherent in the process is the observer, who experiences, interprets, and makes decisions (formative) to help guide the teacher in improving instruction (Macdonald, 1979).

The coach or counselor role of the instructional supervisor during the formative phase of teacher evaluation is ongoing. The purpose of the formative phase is to help teachers improve or upgrade their teaching skills or add to their teaching repertoire. It is later in the evaluation process that the supervisor collects all pertinent data, reviews teacher progress, reflects on changes, and engages in the summative phase of teacher evaluation by making a decision or judgment about the teacher's overall performance.

Of the two phases of teacher evaluation, we believe that the formative should take precedence. It is during the formative evaluation phase that change, if it is going to take place, will occur. Helping teachers improve instruction is a challenging task for instructional supervisors. According to Wiles and Bondi (1980):

> During the process of significant instructional improvement . . . building trust and [building] clear communication are essential to . . . change. The traditional model of supervision . . . can make assessment of instructional improvement . . . subjective, artificial

2.0 Management of Student Conduct				
Category	Effective indicators	Frequency	Frequency	Ineffective indicators
2.1 Rule explication and monitoring	Specifies a rule			Does not specify when rule needed
	Clarifies a rule			Does not clarify rule
	Practices rule			
	Reprimands rule infraction			Does not correct rule infraction
2.2–2.4 With-itness: Desist, quality, overlapping	Stops deviant behavior			Does not stop deviancy/ deviancy spreads
	Corrects worse deviancy			Corrects lesser deviancy
	Desists student causing disruption			Desists onlooker or wrong student
	Suggests alternative behavior			Uses rough, angry, punitive desists
				Uses approval-focused desist
	Attends to task and deviancy simultaneously			Ignores deviancy, continues task/ignores task, engrosses in deviancy
	Attends to two instructional tasks simultaneously			Ignores other students needing help/drops task, engrosses in intrusion
2.5 Group alert	Poses question— selects reciter			Selects reciter— poses question
	Alerts class/calls on one reciter			Alerts group— unison response
	Alerts nonperformers			Ignores nonperformers
2.6–2.7 Movement Smoothness/Slowdown	Ignores irrelevancies/ continues on task			Reacts to or interjects irrelevancies/ flipflops/dangles
	Gives short, clear, nonacademic directions			Overdwells or fragments nonacademic directions
	Moves whole/ subgroup			Fragments group movement
2.8 Praise	Praises specific conduct			Uses general conduct praise
	Praises nondeviant, on-task behavior			
	Gives low-key, quiet praise			Uses loud praise
	Uses contingency praise			
	Uses authentic, varied, warm praise			
	Controls class reaction to misconduct			Allows class to reinforce misconduct

Figure 10.4 Formative classroom observation instrument—management of student conduct. (*Source:* Smith, B. O., Peterson, D., and Micceri, T. [1987]. Evaluation and professional improvement aspects of the Florida Performance Measurement System. *Educational Leadership, 44,* 7, 18. Used with permission of the Association for Supervision and Curriculum Development. Copyright © by ASCD. All rights reserved.)

and nonproductive. . . . What is needed . . . is a form of classroom supervision that is positive in its orientation, nonthreatening in its manner, open in its communication, and continuous in its application. (p. 132)

Instructional supervisors all too often "are like angels making visitations not visits" (Manatt, 1987, p. 12). They need to be trained to collect information that is bias-free and valid. The observation data should be used in meaningful ways. In some districts teachers, after receiving their observation results, are referred to specific staff development programs (Leach and Solomon, 1984; Caldwell, 1986). These staff development programs vary from receiving guidance in employing specific techniques to being teamed with a successful teacher.

Another approach suggested by Beach and Reinhartz (1982) that can be used during formative evaluation is to help teachers develop diagnostic skills relative to personal instructional abilities. Teachers "using inventories or self-diagnostic tools to study their own classroom teaching behavior" have a data base to develop an instructional profile (p. 8).

Once data have been collected and teachers have had opportunities to modify their instructional behavior(s), formative evaluation comes to an end and the summative or decision-making phase begins. Depending upon the individual evaluation system a district uses, the formative phase frequently concludes at the end of a major reporting period such as a semester or school year. For more experienced teachers who have consistently received good evaluations, the formative process may occur every two or three years. Summative evaluation is the final phase in the evaluation process and requires that judgments be made about the quality of a teacher's instructional performance. Figure 10.5 is an example of a summative observation instrument that was developed as a part of the Florida Performance Measurement System.

Figure 10.5 is one example of a lesson assessment instrument that is based on the formative instrument presented in Figure 10.4. It contains specific domains of teaching behaviors that provide a focus for the observation and give specific data for feedback to teachers. According to Smith, Peterson, and Micceri (1987), "The summative instrument [Figure 10.5] . . . serves as a screening function, enabling a trained observer to identify the problem areas such as management of student conduct or organization and conduct of instruction" (p.16).

Domain	Effective indicators		Frequency	Frequency	Ineffective indicators
3.0 Instructional organization and development	1. Begins instruction promptly				Delays
	2. Handles materials in an orderly manner				Does not organize or handle materials systematically
	3. Orients students to classwork/maintains academic focus				Allows talk/activity unrelated to subject
	4. Conducts beginning/ending review				
	5. Questions: academic comprehension/lesson development	asks single factual (Domain 5.0)			Poses multiple questions asked as one; unison response
		requires analysis/reasons			Poses nonacademic questions/nonacademic procedural questions
	6. Recognizes response/amplifies/gives corrective feedback				Ignores student or response/expresses sarcasm, disgust, harshness
	7. Gives specific academic praise				Uses general, nonspecific praise
	8. Provides for practice				Extends discourse, changes topic with no practice
	9. Gives directions/assigns/checks comprehension of homework, seatwork assignment/gives feedback				Gives inadequate directions/no homework/no feedback
	10. Circulates and assists students				Remains at desk/circulates inadequately
4.0 Presentation of subject matter	11. Treats concept—definition/attributes/examples/nonexamples				Gives definition or examples only
	12. Discusses cause-effect/uses linking words/applies law or principle				Discusses either cause or effect only/uses no linking word(s)
	13. States and applies academic rule				Does not state or does not apply academic rule
	14. Develops criteria and evidence for value judgment				States value judgment with no criteria or evidence
5.0 Communication: Verbal and nonverbal	15. Emphasizes important points				
	16. Expresses enthusiasm verbally/challenges students				
	17.				Uses vague/scrambled discourse
	18.				Uses loud-grating, high-pitched, monotone; inaudible talk
	19. Uses body behavior that shows interest—smiles, gestures				Frowns; deadpan or lethargic
2.0 Management of student conduct	20. Stops misconduct				Delays desist/doesn't stop misconduct/desists punitively
	21. Maintains instructional momentum				Loses momentum—fragments nonacademic directions, overdwells

Figure 10.5 Summative observation instrument—effective and ineffective indicators. (*Source:* Smith, B. O., Peterson, D., and Micceri, T. [1987]. Evaluation and professional improvement aspects of the Florida Performance Measurement System. *Educational Leadership, 44,* 7, 17. Used with permission of the Association for Supervision and Curriculum Development. Copyright © by ASCD. All rights reserved.)

In summative evaluation, the instructional supervisor is involved in a process that requires judgments to be made concerning teacher instructional performance, progress toward predetermined goals—or what Manatt (1981) calls job improvement targets—merit pay increments, retention, or dismissal. As noted earlier, the supervisor's dual role is not an easy one, since the formative and summative functions can conflict with each other. According to Sergiovanni and Starratt (1983), instructional supervisors, because of the numerous titles, functions, and roles, are faced with the following basic question:

> How can I evaluate a teacher's performance (with the assumption that it will inevitably result in some critical judgments) and at the same time retain my [formative] role as a facilitator of teacher growth? (p. 318)

This question poses a real dilemma for the instructional supervisor. Because, after working to develop a relationship built on trust and collegiality, he or she is then asked to make a judgment about a teacher's performance that may undermine the trust and hinder the supervisors ability to promote the teachers' professional growth. Perhaps this is why instructional supervisors have avoided the role of evaluator (Sergiovanni and Starratt, 1983). For McNergney and Medley (1984),

> supervisors, like teachers, are often expected both to support people and to make hard decisions about competence. It is unlikely that these expectations will change any time in the near future. . . . What this means is that in most situations supervisors cannot trade away their responsibilities for making summative decisions in hopes of winning the trust of those with whom they work; they must learn instead to take on both sets of responsibilities. (p. 150)

As instructional supervisors are called on more and more to participate in the summative phase of teacher evaluation, they will be required to make judgments regarding a teacher's performance based on information gathered during previous formative classroom observations and conferences (Manatt, 1981). As Sergiovanni and Starratt (1983) explain, "Pointing only to the growth and development side of evaluation and not admitting that teachers also receive grades or performance ratings every year is not facing the realities of the school setting" (p. 324). When viewed as complementary to each other, formative and summative evaluations can lead to improved teacher performance and professional growth; they need not interfere with the supportive collegiality and trust necessary for such improvement and growth.

To maximize the impact of both phases of evaluation, it is essential that the teacher and the supervisor work together as a team and that the rules of the game be clearly understood. In order for teachers to learn these rules and to feel that the system is fair, they have the right, according to Hoyle, English, and Steffy (1985), to ask the following questions:

1. What are the standards of evaluation?
2. Who will do the evaluating?
3. What types of instruments will be used?
4. How will the evaluation results be used?
5. How many times will I be evaluated?
6. What are the appeal procedures if I disagree with the evaluation results?

The overall evaluation system can be successful if teachers feel that the summative as well as the formative phases are fair and equitable and educationally sound.

SUMMARY

Evaluating teachers is the focus of this chapter. There are many difficulties associated with teacher evaluation, ranging from teacher performance criteria that are not consistently applied, to a lack of an adequate training program for both teachers and supervisors. The chapter provides instructional supervisors with a broad view of the topic, which includes perceptions of teaching and teachers, the purposes and assumptions related to evaluation, the characteristics of effective teacher evaluation systems, and a general overview of the formative and summative evaluation phases.

Teacher evaluation, as noted earlier, is a multifaceted endeavor. The goal is the improvement of instruction, which ultimately leads to increased student achievement in the classroom. The basis for teacher evaluation is the belief that all professionals are capable of improving their behavior. This assumption becomes a reality if the evaluation process is systematically implemented, is research-based, has established procedures, has goals linked to district mission and philosophy, involves teachers in the process, and has training programs for teachers and supervisors.

The recommendation that the evaluation criteria be linked to specific teacher behaviors, as supported in the literature, is a promising practice in evaluating teachers. Another promising change is the collaboration that is occurring between teachers and supervisors in the development of evaluation systems at the school district and state levels. As teachers become more involved in the planning, development, implementation, and follow-up of the teacher evaluation system, the greater the level of collaboration.

As stated in the introduction to the chapter, teacher evaluation is indeed complicated, but it is essential to both teacher improvement and school improvement. Professional improvement results in increasing the quality of education in schools and ultimately the entire school system. If the evaluation of teaching is viewed from an improvement perspective, the role of the instructional supervisor seems appropriate and valid.

YOUR TURN

10.1. Interview at least three teachers and three evaluators using four questions related to teacher evaluation. For example, you might ask (a) What makes a teacher evaluation system effective? (b) What do you think about linking evaluation results with monetary incentives or promotion? What pluses and minuses would you cite? Compile the responses of the teachers and the evaluators in a summary statement that could be helpful to you and to your school district in developing and implementing a teacher evaluation system.

10.2. Review three journal articles related to state or district teacher evaluation systems. Then explain how the teacher evaluation system in your district or state differs from the ones you read about.

10.3. If you were in charge of designing the training program for evaluators regardless of the evaluation system used, what type of program would you design? Include specific components, titles of presentations, and possible presenters.

10.4. What efforts would you make to involve teachers in the development and implementation of the evaluation system?

    a. How would you begin?

    b. How would you decide on the number of teachers, representative subject areas, and levels?

    c. What role would teachers play?

10.5. The superintendent has asked you to chair a committee in the district that will develop a comprehensive teacher evaluation system. Who should be on the committee with you? What areas should the committee consider in evaluating teachers? How often will teachers be evaluated? By whom will they be evaluated? And how does the evaluation affect pay and promotion?

10.6. If asked to address a teacher organization concerning the role of instructional supervisors in formative and summative teacher evaluation, how would you respond? If you were asked to address a group of principals or other administrators on the same topic, what would your position be?

10.7. Select a period in American history and research the topic of teacher evaluation. List the common characteristics of the evaluation system(s) cited, the negatives and the positives expressed, and compare these findings with those presented in this chapter.

    a. What similarities and differences did you find?

    b. In what ways are the issues and the concerns of teachers the same or different?

REFERENCES

A nation at risk: The imperative for educational reform. (1983). Washington, D.C.: National Commission on Excellence in Education.

Beach, D. M., and Reinhartz, J. (1982). Improving instructional effectiveness: A self-assessment procedure. *Illinois School Research and Development Journal, 19,* 1, 5–12.

Brandt, R. (1987). Proceed with caution. *Educational Leadership, 44,* 7, 3.

Brown, R. D. (1983). Helpful and humane teacher evaluations. In W. R. Duckett (Ed.), *Teacher evaluation: Gathering and using data.* Bloomington, Ind.: Phi Delta Kappa.

Buttram, J. L., and Wilson, B. L. (1987). Promising trends in teacher evaluation. *Educational Leadership, 44,* 7, 4–6.

Caldwell, M. (1986). *Status report on Virginia beginning teacher assistance program.* Charlottesville: University of Virginia.

Conley, D. T. (1987). Critical attributes of effective evaluation systems. *Educational Leadership, 44,* 7, 60–64.

Delaware Performance Appraisal System. (1986). Dover: Delaware Department of Public Instruction.

Dillon-Peterson, B. (1986). Trusting teachers to know what is good for them. In K. Zumwalt (Ed.), *Improving teaching.* Alexandria, Va.: Association for Supervision and Curriculum Development.

Duke, D. L., and Stiggins, R. J. (1986). *Teacher evaluation: Five keys to growth.* Washington, D.C.: National Education Association.

Duvall, L. A. (1983). An administrator views the evaluation of teaching. In

W. R. Duckett (Ed.), *Teacher evaluation: Gathering and using data.* Bloomington, Ind.: Phi Delta Kappa.

Florida Coalition for the Development of a Performance Measurement System. (1983). *Domains: Knowledge base of the Florida Performance Measurement System.* Chipley, Fla.: Panhandle Educational Cooperative.

Gage, N. L. (1984). What do we know about teaching effectiveness? *Phi Delta Kappan, 66,* 2, 87–93.

Gephart, W. J., and Ingle, R. B. (1983). Introduction. In W. R. Duckett (Ed.), *Teacher evaluation: Gathering and using data.* Bloomington, Ind.: Phi Delta Kappa.

Glatthorn, A. A., and Holler, R. L. (1987). Differentiated teacher evaluation. *Educational Leadership, 44,* 7, 56–58.

Good, T. L., and Brophy, J. E. (1987). *Looking in classrooms* (4th ed.). New York: Harper & Row.

Harris, B., and Hill, J. (1982). *The developmental teacher evaluation kit* (DeTEK). Austin, Tex.: Southwest Educational Development Laboratory.

Hoyle, J. R., English, F. W., and Steffy, B. E. (1985). *Skills for successful school leaders.* Arlington, Va.: American Association of School Administrators.

Iwanicki, E. (1981). Contract plans: A professional growth-oriented approach to evaluating teacher performance. In J. Millman (Ed.), *Handbook of teacher evaluation.* Beverly Hills, Calif.: Sage Publications.

Leach, J., and Solomon, L. (1984). *Performance-based certification in Georgia: Present and future.* Atlanta: Georgia State Department of Education. [ERIC Document Reproduction Service No. ED 253-540.]

Macdonald, J. B. (1979). Evaluation of teaching: Purpose, context, and problems. In W. R. Duckett (Ed.) *Planning for the evaluation of teaching.* Bloomington, Ind.: Phi Delta Kappa.

Manatt, R. P. (1976) *Developing a teacher performance evaluation system as mandated by Senate File 205.* Des Moines: Iowa Association of School Boards.

Manatt, R. P. (1981). *Evaluating teacher performance.* Alexandria, Va.: Association for Supervision and Curriculum Development. [Videotape.]

Manatt, R. (1987). Lessons from a comprehensive performance appraisal project. *Educational Leadership, 44,* 7, 8–14.

McGreal, T. (1983). *Successful teacher evaluation.* Alexandria, Va.: Association for Supervision and Curriculum Development.

McNergney, R. F., and Medley, D. M. (1984). Teacher evaluation. In J. M. Cooper (Ed.), *Developing skills for instructional supervision.* New York: Longman.

Medley, D. M. (1979). The effectiveness of teachers. In P. Peterson and H. Walberg (Eds.), *Research on teaching: Concepts, findings and implications.* Berkeley, Calif.: McCutchan.

Peterson, D., and Smith, B. O. (1986). The use of teacher effectiveness research in the preparation of instructional supervisors. *Wingspan, 3,* 1, 15–19.

Pfeiffer, I. L., and Dunlap, J. B. (1982). *Supervision of teachers: A guide to improving instruction.* Phoenix: Oryx Press.

Rand Checklist (January 1985). Santa Monica, Calif.: Rand Corporation.

Scriven, M. (1981). Summative teacher evaluation. In J. Millman (Ed.), *Handbook of teacher evaluation.* Beverly Hills, Calif.: Sage Publications.

Sergiovanni, T. J., and Starratt, R. (1983). *Supervision: Human perspectives* (3rd ed.). New York: McGraw-Hill.

Shannon, T. A. (1982). Teacher evaluation: Some points to ponder. *CEDR Quarterly, 15,* 4, 18.

Smith, B. O., Peterson, D., and Micceri, T. (1987). Evaluation and professional improvement aspects of the Florida Performance Measurement System. *Educational Leadership, 44,* 7, 16–19.

Tanner, D., and Tanner, L. (1987). *Supervision in education: Problems and practices.* New York: Macmillan.

Texas Teacher Appraisal System, Teacher orientation manual. (1986–1987). Austin: Texas Education Agency.

Travers, R. M. W. (1981). Criteria of good teaching. In J. Millman (Ed.), *Handbook of teacher evaluation.* Beverly Hills, Calif.: Sage Publications.

Wiles, J., and Bondi, J. (1980). *Supervision: A guide to practice.* Columbus, Ohio: Charles E. Merrill.

Wise, A., et al. (1985). Teacher evaluation: A study of effective practices. *Elementary School Journal, 83,* 287–312.

Wise, A., and Darling-Hammond, L. (1984–1985). Teacher evaluation and teacher professionalism. *Educational Leadership, 42,* 4, 28–33.

chapter 11

Working with People: Staff Development

Throughout this book we have emphasized the importance of working with people in the instructional supervision process. The emphasis on working with people culminates in this chapter, which examines the role of the instructional supervisor in planning and implementing inservice and staff development programs. The concern for teachers as individuals becomes the focus of what supervisors do when fostering professional growth and development. For us, inservice education and staff development activities are not just for teachers who are having difficulties in delivering instruction; rather, these activities are for all teachers. Within the school organization, the need for inservice and staff development programs is heightened by two factors: the relative stability of the teaching profession and a young group of beginning teachers. Sergiovanni and Starratt (1983) sum up the situation this way:

> . . . when teachers land a decent job they are likely to stay. Combine this phenomenon with a relatively young teaching force and many districts are faced with large numbers of teachers who are likely to stay employed in the same school and system for the next 2 or 3 decades. (p. 326)

Inservice and staff development are crucial, then, in promoting instructional competency and enhancing the appreciation that teachers have for their work.

On the average, teachers in the United States participate in approximately three days of inservice activities each year, and only rarely are these inservice sessions scheduled for more than one day at a time (Joyce and Showers, 1983). And although sessions are regularly scheduled, teachers do not always have a high regard for inservice education and staff development programs. Wood and Thompson (1980) have gone so far as to say that staff development is the "slum of education" because it is riddled with broken promises and contradictions. Andrews (1981) further describes the problems associated with inservice/staff development programs when he states:

> Educational programs are not designed for adults. They are designed primarily by instructors who use what they have learned (or more likely have experienced) about teaching children, adolescents, or college students. While many of the principles of learning are the same for adults and children, differences do exist, and only by careful attention to those differences will consistently successful learning programs for adults be offered. (pp. 11–12)

A great many teachers are not enthusiastic about inservice/staff development programs because they often perceive these activities as formal, bureaucratic "dog and pony shows."

A fundamental question for supervisors to seek an answer to is, "What motivates teachers to attend inservice/staff development sessions?" Howey (1977) has identified six factors that help provide answers to this question. According to Howey, teachers may rely on inservice/staff development programs to obtain assistance in the following areas:

1. handling the transition from a preservice role as student to an inservice role as teacher (transitional)
2. meeting specific classroom needs (job-specific)
3. meeting mandates of local school districts and/or states (system-related)
4. remaining current (general professional development)
5. progressing in career-related matters (career progression)
6. meeting the personal need to improve (personal development)

An inventory of staff development sessions reveals the typical kinds of options that teachers are given. Some sessions primarily offer inspiring speeches; others are make-and-take workshops; and still others feature presentations on specific skills and/or particular curriculum programs. Although these efforts should be applauded as a way of bringing about professional improvement, the results have been only marginal (Dillon-Peterson, 1981; Yarger, Howey, and Joyce, 1980; Showers, Joyce, and Bennett, 1987). "If behavioral change is the goal of inservice education, the limited one-shot format will not suffice" (Van Cleaf and Reinhartz, 1984, p. 167). Instructional supervisors are going to have to assume much of the responsibility for improving inservice/staff development programs. As stated earlier in the assumptions in Chapter 1, change is possible for teachers if the relationship with the supervisor is collegial. Such a relationship is based on cooperation and mutual respect as both the supervisor and the teacher work toward common goals.

If this description accurately reflects the state of staff development activities found in the literature and in practice, then clearly change is needed to energize inservice and staff development procedures. Such a change will require new and bold thinking on the part of instructional supervisors who are responsible for planning, organizing, and implementing inservice/staff development activities. It is important, then, that instructional supervisors understand the present shortcomings associated with teacher professional growth in order to plan for more meaningful experiences based on what research says about current inservice/staff development programs. In doing so, supervisors will need to know about the professional and developmental characteristics of the teachers they work with as well as their own personal and professional qualities, namely their supervisory style.

This chapter will examine definitions and purposes of inservice and staff development, review what research says about effective inservice/staff development, examine the professional and developmental characteristics of teachers, consider the professional development of instructional supervisors, and outline steps for initiating staff development programs. The chapter will also provide an example of a management approach that has been implemented in business and industry and has applicability for teacher staff development. The chapter concludes with thoughts about the future of supervision and staff development with particular attention given to collegial, cooperative supervision.

DEFINITIONS AND PURPOSES OF INSERVICE
EDUCATION AND STAFF DEVELOPMENT

Inservice education and staff development are not unique to the teaching profession and are widely recognized by other professional organizations as important means of maintaining and upgrading the quality of personnel. For teachers, supervisors, and administrators, inservice and staff development provide an opportunity continually to expand their repertoire of teaching, supervisory, and/or administrative abilities. However, Hammond and Foster (1987) note that "designers of staff development often forget that adults learn when they perceive there is a need to learn" (p. 42). It is important to focus on professional needs when examining the concerns that are currently being raised about the nature of inservice/staff development programs. The present concerns point out the need to (1) reflect on the purposes of inservice/staff development, (2) develop methods for successful program implementation, and (3) restructure professional development (Beach and Reinhartz, 1980).

With a better understanding of the definitions and purposes of inservice education and staff development, instructional supervisors will be in a better position to identify the specific objectives to be accomplished. Edefelt and Johnson (1975) state:

> Inservice education of teachers (or staff development, continuing education, professional development) is defined as any professional development activity that a teacher undertakes singly or with other teachers after receiving his or her initial teaching certificate and after beginning professional practice. (p. 5)

Such a definition is important as a means of understanding the purposes of inservice education, but Edefelt (1979) indicates that the definition is too limited and should be expanded to include all personnel in a school if program development and professional performance are to improve. He notes that teaching staff as well as administrators influence the quality and climate of schools. Inservice education also must be designed to include other professionals, college faculties, state department personnel, and teacher organization staff who play important roles in the total professional development process. Figure 11.1 provides a more comprehensive view of the purposes and conditions related to inservice education. Edefelt (1979) identifies not only the purposes, processes, and settings of inservice education but also

Purpose	Process	Setting	Legal Sanction and/or Administrative Authority	Responsible Agency and/or Standard of Control	Reward	Motivation
Personal/professional development	Choice of individual teacher	Setting appropriate to choice	None, but personal standards and peer pressure influence	Personal/professional standard self-satisfaction	New knowledge, improved competence, satisfaction	Personal desire or commitment
School improvement	Workshops, local seminars, analysis of professional practice with help	School district, teacher center, professional development center, training complex, school building, teaching station	Local school board policy, special state or federal legislation	School district policy collective-bargaining contract	Improved school program, personal satisfaction, parent satisfaction, student satisfaction, salary increment	School board or district requirement, collective bargaining
Degree, credential licensure	Formal college or university study	College or university campus, extension center	State law, state board policy, state department regulation, state professional licensure, commission regulation	State board policy, state department regulation, state professional licensure, commission standard	Degree credential, license, better job opportunities	Legal and professional requirement

Figure 11.1 Purposes and conditions of inservice education. (*Source:* Edefelt, R. A. [April 1979]. Inservice teacher education: A concept, an overview. *Inservice*. Syracuse, N.Y. James F. Collins [Ed.], National Council of States on Inservice Education. Used with permission.)

the legal sanctions, the agencies responsible, the rewards, and the motivations for developing or participating in the programs.

Other researchers have characterized inservice programs in a variety of ways. Dillon-Peterson (1980) has identified five purposes of inservice activities. These purposes include enabling the participants to do the following:

1. Identify key components of an effective staff improvement program;
2. Identify free and inexpensive resources available to school districts;
3. Examine successful models that fit a variety of situations and people;
4. Plan for human needs;
5. Develop a practical staff improvement plan which is applicable to the local situation. (pp. 125–126)

Orlich (1984) views inservice education differently. He sees inservice education as consisting of

programs that are based on identified needs, planned and designed for a specific group of individuals in school districts, have a specific set of learning objectives, and are designed to extend, add, or improve job-oriented skills or knowledge. (p. 34)

Yet another perspective is offered by Howsam (1977), who regards inservice education/staff development as continuing education for teachers. For him, continuing education is

the deliberate effort made by teachers and professional organizations to provide for keeping up to date and expanding the professional knowledge and skills throughout the career of the teacher regardless of where the teacher teaches. (p. 1)

For us, inservice/staff development is a process that should be viewed more comprehensively. Inservice/staff development includes the following aspects.

1. the exploration of knowledge, techniques, and curriculum
2. a way of keeping up with new developments in one's field
3. a means of expanding one's own knowledge and ideas and remaining intellectually alert
4. an effort to achieve professional/intellectual excellence

5. the pursuit of personal and professional goals
6. the opportunity to link inservice education with preservice education
7. an activity intended for all teachers regardless of professional and/or developmental level
8. a systematic, long-term, individualized, and eclectic procedure oriented toward improving classroom instruction

Moreover, according to Sergiovanni and Starratt (1983), it is helpful if instructional supervisors think of staff development as "not something the school does to the teachers but something the teacher does for himself or herself" (p. 327).

WHAT RESEARCH SAYS ABOUT INSERVICE/STAFF DEVELOPMENT PROGRAMS

There are over 9000 documents on the topic of inservice education in the Education Resources Information Clearinghouse (ERIC). According to Showers, Joyce, and Bennett (1987), "Nearly all the research relevant to staff development has been conducted during the last 20 years" (p. 78). It is a difficult if not impossible task to keep up with the growing research on inservice education and staff development. Within this vast array of information on the topic, studies often tend to contradict each other, leaving readers confused about the right thing to do (Brandt, 1980). Even with some contradictory data the "results have been integrated with studies of curriculum and innovation to enlarge the knowledge base" (Showers, Joyce, and Bennett, 1987, p. 78), which has helped to improve some aspects of professional development. For Baden (1982) and Loucks and Melle (1982), the success of staff development programs often rests with participants and their level of satisfaction and with the developer's attempt to bring about behavioral changes in both teachers and students.

According to Joyce and Showers (1980), there are messages from research on inservice training that can be used to guide and improve inservice/staff development programs. These messages are as follows:

1. Teachers are good learners.
2. Certain conditions are needed in order for teachers to learn.
3. Research has revealed what these conditions are.

Wade (1984–1985), after reviewing many articles and documents published or presented between the years 1968 and 1983, selected 91 for statistical analysis. Her findings are consistent with other studies conducted by Joslin (1980) and Lawrence and Harrison (1980). When the data were grouped by grade level, inservice training was found to be effective as indicated by increased teacher learning. Training was moderately effective as measured by changes in teacher behavior; the impact of staff development on students was judged to be only mildly effective.

The findings from Wade's meta-analysis indicate specific factors that helped determine the effectiveness of the programs studied. For instance, groups with both elementary and secondary teachers worked particularly well. (Combining grade levels for inservice sessions suggests new inservice program possibilities.) Factors such as voluntary or mandatory participation, the size of group, the location, or scheduling, were not found to have a significant impact on training outcomes. What did seem to make a difference in the results was who or what agency sponsored the sessions. If agencies other than the school (for instance, the state, federal government, or a university) did, then sessions tended to be more effective. These findings appear to contradict the belief that teacher-conducted sessions have more of an impact. Incentives, such as being designated to represent a group or being selected in a competitive fashion to attend, also had a positive effect. College credit and released time resulted in a moderate effect. Finally, Wade concludes that observing actual classroom activities, microteaching, receiving feedback from video and audio taping, and gaining actual practice are the most successful techniques to use in an inservice presentation. It is in these last activities that teacher-conducted sessions could play an important role.

What implications do Wade's findings have for planning the most effective inservice programs? The following list of suggestions have implications for planning inservice programs:

1. Include elementary and secondary teachers in the same training session when appropriate.
2. Offer participants incentives to attend (for example, a selection process, college credit, released time).
3. Use instructional strategies such as observation, microteaching, video or audio taping, and practice along with lecture and discussion.
4. Have leaders/presenters who are responsible for giving in-

formation and participants who are expected to receive that information.
5. Use "coaching" to enhance the application of newly learned material and the overall instructional effectiveness.

After reviewing many research studies, another investigator, Griffin (1983), constructed a profile of an "ideal" staff development program. The ideal program includes eight features that have brought about positive changes both in the teachers and in the schools. An inservice program will have the following related and sometimes overlapping features:

1. be designed as a consequence of systematic problem identification by those most directly related to the problem.
2. be interactive.
3. mitigate to some degree status differences between teachers and administrators.
4. depend less on consultants and more on teachers and administrators for substantive and procedural guidance.
5. be formulated and monitored largely according to perceptions of the participants.
6. be formulated, in part, in terms of a careful analysis of the organization and the people for whom it is intended.
7. be flexible and responsive to the changes in participants and the changes in the setting.
8. be, within reasonable limits, situation specific. (p. 242)

This information, resulting from a careful study of the research on staff development, can prove helpful to instructional supervisors as they plan for inservice/staff development sessions within their own districts. Supported by this information, supervisors are in a better position to help teachers by providing sessions that will improve instructional effectiveness and meet the needs of the teacher.

TEACHER CHARACTERISTICS—KNOW YOUR TEACHERS

When planning and implementing staff development activities, instructional supervisors also need to consider the demographic makeup of the teachers they work with and the different stages of the teachers' adult development. When viewing teachers as learners, supervisors should keep in mind the general principles of development:

1. Unique, identifiable stages or periods of development exist for adults as well as children.
2. The movement from one stage or period to another is sequential.
3. The rate of development and movement from one period or stage to the next is unique for each individual.

Teachers, then, like students, go through developmental stages that have distinct characteristics and involve distinct tasks. Levine (1987) suggests that an understanding of the life cycles can be an important resource for supervisors and other school leaders because seldom, if ever, will all the teachers a supervisor works with be at the same stage of development. Three distinctive periods of adult development (Helms and Turner, 1986) and the corresponding developmental tasks (Newman and Newman, 1987) are summarized in Figure 11.2

By combining the basic principles of development with the periods of adult development, Andrews (1981) cites the work of Warnat (1979) in summarizing characteristics of adult learners:

1. In terms of intelligence, adult learners are the smartest between the ages of 18 to 25 years, but they become wiser and more experienced with increasing age.

Period of development	Age	Task/Characteristics
Early adulthood	20–30/40	Seek intimacy versus isolation through marriage, work, and life style; is idealistic and motivated
Middle adulthood	30/40–65	Seeks generativity versus stagnation through management of career and/or household, nurturing marriage or other intimate relationships, raising children; has conformist behavior and seeks to belong
Later adulthood	65 to death	Seeks integrity versus despair by redirecting energy toward new roles and interests, accepting one's position in life, coping with physical and physiological changes, and developing a perspective about death.

Figure 11.2   Stages of adult development.

2. The vocabulary of a 45-year-old adult learner is about three times greater than that of an individual just graduating from college.
3. The brain of the adult learner at age 60 possesses about four times more information than when the individual was 21.
4. In terms of happiness and satisfaction with life, adult learners have the best sense of their physical self from ages 15 to 24.
5. Adult learners have the best sense of their professional self between the ages of 40 to 45.
6. For the adult learner, pessimism peaks between the ages of 30 and 39.
7. After age 30, adults become more realistic about achieving happiness; they realize that talent and determination are not always enough to guarantee success and that happiness is no longer an aim in and of itself but encompasses their health, professional achievement, and emotional goals.
8. In terms of creativity, generally the peak period is between the ages of 30 and 39 but varies according to the profession.
9. For the well-conditioned mind of the adult learner, there is no peak.
10. While the peak in most fields comes early, creative people continue to produce quality work throughout their lives. (If supervisors view teaching as a creative act, then this principle is quite encouraging for both supervisors and teachers.)

Because of the numbers of teachers who participate in inservice sessions and the differences in their ages, many, if not most, function at different developmental levels. Instructional supervisors, therefore, should pay particular attention to the teachers' level of cognitive functioning (Harvey, Hunt, and Schroder, 1961; Santmire, 1979; Glickman, 1985). Supervisors must recognize that teachers, like students, are individuals with varying cognitive abilities, and that they have different levels of professional commitment to personal growth and change.

Differences in cognitive functioning influence the degree to which teachers will process the information presented and the degree to which they will implement the information in their classrooms. Some teachers can, with little assistance, absorb information from inservice/staff development sessions and use it the next day in their classrooms because they have the background, experience, and ability to think at a high abstract or cognitive level (Glickman, 1981; Wilsey and Killion, 1982). According to Van Cleaf and Reinhartz

(1984), these teachers are called P-1 perceivers. They have the skills necessary to take advantage of inservice sessions with minimal, if any, assistance from supervisors and others. However, the P-1 perceiver is not the only type of teacher who is in the audience.

Van Cleaf and Reinhartz (1984) identified another group of teachers, the P-2 perceivers. These teachers are interested in the information being presented, but they need assistance and guidance from supervisors, peers, or others to integrate the information or strategy into their teaching repertoire. In addition, P-2 perceivers usually need follow-up and coaching sessions to help them in applying the information to their particular grade level, content or subject area, and/or group of students. As illustrated in Figure 11.3, P-1 perceivers can benefit the most if information presented relates to their developmental level. P-2 perceivers, on the other hand, will not be able to implement the information from the staff development session without additional assistance.

As shown in Figure 11.3, a third group of teachers, the non-perceivers, are also present at inservice sessions. These teachers do not recognize the need for the training that is presented. Generally,

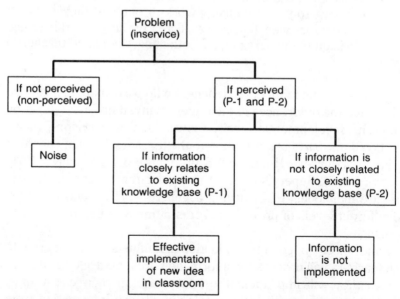

Figure 11.3 Adaptive inservice model. (*Source:* Van Cleaf, D., and Reinhartz, J. [December 1984]. Perceivers and non-perceivers. *The Clearing House, 58,* 4, 168. Reprinted with permission of the Helen Dwight Reid Educational Foundation. Published by Heldref Publications, 4000 Albemarle St., N.W., Washington, D.C. 20016. Copyright © 1984.)

these non-perceiving teachers are not able to think abstractly and are unable to process the information and apply it to their classes. For the non-perceiving teachers, the inservice program is just "noise." Therefore, non-perceivers do not and will not benefit from inservice/ staff development sessions that fail to take into account each teacher's level of cognitive functioning, background, experience, and current teaching situation. As instructional supervisors develop inservice/staff development programs to meet the needs of all teachers, these non-perceivers present a special challenge.

The challenge for supervisors is to initiate inservice/staff development activities that provide the conditions under which the adaptation process (change) can occur. According to Bents and Howey (1981), for behavioral or developmental change to occur the teacher's mental structure must be affected. As instructional supervisors plan inservice/staff development programs, they should view teachers as individuals who have different instructional needs, interests, and cognitive abilities. Instructional supervisors should therefore identify teachers who are perceivers and non-perceivers and keep these two groups in mind as they plan and conduct inservice/staff development sessions and follow-up activities. Without a comprehensive plan that accommodates these cognitive differences among teachers, non-perceivers are not likely to adopt any new ideas or implement any new strategies in their classrooms. If change, in the form of improved instruction, is the objective of inservice/staff development, the entire process is often seen as useless and meaningless when change does not occur. Teachers return to their classrooms, remain isolated and do not benefit from the very programs that were designed expressly to help meet their professional needs.

SUPERVISOR CHARACTERISTICS—KNOW YOURSELF

Throughout this book, activities and inventories have been included as a way of providing opportunities for self-assessment and involvement. We have tried to identify personal and professional characteristics as well as practices and procedures that are associated with effective instructional supervisors. Prospective supervisors should now be able to reflect on the type of supervisor they would like to become. To become truly effective, supervisors need to be in control of their own learning, capitalize on their abilities, and have a keen sense of their own strengths as well as their liabilities and deficiencies. By knowing the characteristics of the teachers they work with and their own strengths and weaknesses, supervisors will be more effective in selecting and conducting inservice/staff development activities.

In order for instructional supervisors to be the best they can be, a focus on "self" is encouraged. According to Eble (1978), the supervisor's ability to develop "his or her own self lies in bringing out and using wisely those qualities of personality and character essential to the complex task of bringing out the best in others" (p. 81). With the foundations and practice components of supervision presented in earlier chapters, introspection now becomes the key to the supervisor's professional development and ultimate effectiveness. Before supervisors confront realistic situations in school settings, introspection provides a way of assessing their supervisory style, leadership skills, attitudes about the teaching–learning process, and ability to work with teachers and others.

As individuals involved in a professional field of human resource management, supervisors should understand themselves and their roles. One way of helping supervisors understand their personality traits is through the use of the "Johari Window," which was developed by Joseph Luft and Henry Ingham (1955) and gets its name from the names of its authors. This framework serves as a way of focusing on known and unknown personality traits. Using this conceptual framework, we have shown in Figure 11.4 the relationship between the supervisor and teachers concerning known and unknown behavior traits.

	What the teacher knows about the supervisor	What the teacher does not know about the supervisor
What the supervisor knows about himself or herself	Public or Open self	Hidden or Private self
What the supervisor does not know about himself or herself	Blind self	Undiscovered or Unknown self

Figure 11.4 The Johari Window.

According to Figure 11.4, there are some personality traits or personal characteristics of the supervisor that are known to both the supervisor and the teachers. This part of the window is called the "public self." Some traits of a supervisor are known only to the individual himself or herself. This area of the window is called the "private" or "hidden self" and consists of personal assessments the supervisor makes about how he or she relates to others. There are traits that are known to the teachers, but are unknown to the supervisor. This area of the window is called the "blind self" because the supervisor is not receiving or does not understand the feedback from others. Finally, there are traits that are unknown to both the supervisor and to teachers. This area of the window is called the "unknown or undiscovered self" because this is a part of the supervisor's personality or behavior that remains unknown. Supervisors can modify the shapes of the different window "panes" by disclosing or withholding information or guarding information. The Johari Window provides a useful mechanism for self-recognition as supervisors reflect on the insights about their behavior coupled with a willingness to seek out new information and to see themselves as others see them.

For instance, at an inservice session a supervisor may overlook useful feedback, in the form of questions from teachers, about the supervisor's handling of the program. Instead of becoming defensive, a supervisor with an awareness of the Johari Window's "blind" pane might be more attuned to information from others so that he or she could assess behaviors and improve professional competence.

Another way for supervisors to begin the self-assessment process is to focus on supervisory style. Glickman (1981) has developed a simple inventory to assist supervisors in determining their supervisory style. Figure 11.5, the Supervisor Beliefs Inventory, may prove helpful to supervisors as they reflect on their style. To review the basic description of each supervisory style, see Chapter 8.

Introspection, coupled with the information about specific supervisory roles, responsibilities, and skills, can assist supervisors in their quest for excellence. Bruner (1966) suggests that in obtaining knowledge, "unless the learner [supervisor] also masters himself [or herself], disciplines his [or her] taste, deepens his [or her] view of the world, the 'something' learned . . . is hardly worth the effort of transmission" (p. 73).

Professional growth should be viewed from a learning perspective. For supervisors to develop professionally, they need the freedom to determine their own direction for growth, to interact with other supervisors in a cooperative manner, and to discuss new ideas and break the feeling of isolation. They also need time to talk, listen, and reflect on new learning.

The Supervisor Beliefs Inventory

This inventory is designed for supervisors to assess their own beliefs about teacher supervision and staff development. The inventory assumes that supervisors believe and act according to all three of the orientations of supervision, yet one usually dominates. The inventory is designed to be self-administered and self-scored. Supervisors are asked to choose one of two options. A scoring key follows.

Instructions: Circle either A or B for each item. You may not completely agree with either choice, but choose the one that is closer to how you feel.

1. A. Supervisors should give teachers a large degree of autonomy and initiative within broadly defined limits.
   B. Supervisors should give teachers directions about methods that will help them improve their teaching.

2. A. It is important for teachers to set their own goals and objectives for professional growth.
   B. It is important for supervisors to help teachers reconcile their personalities and teaching styles with the philosophy and direction of the school.

3. A. Teachers are likely to feel uncomfortable and anxious if the objectives on which they will be evaluated are not clearly defined by the supervisor.
   B. Evaluations of teachers are meaningless if teachers are not able to define with their supervisors the objectives for evaluation.

4. A. An open, trusting, warm, and personal relationship with teachers is the most important ingredient in supervising teachers.
   B. A supervisor who is too intimate with teachers risks being less effective and less respected than a supervisor who keeps a certain degree of professional distance from teachers.

5. A. My role during supervisory conferences is to make the interaction positive, to share realistic information, and to help teachers plan their own solutions to problems.
   B. The methods and strategies I use with teachers in a conference are aimed at our reaching agreement over the needs for future improvement.

6. In the initial phase of working with a teacher:
   A. I develop objectives with each teacher that will help accomplish school goals.
   B. I try to identify the talents and goals of individual teachers so they can work on their own improvement.

7. When several teachers have a similar classroom problem, I prefer to:
   A. Have the teachers form an ad hoc group and help them work together to solve the problem.
   B. Help teachers on an individual basis find their strengths, abilities, and resources so that each one finds his or her own solution to the problem.

Figure 11.5 Self-assessment instrument—Supervisor Beliefs Inventory. (*Source:* Glickman, C. D. [1981]. *Developmental Supervision: Alternative practices for helping teachers improve instruction,* pp. 13–15. Alexandria, Va.: Association for Supervision and Curiculum Development. Used with permission of the Association for Supervision and Curriculum Development. Copyright © by ASCD. All rights reserved.)

Figure 11.5 continued

8. The most important clue that an in-service workshop is needed is when:
   A. The supervisor perceives that several teachers lack knowledge or skill in a specific area which is resulting in low morale, undue stress, and less effective teaching.
   B. Several teachers perceive the need to strengthen their abilities in the same instructional area.

9. A. The supervisory staff should decide the objectives of an in-service workshop since they have a broad perspective of the teachers' abilities and the school's needs.
   B. Teachers and the supervisory staff should reach consensus about the objectives of an in-service workshop before the workshop is held.

10. A. Teachers who feel they are growing personally will be more effective than teachers who are not experiencing personal growth.
    B. The knowledge and ability of teaching strategies and methods that have been proven over the years should be taught and practiced by all teachers to be effective in their classrooms.

11. When I perceive that a teacher might be scolding a student unnecessarily:
    A. I explain, during a conference with the teacher, why the scolding was excessive.
    B. I ask the teacher about the incident, but do not interject my judgments.

12. A. One effective way to improve teacher performance is to formulate clear behavioral objectives and create meaningful incentives for achieving them.
    B. Behavioral objectives are rewarding and helpful to some teachers but stifling to others; also, some teachers benefit from behavioral objectives in some situations but not in others.

13. During a pre-observation conference:
    A. I suggest to the teacher what I could observe, but I let the teacher make the final decision about the objectives and methods of observations.
    B. The teacher and I mutually decide the objectives and methods of observation.

14. A. Improvement occurs very slowly if teachers are left on their own; but when a group of teachers work together on a specific problem, they learn rapidly and their morale remains high.
    B. Group activities may be enjoyable, but I find that individual, open discussions with a teacher about a problem and its possible solutions leads to more sustained results.

15. When an in-service or staff development workshop is scheduled:
    A. All teachers who participated in the decision to hold the workshop should be expected to attend it.
    B. Teachers, regardless of their role in forming a workshop, should be able to decide if the workshop is relevant to their personal or professional growth and, if not, should not be expected to attend.

Scoring Key

Step 1. Circle your answer from the inventory in the columns below:

Column I	Column II	Column III
1B 1A		
	2B 2A	
3A 3B		
4B 4A		
	5B 5A	

Figure 11.5 continued

```
6A ........................................ 6B
              7A .................... 7B
8A ........................................ 8B
9A .................... 9B
10B ........................................ 10A
11A ........................................ 11B
12A ................ 12B
              13B ................ 13A
14B ................ 14A
              15A ................ 15B
```

Step 2. Tally the number of circled items in each column and multiply by 6.7.

2.1 Total response in Column I _____ × 6.7 = _____
2.2 Total response in Column II _____ × 6.7 = _____
2.3 Total response in Column III _____ × 6.7 = _____

Step 3. Interpretation

The product you obtained in step 2.1 is an approximate percentage of how often you take a directive approach to supervision, rather than either of the other two approaches. The product you obtained in step 2.2 is an approximate percentage of how often you take a collaborative approach; and step 2.3 is an approximate percentage of how often you take a nondirective approach.

STEPS IN DEVELOPING INSERVICE/STAFF DEVELOPMENT PROGRAMS

Not only must supervisors have a knowledge of their own strengths and weakness as well as of the developmental characteristics of the teachers they work with; they must also be aware of the aspects of successful staff development programs. A comprehensive and continuous plan for the improvement of instruction is a prerequisite if staff development is to be effective. As most districts are currently constituted, supervisors, in addition to their other roles, also serve as the person in these districts with primary responsibility for inservice/staff development programs. Even with a large investment of time and effort from supervisors, as well as a commitment of other resources, staff development may frequently appear to be disorganized, with unclear goals and objectives (Wood and Thompson, 1980; Orlich, 1984).

Perhaps one reason for this disorganized appearance is that supervisors have often been accused of supporting McGregor's Theory X, as described in Chapter 4, in that they view teachers as disliking and avoiding inservice sessions. The supervisors' views of teachers in this regard are communicated to teachers, who then consider inservice sessions a waste of time. Consequently, in many districts, Theory X becomes a self-fulfilling prophecy. How can staff development become the primary vehicle for improving instruction? What does it take to make staff development effective? Several investigators have provided some insights into these questions.

Orlich (1984) has identified the following six methods for achieving successful staff development programs:

1. Involve the participants during the presentations.
2. Incorporate sessions into an overall plan to improve instruction.
3. Offer specific, concrete training that takes place over an extended period of time.
4. Observe similar skills or programs in action.
5. Provide sessions that focus on concrete, practical problems.
6. Use logically developed materials.

Earlier in the chapter we discussed Wade's helpful suggestions based on her research findings (1984–1985). For Sparks (1983), staff development also offers a promising road to teacher growth and instructional improvement. And although teacher growth is the objective, according to Sergiovanni and Starratt (1983), inservice/staff development should be

> less a function of polishing existing teaching skills or keeping up with the latest teaching developments and more a function of the teacher's changing as a person—of seeing himself or herself, the school, the curriculum and students differently. (p. 327)

When instructional supervisors are ready to plan and implement staff development programs, all the information gleaned from research, adult learning theory, and introspection may prove helpful. The supervisor can add to this body of information a format that provides the steps for putting together an inservice/staff development workshop. Figure 11.6 identifies critical steps that supervisors can follow as they plan inservice/staff development programs for teachers. Figure 11.6 suggests that supervisors consider the audience for the program, the competencies to be developed, the objectives of the sessions, a time line for implementation, and evaluation procedures to determine the effectiveness of the program(s). To do

Steps in Implementing Staff Development Program
1. Identify target group.
a. Select the grade level(s).
b. Choose buildings, schools.
c. Choose teachers, support staff.
2. Assess baseline competencies.
a. Administer a pretest on content.
b. Administer a values assessment.
c. Determine the knowledge and value level.
3. Based on baseline data, make decision to initiate the inservice session.
a. Involve appropriate levels in decision.
b. Demonstrate commitment to workshop decision through tangible support.
4. Determine objectives and assign priorities based on assessed needs.
a. Determine cognitive objectives.
b. Determine affective objectives.
c. Determine program objectives.
5. Establish a time line for inservice workshop.
a. Schedule a date for workshop.
b. Attend to details of planning for events leading to workshop.
6. Select leadership, activities, and resources to accomplish objectives.
7. Conduct formative and summative evaluations.
a. Determine success of workshop planning and implementation.
b. Determine degree of cognitive and affective gains.
8. Provide feedback.

Figure 11.6   Format for preparing an inservice / staff development program for teachers.

a good job in planning and conducting inservice/staff development activities, the instructional supervisor will clearly need to devote considerable time and effort to the project.

A MANAGEMENT APPROACH TO STAFF DEVELOPMENT

While not necessarily presented as a staff development model per se, one of the most widely recognized approaches for people development has been proposed by Blanchard and Johnson (1982) in their book *The One Minute Manager.* This model has a business orientation; it focuses on ways of increasing profits while improving the productivity of people within the organization. The concepts presented, however, provide a sound basis for a generalizable model that instructional supervisors can use in working with teachers. The "One Minute Manager" approach places an emphasis on principles of people management and is designed to get quality results from the people in any organization. Perhaps this emphasis on people is best summarized when Blanchard and Johnson (1982) note:

> The One Minute Manager's symbol—a one minute readout from the face of a modern digital watch—is intended to remind each of

us to take a minute out of our day to look into the faces of the people we manage [supervise]. And to realize that *they* are our most important resources. (p.5)

In applying this view to schools, instructional supervisors must realize that teachers are our greatest resources. The following discussion outlines how the One Minute Manager technique can be used with teachers.

The first step in the approach is called One Minute Goal Setting. In this step, the supervisor works with the teachers by

1. establishing and agreeing upon goals
2. demonstrating and showing what good behavior/performance looks like
3. writing out goals using less than 250 words
4. reading and focusing on each goal

The second step, designed to help people reach their full potential, is especially important during training and development. This step is called One Minute Praising. In implementing this step, the supervisor incorporates the following components:

1. telling teachers *up front* how they are doing
2. giving praise immediately and being specific about what was done right
3. telling teachers how good you feel about their performance
4. pausing to allow teachers to feel the praise and feel how good you feel
5. encouraging teachers to do more of the same and shaking hands or touching in a way that makes it clear that you support their success

Within the One Minute Manager approach, the key to developing people is to catch them doing something right and praising them for it. As teachers become successful, supervisors don't have to catch them doing something right very often, because they are able to reinforce themselves.

The final step in this approach involves the One Minute Reprimand. This step is to be used *only* for good teachers: those who are successful and have consistently been praised. The reprimand should never be used for those who are learning and developing and need reinforcement when they do things right or approximately right. The supervisor should use the reprimand *only* when working with experienced, successful teachers. In implementing this step, the supervisor should include the following components by

1. telling teachers in advance that they will be given both negative and positive feedback on their performance
2. providing the reprimand immediately
3. being specific about what was done incorrectly
4. telling teachers how you feel about what they did wrong
5. pausing to let teachers feel your dissatisfaction with their performance
6. reaffirming that you think well of them and that while you are not pleased with their performance in this situation, you value them as members of the school organization
7. realizing that when the reprimand is over, it is over

Figure 11.7 provides a brief summary and overview of the One Minute Manager approach that instructional supervisors can use in working with teachers.

The *One Minute Manager* provides an approach that can be a tool for instructional supervisors to use as they assist teachers in improving their performance in the classroom. Three principles from this model further serve to guide supervisors in staff development. First, Blanchard and Johnson (1982) state: "Everyone is a potential winner. Some people are disguised as losers; don't let their appearances fool you" (p. 71). They also say: "People who feel good about themselves produce good results" (p. 19). And, finally, the One Minute Manager emphasizes that the best minute that supervisors can spend is the one that is invested in people.

FUTURE TRENDS: COOPERATIVE AND COLLABORATIVE SUPERVISION

One of the most promising trends in supervision and staff development involves a cooperative, collaborative interaction between instructional supervisors and teachers. In schools where a collaborative approach is implemented, teachers learn to view each other as resources for professional growth and work together with instructional supervisors toward common instructional goals (Smith, 1987). Thus what has sometimes been seen as an adversarial relationship in the past has become a cooperative, collegial endeavor.

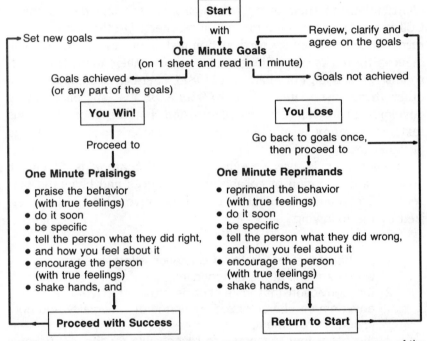

A very brief summary of
The One Minute Manager's "Game Plan"
How to give yourself and others "the gift" of getting greater results in less time.
Set goals; praise and reprimand behaviors; encourage people;
speak the truth; laugh; work; enjoy;
and encourage the people you work with to do the same as you do!

Figure 11.7 A people-oriented approach to management—a summary of the One Minute Manager's game plan." (*Source:* Blanchard, K., and Johnson, S. [1982]. *The one minute manager*, p. 101. New York: William Morrow. Copyright © Communications Corporation. By permission of William Morrow and Company, Inc.

A collaborative approach to staff development, in which teachers work together, is different from schools that Rosenholtz (in press) has described, where teachers work in isolation. In collaborative schools, then, teachers have the freedom to work with other teachers and supervisors in experimenting with alternative practices and procedures. To be effective in implementing a cooperative, collaborative approach to staff development, instructional supervisors need to understand the characteristics of cooperative supervision, collaborative schools, and coaching. Supervisors must also be skilled in ways to foster and enhance those characteristics among teachers. This section will briefly discuss these promising practices and describe ways instructional supervisors can utilize a collaborative approach to facilitate instructional improvement.

When we speak of collaboration, it is important to note that there is no single model of collaboration. The term *collaboration* in this text refers to a range of practices and procedures that involve teachers in making decisions about curriculum and instructional activities within individual schools and involves teachers in making contributions to their own professional growth and development. Collaboration cannot be imposed on teachers. On the contrary, the term connotes voluntary participation and involvement and the willingness to work with colleagues to improve their individual classrooms and school. For Glatthorn (1987), peer-centered options, another term associated with *collaboration,* is an encouraging development for instructional supervision. For the purpose of this text, *collaboration* is an all-inclusive term that encompasses a range of behaviors.

Since a single, precise definition of *collaboration* is difficult to provide, a description of collaborative practices and beliefs is presented. According to Smith (1987), a collaborative school is characterized by the following:

1. the belief that the quality of education is largely determined by what happens at the school site;
2. the conviction that instruction is most effective in a school environment characterized by norms of collegiality and continued improvement;
3. the belief that teachers are responsible for the instructional process and accountable for its outcomes;
4. the use of a wide range of practices and structures that enable administrators [supervisors] and teachers to work together on school improvement; and
5. the involvement of teachers in decisions about school goals and the means for implementing them. (p. 5)

Collaboration, then, requires teachers to make an investment of their time and skills as they work in small cooperative teams. As teachers invest their time and energy to ensure that the best academic climate is provided for their students, so teachers must also "make a similar investment in their own personal and professional growth" (Paquette, 1987, p. 37). However, it is not enough that teachers interact; it is the quality and the nature of that interaction that bear a relationship to school effectiveness (Little, 1982; Rosenholtz, in press).

The role of supervisors in collaborative settings is one of halting the spread of isolationism and of assisting teachers in establishing new ways of cooperating with co-workers. For example, supervisors can help teachers learn to monitor their collegial progress, take responsibility for mentoring activities, and develop cooperative learning skills. In effect, supervisors coordinate the efforts of professionals in a collegial, supportive school-based environment (Alfonso and Goldsberry, 1982). According to Smith (1987), "a collaborative school requires a higher calibre of leadership than does a bureaucratic school" (p. 6).

Within this context, supervisors develop cooperative structures that lead to a new way of perceiving collegial support. Within a cooperative structure, group members function as a team and work together to achieve group goals. When the group's goals are achieved, so too are those of the individual members. These cooperative structures rely on teachers to manage any conflict constructively. In such a school setting, supervisors are often called upon to assist teachers in building collaborative skills—which simply means being a good colleague. For Johnson and Johnson (1987a), building more collegiality among teachers involves five basic elements: (1) deliberately structuring sink-or-swim-together situations, (2) arranging for a number of face-to-face interactions to occur in small decision-making groups, (3) having each person accountable for what occurs, (4) making sure the teachers possess social skills, and (5) making sure that the group members think constructively about "how well they are operating and how they might do better in the future" (p. 19).

As a staff development strategy, "collegial support groups offer a formal structure for learning from colleagues" which complements on-the-job learning (Johnson and Johnson, 1987b, p. 27). Each support group consists of three to five teachers who are responsible for planning, designing, and evaluating teaching practices, curriculum, and materials. Members of these teams work together in the areas of professional dialogue, curriculum development, peer supervision, peer coaching, and action research. As they work together, the teachers are enhancing their own professional development (Glatthorn, 1987). In addition, the team members co-teach, observe each other's teaching, and provide feedback. Staff cooperation, as envisioned by Johnson and Johnson (1987b), is likely to improve the quality of teaching and learning in the schools, and instructional supervision will play an important role in fostering adult (teacher) cooperation and development as well.

If the ultimate goal of instructional supervision is to increase student achievement or promote student learning, then the research data give support to the collaborative professional development process. According to Glatthorn (1987), "students of coached teachers had greater achievement on a model-relevant test than did students of uncoached teachers" (p. 34). In addition, meta-analysis of research has been done comparing the effectiveness of cooperative, competitive, and individualistic efforts among adults (Johnson and Johnson, in press). From the results of the meta-analysis of adult samples, cooperation promoted achievement, more positive interactions, greater social support, and higher self-esteem than did competitive or individualistic efforts.

A word of caution, however, should be sounded. In order to achieve these results, supervisors should be sure that teachers have the following characteristics: (1) skills to make decisions, (2) ability to deal with conflict, (3) communication skills that build trust, and (4) ability to work with other group members. Therefore, groups should be carefully structured and have schedules and assignments that foster cooperative interaction. Teachers also need to be rewarded when they demonstrate these cooperative skills as they work with teachers, administrators, and students (Glatthorn, 1987). By taking time to attend to these procedures, supervisors will be in a better position to reap the benefits of professional collaboration and collegiality.

The response from teachers to a collaborative approach to staff development has been quite encouraging. In one high school in Alberta, Canada, "the positive response from the staff exceeded even . . . optimistic expectations" (Paquette, 1987, p. 38). In interview data from a high school in New York State, the collegial process has helped alleviate some of the isolation common among secondary teachers. As one teacher put it, "Coaching and critiquing develop trust and the more you interact and share, the better the environment is for kids and for teachers" (Anastos and Ancowitz, 1987, p. 42). In Wisconsin's Regional Staff Development Center, educators from all grade levels and disciplines work together to learn with and from one another, and "the collegiality resulting from educators' sharing their knowledge and love of subject matter has transcended the levels at which they teach" (Gould and Letven, 1987, p. 50).

When employing a cooperative, collaborative approach to staff development, teachers share success and failures, and problems become a challenge as teachers work together to solve them. According to Gould and Letven (1987), it is through these newly formed alliances and networks that teachers maintain a spirit of inquiry that is "crucial to the healthy life of all faculty members" (p. 51).

For the immediate future, both circumstances and the data suggest that supervisors will need to help teachers to form peer support groups to pool their knowledge, talents, and abilities and to contribute to each other's professional growth (Paquette, 1987). The instructional supervisor can be the key person who helps teachers cooperate and collaborate as they pool their skills and grow professionally.

SUMMARY

This chapter focuses on the staff development process, which can serve to enhance the professional skills of teachers. It is important to note that inservice/staff development is for all teachers, not just for those with instructional problems. Such goals as improved skills and professional commitment are possible to accomplish if instructional supervisors attend to what the research literature says about staff development and view teachers as learners. Supervisors must also be committed to a long-term process of staff development.

The instructional supervisor should consider the purposes of staff development, the research data, the principles of adult learning and development, and their own strengths and weaknesses when planning meaningful inservice/staff development programs for all teachers. The concerns being raised about the present state of inservice and staff development programs point out the need to define accurately and state the purposes of such activities. There is also a need to develop a process for restructuring the delivery and implementation of professional development programs so that their potential can be more fully realized.

For inservice to be considered a success, sessions should be designed with teachers in mind. Teachers need to perceive the worthwhileness of staff development, cognitively accommodate the information, and have opportunities for active involvement. Next, each supervisor needs to take a look at who he or she is and what his or her role is in helping teachers to grow professionally. Instructional supervisors need to know their audience—the teachers and other school personnel with whom they work.

Instructional supervisors may find these guidelines generated from research studies helpful in developing, implementing, and evaluating future staff development programs. From the literature and current practices, it is evident that what is presented, to whom it is presented, and how it is presented are key components of an effective staff development program. Instructional supervisors should keep these factors in mind as they work with teachers in promoting more effective teaching through staff development efforts.

The chapter presents an example of a staff development approach used in the corporate community along with an outline of how it can be used with teachers in schools. The *One Minute Manager* has three major components for the supervisor. These include goal setting, providing praise, and reprimanding when appropriate. These steps, when used according to the guidelines presented, can be helpful tools for instructional supervisors as they conduct staff development on a daily basis and as they work with teachers in their classrooms.

The chapter ends by describing promising trends, especially cooperative and collegial approaches to supervision and staff development. The role of supervisors in a collaborative setting is one in which they build cooperative structures between and among teachers and colleagues. Supervisors, as perceived in such a setting, are responsible for fostering the collaborative professional growth of teachers.

YOUR TURN

11.1 Reflect on the following questions that focus on how you, as an instructional supervisor, will help teachers grow professionally even though your school district might not have the financial resources for a well-developed, long-range program.
  a. What steps will you take to promote and ensure growth?
  b. What plan(s) would you implement?
  c. List possible programs and presenters that could help your teachers grow professionally.
11.2 You are planning inservice sessions to explain the implementation of a new reading program for the school district. Some teachers are skeptical about the new program and are reluctant to participate in the sessions you have planned. Not only do they have a negative attitude, but they have difficulty handling abstract concepts. Prepare an outline of topics, including goals, instructional objectives, materials, and speakers of inservice and follow-up activities to use throughout the year that could help these teachers modify their attitudes about the new reading program and, at the same time, help them understand and implement it effectively with their students.
11.3. You have been asked by the superintendent to prepare a "white paper" report on the status and needs of staff development in your district.

As you plan for your assignment, identify specifically how you would obtain input from both elementary and secondary levels, from the central administration staff, and from members of professional organizations, regarding the perceptions among these various individuals and groups of the status and needs of staff development in the district.

11.4. The next time there is an inservice/staff development workshop in your district, attend and take note of the following characteristics.

  a. length of session
  b. composition of the group (including teachers, administrators, grade levels/subject areas)
  c. strategies used by the presenter(s)
  d. tasks or participation required of the participants
  e. overall effectiveness of the session

Write a report of your findings that include these elements.

11.5. Complete the Supervisor Beliefs Inventory (Figure 11.5). What was your dominant style? Did you learn something about yourself? If so, what? Will you need to make any changes in your supervisory behavior? If so what? If not, why not?

REFERENCES

Alfonso, R. J., and Goldsberry, L. (1982). Colleagueship in supervision. In T. J. Sergiovanni (Ed.), *Supervision of teaching.* Alexandria, Va.: Association for Supervision and Curriculum Development.

Anastos, J., and Ancowitz, R. (1987). A teacher-directed peer coaching project. *Educational Leadership, 45,* 3, 40–42.

Andrews, T. E. (1981). Improving adult learning programs. In T. E. Andrews, W. R. Houston, and B. L. Bryany (Eds.), *Adult learners (A research study).* Washington, D.C.: Association of Teacher Educators.

Baden, D. J. (1982). A user's guide to the staff development. In F. J. McDonald, W. J. Papham, and D. J. Baden (Eds.) *Assessing the impact of staff development programs.* Syracuse, N.Y.: National Council of States on Inservice Education.

Beach, D. M., and Reinhartz, J. (1980). Inservice education: Definition and direction for renewing professional vigor. *Centering Teacher Education, 2,* 1, 3–4.

Bents, R. H., and Howey, K. R. (1981). Staff development = change in individual. In B. Dillon-Peterson (Ed.), *Staff development/organization development.* Alexandria, Va.: Association for Supervision and Curriculum Development.

Blanchard, K., and Johnson, S. (1982). *The one minute manager.* New York: William Morrow.

Brandt, R. (1980). Overview. *Educational Leadership, 37,* 5, 371.

Bruner, J. (1966). *Toward a theory of instruction.* New York: W. W. Norton.

Dillon-Peterson, B. (1980). Conducting a workshop program/staff improvement. In W. R. Houston and R. Pankratz (Eds.), *Staff development and educational change.* Reston, Va.: Association of Teacher Educators.

Dillon-Peterson, B., ed. (1981). *Staff development/organization development.* Alexandria, Va.: Association for Supervision and Curriculum Development.

Eble, K. (1978). *The art of administration.* San Francisco: Josey-Bass Publishers.

Edefelt, R. A. (1979). Inservice teacher education: A concept, an overview. *Inservice.* Syracuse, N.Y.: National Council of States on Inservice Education.

Edefelt, R. A., and Johnson, M., eds. (1975). *Rethinking in-service education.* Washington, D.C.: National Education Association.

Glatthorn, A. A. (1987). Cooperative professional development: Peer-centered options for teacher growth. *Educational Leadership, 45,* 3, 31–35.

Glickman, C. D. (1981). *Developmental supervision: Alternative practices for helping teachers improve instruction.* Alexandria, Va.: Association for Supervision and Curriculum Development.

Glickman, C. (1985). *Supervision of instruction: A developmental approach.* Boston: Allyn and Bacon.

Gould, S., and Letven, E. (1987). A center for interactive professional development. *Educational Leadership, 45,* 3, 49–52.

Griffin, G. (1983). Implications of research for staff development programs. *The Elementary School Journal, 83,* 4, 414–425.

Hammond, J., and Foster, K. (1987). Creating a professional learning partnership. *Educational Leadership 44,* 5, 42–44.

Harvey, O. J., Hunt, D., and Schroder, H. M. (1961). *Conceptual systems and personality organization.* New York: Wiley.

Helms, D. B., and Turner, J. S. (1986). *Exploring child behavior* (3rd. ed.). Monterey, Calif.: Brooks/Cole.

Howey, K. R. (March 1977). Organization for inservice teacher education. *Inservice.* Syracuse, N.Y.: National Council of States on Inservice Education.

Howsam, R. B. (March 1977). Reconceptualizing inservice education. *Inservice.* Syracuse, N.Y.: National Council of States on Inservice Education.

Johnson, D. W., and Johnson, R. T. (1987a). On cooperation in schools: A conversation with David and Roger Johnson. *Educational Leadership, 45,* 3, 14–19. [Interview with Ron Brandt, editor of *Educational Leadership*].

Johnson, D. W., and Johnson, R. T. (1987b). Research shows the benefits of adult cooperation. *Educational Leadership, 45,* 3, 27–30.

Johnson, D. W., and Johnson, R. T. (In press). *A meta-analysis of cooperative, competitive and individualistic goal structures.* Hillsdale, N.J.: Lawrence Erlbaum.

Joslin, P. A. (1980). Inservice education: A meta-analysis of the research (doctoral dissertation, University of Minnesota).

Joyce, B. R., and Showers, B. (1980). Improving inservice training: The message from research. *Educational Leadership, 37,* 379–385.

Joyce, B. R., and Showers, B. (1981). Transfer of training: The contribution of coaching. *Journal of Education, 163,* 2, 163–172.

Joyce, B., and Showers, B. (1983). *Power in staff development through research on training.* Alexandria, Va.: Association for Supervision and Curriculum Development.

Lawrence, G., and Harrison, D. (1980). Policy implications of research on the professional development of education personnel: An analysis of fifty-nine studies. In *Report on education personnel development.* Washington, D.C.: Feistritzer Publications.

Levine, S. L. (1987). Understanding life cycle issues: A resource for school leaders. *Journal of Education, 169,* 1, 7–19.

Little, J. W. (1982). Norms of collegiality and experimentation: Workplace conditions of school success. *American Educational Research Journal, 19,* 3, 325–340.

Loucks, S. F., and Melle, M. (1982). Evaluation of staff development: How do you know it took? *The Journal of Staff Development, 3,* 102–117.

Luft, J., and Ingham, H. (1955). The Johari window: A graphic model of interpersonal awareness. *Proceedings of the Western Training Laboratory in Group Development.* University of California, Los Angeles Extension Office.

Manatt, R. P. (1981). *Evaluating teacher performance.* Alexandria, Va.: Association for Supervision and Curriculum Development. [Videotape.]

Newman, B. M., and Newman, P. R. (1987). *Development through life: A psychosocial approach* (4th ed.). Chicago: Dorsey Press.

Orlich, D. C. (1984). Inservice education: A problem or a solution? *Science and Children, 21,* 5, 33–35.

Paquette, M. (1987). Voluntary collegial support groups for teachers. *Educational Leadership, 45,* 3, 36–39.

Rosenholtz, S. J. (In press). *Teacher's workplace: A study of social organizations.* New York: Longman.

Santmire, T. E. (1979). *Developmental differences in adult learners: Implications for staff development.* Lincoln: University of Nebraska. [Mimeograph.]

Sergiovanni, T. J., and Starratt, R. J. (1983). *Supervision: Human perspectives* (3rd ed.). New York: McGraw-Hill.

Showers, B., Joyce, B., and Bennett, B. (1987). Synthesis of research on staff development: A framework for future study and a state-of-the-art analysis. *Educational Leadership, 45,* 3, 77–87.

Smith, S. C. (1987). The collaborative school takes shape. *Educational Leadership, 45,* 3, 4–6.

Sparks, G. M. (1983). Synthesis of research on staff development for effective teaching. *Educational Leadership, 41,* 3, 65–72.

Sparks, G. M. (1983). Inservice training activities, teacher attitude, and behavior change (doctoral dissertation, Stanford University).

Van Cleaf, D., and Reinhartz, J. (1984). Perceivers and non-perceivers: Adaptation through inservice. *The Clearing House, 58,* 4, 167–170.

Wade, R. K. (1984–1985). What makes a difference in inservice teacher education? A meta-analysis of research. *Educational Leadership, 42,* 4, 48–54.

Warnat, W. I. (April 1979). A new dimension of adult learning: Inservice education. *Inservice.* Syracuse, N.Y.: National Council of States on Inservice Education.

Wilsey, C., and Killion, J. (1982). Making staff development programs work. *Educational Leadership, 40,* 1, 36–43.

Wood, F. H., and Thompson, S. R. (1980). Guidelines for better staff development. *Educational Leadership, 37,* 5, 374–378.

Yarger, S. J., Howey, K. R., and Joyce, B. R. (1980). *Inservice Teacher Education.* Palo Alto, Calif.: Booksend Laboratory.

chapter 12

Making Decisions and Facilitating Educational Change

Two aspects of instructional supervision that are vital to the supervisor are the ability to make decisions and the capacity to foster change. School personnel are involved in making decisions on a daily basis; their ability to make rational, logical choices is essential to the operation of the schools (Alfonso, Firth, and Neville, 1981). Likewise, skill in initiating and facilitating change, and at the same time helping others, especially teachers, deal with change, is crucial for instructional supervisors. We agree with Lovell and Wiles (1983), who state that instructional supervision exists for the purpose of improving instruction and thereby raising the chances that student achievement (learning) will also increase. "Since instructional improvement implies change, it is our assumption that the coordination and facilitation of instructional and curricular change are fundamental dimensions of instructional supervision" (p. 114). Clearly, decision making is not separate from but is a component of the change process. Without sound decisions, changes may be made that are not in the best interests of those involved.

This chapter will focus first on the decision-making process, the steps involved in making good decisions, and some general principles related to decision making. Next we will examine the change process by providing a rationale for the need for change, steps in promoting and adopting change, and ways of facilitating change in light of the concerns raised and resistance expressed by teachers and others. We will look at the reasons behind resistance to change. Finally we will provide a brief description of a change model.

THE DECISION-MAKING PROCESS

Decisions made in schools about the delivery of instruction are not routine but should involve careful analysis. Research into the decision-making process reveals, however, a different pattern. According to Gorton (1987):

> The picture that emerges from these [research] studies is that most administrators [and supervisors] tend to "muddle through" when faced with a decision, and end up with an action that may have little relationship to the original situation that called for a decision. (p. 4)

This type of decision making, as it is found in education, has been called the "garbage can model" (Cohen, March, and Olson, 1972; Gorton, 1987) and suggests that unless supervisors are constantly monitoring the decision-making process, they are candidates for being "dumped on" and may be left with the task of sorting through the garbage.

Two views of the decision-making process have emerged from research studies. One view, the *normative,* or rational, view (Draft, 1986) sees decision making "as a process that begins with a problem or need which the decision maker then logically addresses by engaging in a series of . . . steps that culminate in an effective solution or decision" (Gorton, 1987, p. 3). Thus, in the normative approach, decisions are made according to sound principles of analyses performed in prescribed stages. The second view, the *descriptive,* examines the actual practice of decision making as determined by organizational circumstances rather than by "ideal" conditions (Gorton, 1987). The second view reveals the "garbage can" approach to decision making and therefore often reflects what *is* done instead of what *should be* done.

Current perspectives on decision making generally favor the normative view over the descriptive view, and definitions tend to emphasize the rational, problem-solving dimension of good decision

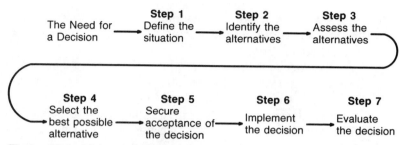

Figure 12.1 Major steps in decision making. (*Source:* Gorton, R. A. [1987]. *School leadership and administration* [3rd ed.]., p. 6. Dubuque, Iowa: Wm. C. Brown. Used with permission.)

making. *Decision making,* then, can be defined as a process in which, after examining a problem or a need, an individual or group incorporates information and values in proposing various solutions that are weighted. A choice is made from among alternatives and then implemented (Lipham and Furth, 1976). We view the rational method as the best view of the decision-making process, although we recognize that, in the pressure of daily routines, people are often forced to take the garbage can approach. It should be noted that instructional supervisors must constantly guard against lapsing into this latter means of decision making.

To help instructional supervisors make good decisions, Gorton (1987) has developed a series of steps that help improve the quality of decision making. Figure 12.1 represents the major steps involved in the decision-making process. As illustrated in Figure 12.1, decision making is a complex process that, when done correctly, requires a great deal of time and thought. The base of decision making is problem solving; therefore, this process can lead to major accomplishments in the instructional program when supervisors have the time to engage in quality decision making.

Some general principles can serve to guide supervisors in the decision-making process. These principles, based on the work of Gorton (1987) and Alfonso, Firth, and Neville (1981), are summarized below.

1. Effective decision making requires that, even in the best of situations, the nature and causes of constraints (including the amount of time, resources, or data available) should be analyzed and efforts to decrease their impact of the decision-making process should be made.
2. Decision making requires the thoughtful, careful analysis of

issues and the actions (consequences) to be taken which become a part of the total attributes that makeup the educational organization.

3. Effective decision making requires that choices be made from among a range of alternatives and that opportunities for growth and refinement should be made available.

4. Effective decision making requires that risks be taken, because the outcome of a decision cannot be determined with total accuracy.

5. Effective decision making requires that judgments be made on the basis of data collected about the school organization, its goals, and its membership.

6. Decision making is more effective when it is encouraged by the organization and when past decisions have been rewarded or reinforced by the organization.

7. Decision making is more effective when it increases the commitment of individuals to the goals and objectives of the school organization.

8. An effective decision maker recognizes the political nature of the decision-making process as it relates to the power structure, control, and resources of the school organization.

9. Decision making can be more responsive to group members when they recognize that decisions are not perfect solutions but merely the best choices from among possible options.

10. Decision making is influenced by the social, political, and historical contexts in which the decision is being made and by the psychological makeup of the person making the decision.

11. Effective decision making requires the limiting of personal bias and prior experience and the establishment of an open and objective mind set.

12. To be an effective decision maker, an individual should not assume more authority than exists.

13. Decision making will be enhanced when the school organization provides an atmosphere of cooperation and problem solving.

14. Decision making will be more effective when there is a continuous process for evaluating decisions and procedures for making decisions.

Gorton (1987) has also observed several personal variables that influence the actions of the decision maker. He has identified five types of personal attitudes or values that may affect the decision maker's choice. Figure 12.2 indicates the kinds of personal thoughts

Personal thoughts	Type of attitude or value
1. "I wonder about the risks involved in pursuing this particular alternative."	Risk orientation
2. "If Hank recommends it, I am sure that it would make a good decision."	Attitude toward people
3. "I question whether adopting a 'far out' innovation like the open classroom is good education."	Educational philosophy
4. "This is the type of decision that an educational leader should make."	Concern about status
5. "It seems to me that if we adopt that alternative, we can no longer 'call the shots' in that area."	Concern about authority and control

Figure 12.2   Attitudes revealed in personal and professional decision making. (*Source:* Gorton, R. A. [1987]. *School leadership and administration,* p. 15. Dubuque, Iowa: Wm. C. Brown Publishers. Used with permission.)

involved in the decision-making process and the values or attitudes that are evident in the thought process.

As Figure 12.2 suggests, there are personal as well as organizational variables to the decision-making process. In order to make good decisions and find solutions to problems, supervisors should be aware of the personal factors—whether positive or negative—that may play a role in the decision-making process. By utilizing the 14 principles and guidelines presented here, supervisors can seek to implement the decision-making process in a rational and thoughtful manner. In so doing, they can increase their likelihood of finding solutions to instructional problems by making good decisions.

A RATIONALE FOR THE NEED TO CHANGE

If change is often difficult to achieve and slow to be implemented, why is there a need for change? What does the change process accomplish? Gorton (1987) provides an excellent description of a rationale for change that he says is based on the following premises:

(1) Although the status quo is not necessarily bad, there is usually room for improvement; (2) while all change does not necessarily lead to improvement, improvement is not likely to occur without change; (3) unless we attempt change, we are not likely to know whether a proposed innovation is better than the status quo; and (4) participation in the change process can result in greater under-

standing and appreciation of the desirable features of the status quo and . . . a better understanding and appreciation of, and skill in, the change process itself. (p. 136)

Infatuation with the change process itself, however, provides a much more compelling rationale. According to Alfonso, Firth, and Neville (1981), a sense of urgency is often associated with change; there seems to be, in fact, "a belief that our survival as a civilized society depends on our willingness to initiate and accept change" (p. 244).

The schools have not been immune to this sense of urgency and rush to change. Knezevich (1984) notes that "the professional behaviors of teachers, . . . methods of instruction, design of facilities . . . are very different now from what they were a generation ago, much less a century ago" (p. 102). Beginning as early as the 1800s and continuing into the present, changes—or innovations, as they have come to be called—have increasingly found their way into the schools in the form of new subject matter and revised content materials; organization of pupils by criteria such as age, grade, or ability; and building designs that have been functional and practical as well as "open."

In order to understand the change process and its impact on the teaching–learning process, Knezevich provides a definition of *innovation*. For him, an *innovation* derives from a practice, procedure, or some other aspect in need of change that is dependent upon a discovery or development—something novel or different—before the change or replacement can be implemented. One example of this is the use of technological innovations in the public schools, such as the use of computer-assisted instruction coupled with interactive video disks to teach developmental reading skills. The trend of introducing innovations into schools and classrooms will continue, and, if the past is any indication, it will be at a much faster rate. Individuals who function in any capacity as an instructional supervisor will be called upon to help manage or facilitate the implementation of the changes or innovations.

STEPS IN PROMOTING AND ADOPTING CHANGE

Instructional supervision plays a vital role in the change process. While many factors determine whether personnel will accept and implement change and their chances of success in doing so, instructional supervisors serve as keys to the process. Gorton (1987) has identified the following steps that are helpful in introducing and initiating change:

Stage I: Conduct a needs assessment. Identify the need for change by examining the present system to determine which aspects ought to be improved. Develop a new approach or evaluate and select a system that will replace the current method(s).

Stage II: Orient the target group to the proposed change. Create in the target group an awareness or interest in the proposed new method or other change. Assist the target group in examining the strengths and weaknesses of the proposed innovation, then pilot-test and refine the change prior to full implementation. With the help of the target group, identify the necessary commitments needed, such as resources, training, or building modifications.

Stage III: Make a decision whether to introduce and implement the change. Identify the individuals who should participate in this decision and determine the process that will be used to make the decision. Decide whether or not to proceed with the implementation of change.

Stage IV: *Plan an implementation program.* Plan and conduct inservice training programs for all individuals involved with or affected by the proposed change. Provide the necessary support and resources to implement the change and anticipate and try to resolve in advance any operational problems that may be encountered.

Stage V: Implement the proposed innovation. Implement the proposed innovation with appropriate target group using established guidelines and procedures.

Stage VI: Conduct an in-process evaluation. Design and utilize a procedure for obtaining feedback on the extent to which the proposed change is accomplishing the objectives or meeting the goals. Diagnose aspects of the innovation that need improvement or additional support.

Stage VII: Refine and institutionalize the innovation. Modify the innovation if necessary and provide additional support (such as training, additional resources). Gain acceptance of the innovation as a regular and ordinary part of the educational program.

To assist the instructional supervisor in the change process, Gorton (1987) suggests some questions that can, depending upon the answers, guide the implementation of the innovation. These modified questions include the following:

1. What are the objectives of the proposed change and what is the change supposed to accomplish?
2. Are the objectives relevant to the needs of the local district?
3. What evidence will be provided that the innovation has accomplished the objectives?
4. How difficult is the proposed innovation to understand and implement?
5. What skills do people need in order to adopt the innovation? If these skills are lacking, how will they be provided?
6. What are the financial obligations involved in the innovation and what other resources will be needed?
7. What are the strengths and weaknesses/advantages and disadvantages of the proposed innovation?
8. How will we know that the innovation has been successful?

It should be clear from these questions and from previously cited stages that the role of the instructional supervisor throughout the change process is critical in planning, organizing, training, diagnosing, and evaluating. Although the terms used to describe the steps are somewhat different from those Gorton employs, this model represents a similar process for initiating and implementing change. Figure 12.3 presents a slightly different model of the innovation process and the steps involved in fostering change.

Once the change or innovation has been proposed, the supervisor must shepherd it through to adoption. Clearly, the first step, the initiation of change, is crucial to the success of the innovation. Assessing the needs and recommending an appropriate alternative to current practice are often risky. But risk is involved in any change because this disequilibrium is created and there is no guarantee that the

MODEL OF THE INNOVATION PROCESS

1. Disequilibrium
   ↓
2. Conceptualization
   ↓
3. Identification or design for invention
   ↓
4. Experimentation
   ↓
5. Evaluation (return to step 2 if necessary)
   ↓
6. Pilot programs
   ↓
7. Diffusion
   ↓
8. Successful installations
   ↓
9. New balance or equilibrium

Figure 12.3 Steps involved in bringing about change. (*Source:* Knezevich, S. J. [1984]. *Administration of public education,* p. 110. New York: Harper & Row. Used with permission.)

change will be an improvement over the status quo. "It is possible to regress . . . change for the worse rather than better" (Knezevich, 1984, p. 103). That is why the initial step—needs assessment and determination of the appropriate innovation—is so important to the overall effectiveness.

Finally, if the innovation is acceptable to the target group in the preliminary stages, the wholesale adoption process becomes the next critical step in the process. Gorton (1987) and Havelock, Huber, and Zimmerman (1970) have identified the following six stages associated with the adoption of an innovation:

1. *Awareness stage.* Teachers are exposed to the proposed innovation, become aware of it, and demonstrate an interest in finding out more about it.
2. *Interest stage.* Teachers develop an interest in the innovation, want to find out more, and begin to have positive and/or negative feelings about the innovation.
3. *Mental stage.* Teachers carefully evaluate the innovation and determine the appropriateness for them, their students, and their situation; they seek out an assessment from other teachers.
4. *Trial stage.* Teachers actually try out the innovation to see if it will work for them in their classroom situation.
5. *Adoption stage.* Teachers adopt the innovation and implement it in their classrooms.
6. *Integration stage.* Teachers internalize the innovation, and it becomes an integral part of their classroom teaching behavior.

In thinking through the steps involved in initiating and adopting change, it is helpful to examine what others have learned about change and innovation. According to Hord and colleagues (1987), the following points can be made about initiating change:

1. Change is a process, not an event.
2. Change is accomplished by individuals.
3. Change is a highly personal experience.
4. Change involves developmental growth.
5. Change is best understood in operational terms.
6. The focus of facilitation should be on individuals, innovations and the context. (pp. 5–6)

These insights into the change process can be valuable to instructional supervisors as they work with teachers individually or in groups to initiate and adopt new strategies, procedures, or materials that will improve classroom instruction. By focusing on the previously identified stages and the above points, supervisors may be able to overcome some of the initial resistance and negative feelings that are often associated with educational change.

FACILITATING CHANGE

Change often seems to surround the school environment and is a concern for teachers as well as instructional supervisors. In fact, Alfonso, Firth, and Neville (1981) note that "change is a condition of human existence . . . and . . . a social organization [the school] must value and provide for change if it is to retain any vitality as an organization" (p. 243). Therefore, supervisors, in working with teachers, play a role in initiating, planning, and directing change for the improvement of instruction.

Change in the schools, when not planned and orderly, may seem chaotic and may seem to take place too fast for some supervisors who become caught up in all the aspects associated with the change process. Yet in spite of the many changes that do occur, Mort and Ross (1957) have expressed concern over the length of time it takes for changes in education to be diffused and accepted in schools. They note that in some schools the lag time for incorporating change may be as much as 25 years behind the best practice. Although the winds of change in education may have blown a little faster in recent years and provided refreshing alternatives, "many may wonder why things cannot move faster and surer" (Owens, 1970, p. 141).

Dealing with change, then, is a part of the instructional supervision process. In fact, the role of the instructional supervisor is often one of giving force, direction, and meaning to changes that occur in schools.

For change to be successful, supervisors are frequently asked to facilitate the implementation and adoption of certain innovations. As noted earlier, the reluctance that others may feel is a reality that supervisors will need to deal with. As testimony to this reluctance, many schools are littered with the failed innovations of the past. In the foreword to the book *Taking Charge of Change* by Hord and colleagues (1987), Knoll notes the problems that have been encountered when trying to facilitate educational changes. She states:

One only has to search obscure storage closets or bookrooms in schools or talk with those who have been involved with education and its improvement over a period of time to understand the frustration involved in changing the status quo. Innovations involved with instructional strategies and curriculum have usually failed. (foreword)

As supervisors work to facilitate change, it is to their advantage to take every necessary precaution to overcome the possible negativism and resistance they may encounter. Supervisors can be encouraged by the research suggesting that (1) change is not always resisted by a target group and (2) an innovation may fail even though initially accepted because the people involved were not given sufficient orientation, training, materials, other prerequisites, or support (Herriott and Gross, 1979; Parish and Arends, 1983; Gorton, 1987). The role of facilitator, then, may be crucial to the ultimate success of the innovation.

What does it take to be a good facilitator or innovator? Rogers (1965) identified the following characteristics of innovators:

1. Innovators are usually young.
2. Innovators usually have some degree of high social status based on education, prestige, and income.
3. Innovators use impersonal and cosmopolitan sources of data and information.
4. Innovators have a sense of worldliness and sophistication (they are cosmopolitan rather than provincial).
5. Innovators demonstrate opinionated leadership.
6. Innovators often see themselves and are viewed by others as unusual, unorthodox, and deviant.

It is clear from this list that innovators are not solid-core, status quo people. That is often the bind in which instructional supervisors find themselves. On the one hand, they are entrusted with routine maintenance activities of the school (such as writing reports, conducting meetings); on the other hand, they are expected to be innovators who not only inspire change but can facilitate innovation in others. There is no easy solution to this dilemma. However, supervisors should seize every opportunity to utilize their creative and innovative abilities to foster and facilitate change in others, especially teachers.

To help supervisors be more effective in facilitating change, Gorton (1987) suggests a series of questions to guide the process. These questions in modified form include the following:

1. What activities or actions are needed in order to produce the innovation?
2. What resources—personnel, facilities, and materials—are needed to accomplish the innovation?
3. What kinds of reactions (problems) can be expected to be generated from the implementation of the innovation?
4. What is the best sequence of activities and the best use of resources to maximize acceptance of the innovation?
5. What is the best possible time line for implementation?
6. What kind of follow-up will be provided to those who implement the innovation?

A well-conceived plan is necessary for facilitating the adoption of change or innovation. The instructional supervisor will need a long-range as well as a short-range game plan if the innovation is to be successful with teachers in the improvement of instruction. Hord and colleagues (1987) have identified different stages of concern that supervisors will face as they work with teachers in accepting change and innovation. Using the concerns expressed, Hord and colleagues have developed ways of dealing with those concerns to expedite the facilitation of change. Figure 12.4 identifies typical statements associated with the various stages of concern, and Figure 12.5 provides

	Stages of concern	Expressions of concern
I M P A C T	6 Refocusing	I have some ideas about something that would work even better.
	5 Collaboration	I am concerned about relating what I am doing with what other instructors are doing.
	4 Consequence	How is my use affecting kids?
T A S K	3 Management	I seem to be spending all my time getting material ready.
S E L F	2 Personal	How will using it affect me?
	1 Informational	I would like to know more about it.
	0 Awareness	I am not concerned about it (the innovation).

Figure 12.4 Stages of concern: Typical expressions of concern about the innovation. (*Source:* Hord, S. M., et al. [1987]. *Taking charge of change,* p. 31. Alexandria, Va.: Association for Supervision and Curriculum Development. Used with permission of the Association for Supervision and Curriculum Development. Copyright © by ASCD. All rights reserved.)

Stage 0—Awareness Concerns

a. If possible, involve teachers in discussions and decisions about the innovation and its implementation.

b. Share enough information to arouse interest, but not so much that it overwhelms.

c. Acknowledge that a lack of awareness is expected and reasonable, and that no questions about the innovation are foolish.

d. Encourage unaware persons to talk with colleagues who know about the innovation.

e. Take steps to minimize gossip and inaccurate sharing of information about the innovation.

Stage 1—Informational Concerns

a. Provide clear and accurate information about the innovation.

b. Use a variety of ways to share information—verbally, in writing, and through any available media. Communicate with individuals and with small and large groups.

c. Have persons who have used the innovation in other settings visit with your teachers. Visits to user schools could also be arranged.

d. Help teachers see how the innovation relates to their current practices, both in regard to similarities and differences.

e. Be enthusiastic and enhance the visibility of others who are excited.

Stage 2—Personal Concerns

a. Legitimize the existence and expression of personal concerns. Knowing these concerns are common and that others have them can be comforting.

b. Use personal notes and conversations to provide encouragement and reinforce personal adequacy.

c. Connect these teachers with others whose personal concerns have diminished and who will be supportive.

d. Show how the innovation can be implemented sequentially rather than in one big leap. It is important to establish expectations that are attainable.

e. Do not push innovation use, but encourage and support it while maintaining expectations.

Stage 3—Management Concerns

a. Clarify the steps and components of the innovation. Information from innovation configurations will be helpful here.

b. Provide answers that address the small specific "how-to" issues that are so often the cause of management concerns.

c. Demonstrate exact and practical solutions to the logistical problems that contribute to these concerns.

d. Help teachers sequence specific activities and set timelines for their accomplishments.

e. Attend to the immediate demands of the innovation, not what will be or could be in the future.

Figure 12.5 Concerns and the facilitation of change. (*Source:* Hord, S. M., et al. [1987]. *Taking charge of change,* pp. 44–46. Alexandria, Va.: Association for Supervision and Curriculum Development. Used with permission of the Association for Supervision and Curriculum Development. Copyright © by ASCD. All rights reserved.)

Figure 12.5 continued

Stage 4—Consequence Concerns
   a. Provide these individuals with opportunities to visit other settings where the innovation is in use and to attend conferences on the topic.
   b. Don't overlook these individuals. Give them positive feedback and needed support.
   c. Find opportunities for these persons to share their skills with others.
   d. Share with these persons information pertaining to the innovation.

Stage 5—Collaboration Concerns
   a. Provide these individuals with opportunities to develop those skills necessary for working collaboratively.
   b. Bring together those persons, both within and outside the school, who are interested in collaboration.
   c. Help the collaborators establish reasonable expectations and guidelines for the collaborative effort.
   d. Use these persons to provide technical assistance to others who need assistance.
   e. Encourage the collaborators, but don't attempt to force collaboration on those who are not interested.

Stage 6—Refocusing Concerns
   a. Respect and encourage the interest these persons have for finding a better way.
   b. Help these individuals channel their ideas and energies in ways that will be productive rather than counterproductive.
   c. Encourage these individuals to act on their concerns for program improvement.
   d. Help these persons access the resources they may need to refine their ideas and put them into practice.
   e. Be aware of and willing to accept the fact that these persons may replace or significantly modify the existing innovations.

several suggestions for handling concerns at various stages of the change process. In addition to the concerns listed and the suggested ways of handling them, Hord and colleagues provide a checklist for change facilitators (CF) to use in developing game plan components (GPC) to support the change process. Figure 12.6 is the checklist developed by Hord and colleagues.

   The suggestions provided in this section are designed to assist the instructional supervisor in serving as a facilitator of change efforts. It is important that supervisors are aware of the stages of the change process and the possible concerns that will be raised about the implementation of an educational change or innovation. The work by Hord and others should provide valuable information and assistance to supervisors as they work with teachers to bring change.

GPC 1: Developing Supportive Organizational Arrangements

Developing innovation-related policies
Establishing global rules
Making decisions
Planning
Preparing
Scheduling
Staffing
Restructuring roles
Seeking or providing materials
Providing space
Seeking/acquiring funds
Providing equipment

GPC 2: Training

Developing positive attitudes
Increasing knowledge
Teaching innovation-related skills
Reviewing information
Holding workshops
Modeling/demonstrating innovation use
Observing innovation use
Providing feedback on innovation use
Clarifying innovation misconceptions

GPC 3: Consultation and Reinforcement

Encouraging people on a one-to-one basis
Promoting innovation use among small groups
Assisting individuals in solving problems
Coaching small groups in innovation use
Sharing tips informally
Providing personalized technical assistance
Holding brief conversations and applauding progress
Facilitating small groups in problem solving
Providing small "comfort and caring" sessions
Reinforcing individuals' attempts to change
Providing practical assistance
Celebrating small successes (or large ones, too)

GPC 4: Monitoring

Gathering information
Collecting data
Assessing innovation knowledge or skills informally
Assessing innovation use or concerns formally
Analyzing/processing data
Interpreting information
Reporting/sharing data on outcomes
Providing feedback on information collected
Administering end-of-workshop questionnaires
Conferencing with teachers about progress in innovation use

GPC 5: External Communication

Describing what the innovation is
Informing others (than users)
Reporting to the Board of Education and parent groups
Making presentations at conferences
Developing a public relations campaign
Gaining the support of constituent groups

GPC 6: Dissemination

Encouraging others (outside the implementing site) to adopt the innovation
Broadcasting innovation information and materials
Mailing descriptive brochures
Providing charge-free demonstration kits
Training innovation representatives
Making regional innovation presentations to potential adopters
Marketing the innovation

Figure 12.6 A checklist of suggested change facilitator actions to support change. (*Source:* Hord, S. M., et al. [1987]. *Taking charge of change,* p. 75. Alexandria, Va.: Association for Supervision and Curriculum Development. Used with permission of the Association for Supervision and Curriculum Development. Copyright © by ASCD. All rights reserved.)

REASONS FOR RESISTANCE TO CHANGE

As has been noted throughout this chapter, whenever change is mentioned, a frequent and natural response is one of resistance. Teachers, and students as well, can become so conditioned to the routine of school that they have come to love the security of the status quo and the limits that enslave them. In implementing a change, supervisors must overcome the status quo—often a difficult task. The statements below are examples of the kinds of reactions that supervisors may receive when they mention "change" or "innovation":

1. Everything is going all right, so why change?
2. People aren't ready for change.
3. Has anyone else tried this yet?
4. It won't work in *this* school (or in *my* class).
5. We've never done it that way before in this school.
6. We (the faculty and/or students) are not ready for that.
7. That's too radical for us.
8. We don't have enough time (or resources) to do it now.
9. It's too complicated.
10. Our students don't need that.

Perhaps as a supervisor you will not encounter too many Negative Nellies or Negative Neds, but the mention of change often brings them out in force. Statements like those in the list above will have to be dealt with in order for the change to be truly effective.

The following factors also serve as a basis for resistance to change (Gorton, 1987):

1. *Habit.* People tend to behave the same way they have always behaved, and a change represents a challenge to their accustomed behavior.
2. *Bureaucratic structure of schools.* As a bureaucracy, the school emphasizes order, rationality, and stability. The uniformity of programs and procedures are valued, while diversity and difference are not.
3. *Lack of incentive.* If a change seems threatening and frustrating, it is difficult to motivate others to consider the innovation unless some form of incentive is offered.
4. *Nature of the proposed change.* Some innovations are more difficult to implement because of their complexity, cost, or other factors.

5. *Teacher, school, and community norms.* Group norms act as effective barriers to change because individual teachers are reluctant to go against their peers or against community expectations.
6. *Lack of understanding.* Many people resist change simply because they do not understand all the aspects, implications, or benefits of the proposed change or they have a misunderstanding of the proposed innovation.
7. *Difference of opinion.* Some changes may be resisted simply because there is an honest difference of opinion and teachers do not feel that the proposed innovation is the proper course of action to take.
8. *Lack of skill.* People often resist change because they do not possess the necessary skills to implement the change and are reluctant to learn new skills.
9. *Fear.* Fear is a strong reason for resistance to change because people fear the unknown, they fear for their jobs, and they fear for their position. Change could disrupt any and all of these areas.

Resistance to change is a complex situation with many causes that vary from individual to individual. The supervisor should work closely with teachers and try to anticipate those individuals who might resist change and then diagnose a possible reason for the resistance.

A CHANGE MODEL

Pfeiffer and Dunlap (1982) have provided a change model incorporating many of the ideas that have been presented in the chapter. This model is represented in Figure 12.7.

The six stages in this model represent the process that individual teachers or groups of teachers go through in making an educational change. Each stage (rapport development, teacher adaptiveness, reality sharing, decision box activity, pro-change/con-change choices, and crystallization) in the model represents a part of the process of adapting to change. Each stage presented in Figure 12.7 is described in detail:

Stage I: Rapport development. In this stage, the members of the group targeted for the change meet together with the supervisor to discuss the proposed change. The purpose of the meeting

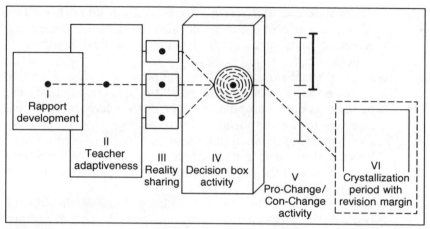

Figure 12.7 The decision process. (*Source:* Pfeiffer, I. L., and Dunlap, J. B. [1982]. *Supervision of teachers: A guide to improving instruction.* Used by permission of the Oryx Press, 2214 North Central Avenue at Encanto, Phoenix, Arizona 85014.

is to encourage open and honest discussion, and the supervisor employs a variety of communication skills, especially active listening (see Chapter 5). The intent of this meeting is to develop a trusting relationship as the supervisor demonstrates patience, understanding, and acceptance of a variety of attitudes. Individuals who feel a need for change or who support a proposed change are afforded the opportunity to express their views.

Stage II: Teacher adaptiveness. During this stage, teachers indicate a willingness to consider change as a way of alleviating instructional concerns. An initial receptivity to change is enhanced if the supervisor has created an environment that is open to alternatives and supports new ideas. As teachers view the possibilities, they reflect on their own behavior and the changes that are needed, in order to incorporate any new suggestions. Teachers begin to personalize the change process by interpreting the proposed changes in terms of their own teaching behaviors.

Stage III: Reality sharing. During this stage, teachers look at the situation as it exists and consider the possible outcomes of continuing with the status quo, initiating a change, or creating other alternatives. Important aspects to consider are the amount of time, teacher effort, and teacher involvement required to implement an innovation. Other considerations that must be viewed realistically are (1) attitudes (in particular, resistance vs. acceptance), (2) necessary resources, and (3) kinds of activities.

Stage IV: Decision box activity. At this stage in the change process, responses are solicited from "significant others." These others include administrators, other supervisors (such as consultants, facilitators, coordinators), parents and/or other members of the community, teachers who work at grade levels or other assignments that interface with proposed implementation areas, and content specialists. This stage should provoke those involved to express opinions and should provide for new insights concerning positive and negative aspects of the change. The results should help the supervisor better define the specifications of the change or innovation.

Stage V: Pro-change/Con-change choices. This is the fundamental decision stage of the model. After the widest possible input and analysis and thoughtful consideration of the choices, group consensus is sought regarding the disposition of the change. The decision is made either to implement or not to implement the change. If the decision is not to initiate the change, the proposal is discarded. If the decision is for change, then implementation begins.

Stage VI: Crystallization period with revision margin. At this point, the supervisors and teachers have implemented the change and the innovation is in place. As the change becomes a part of the teacher's instructional program, the supervisor serves in a helping capacity to secure time, facilities, and resources for the teachers involved. As the change is implemented, revisions or modifications may need to be made based on data from evaluations and feedback. The supervisor should continue to support change activities, coordinate efforts, revise programs, and work out difficulties as well as orient new teachers to the program.

This model places an emphasis on collegial, helping relationships between the supervisor and teachers. The model views the positive interactions that occur between teachers and supervisors and among teachers themselves as crucial to the success of any change effort. All too often the change process has required heroic efforts among participants, but, as Corbett and D'Amico (1986) state:

Educational improvements should not have to rely on heroic efforts. We must begin to think about how to support innovation systematically. At least four organizational conditions can facilitate improvement [change]: (1) available time, (2) cushions against interference, (3) opportunities for encouragement, and (4) recognition of the need for incorporation. (p. 71)

Using the concepts presented in this chapter, supervisors can help ensure that change efforts don't fall apart and that the objectives of instructional and school improvement are attained.

SUMMARY

This chapter has examined the aspects of decision making and change as related to the process of instructional supervision. Both decision making and change are critical aspects of the work of an instructional supervisor. Decision making helps individuals and organizations improve by seeking rational, logical solutions to problems. Both serve to enhance what happens instructionally in schools.

The chapter begins by describing the nature of the decision-making process and listing several steps that are involved in making good decisions. The chapter advocates a proactive model, which involves developing and selecting from among alternative choices, rather than a reactive model, responding to problems after they have developed. This section closes with a list of principles to guide instructional supervisors in the decision-making process.

The chapter then describes a rationale for the need to change. Next, it focuses on the procedures for initiating and fostering change. Several steps are outlined in the change process, with particular emphasis placed on the assessment of needs. Also discussed are the stages in the adoption process, as teachers become involved in the innovation. Several ways of facilitating change are discussed. The chapter also identifies ways that supervisors can deal with resistance to change and the reasons for the resistance are examined. Finally, a model of initiating change is offered. Supervisors should be actively engaged in fostering and facilitating instructional changes in teachers and the total educational program.

YOUR TURN

12.1. You have been asked to make a decision about year-round schools. Your school district is experiencing financial difficulties, and top administrators are looking for ways to save money. One alternative might be year-round schooling. Your superintendent wants your feelings and reasons to support your decision. Research the topic and find six pros for the schooling and six cons. Then decide whether you favor the proposal or not. Prepare the most convincing case you can, based on the decision you made. Are there other viable alternatives you would suggest for saving money for the school district?

12.2. You are working with a teacher who is experiencing a personal problem (it could be substance abuse). In your opinion the problem is affecting the teacher's productivity and effectiveness in the classroom. As a result, the students are receiving less than adequate instruction. You must decide if the situation is serious enough to call it to the attention of the principal or superintendent. Your chief concern is that you have been a friend to this teacher and much of what you know has been told to you in confidence on a personal level. What do you do? Do you let things go or do you bring the situation to someone's attention? You have to make a decision. Outline several alternative courses of action you might take.

12.3. Part of decision making is to establish priorities. Consider completing a time management inventory. It will tell you how you are spending your time and therefore provide insight into some of the "unconscious" decisions you make. A suggested management inventory follows:

Time	Activity/task	Cost to school district	Value (high, none, low)

Develop an inventory using this format and complete the inventory for a day or two. After you have completed the inventory, examine the activities and determine those tasks you feel you can delegate. What activities can someone else do so you can give more time to the priority items?

12.4. You have attended several conferences on a new reading program; you are excited about the prospect of implementing such a program in your district. You have briefly introduced the key components of the new program to the teachers, but you are aware that there is some resistance to adopting and implementing it. Moreover, some teachers as well as other supervisors and administrators have been frank with you and have said, "Why us? We'll change it in five years anyway." Under these circumstances, what steps will you take to facilitate change to implement the new reading program? Consult Gorton's seven stages for introducing and initiating change (page 269). Describe the strategies that you will use to shepherd the process.

12.5. It has been said that teachers as well as students love routine; in fact, "they love the bonds that enslave them." What does this statement mean to supervisors? How could you go about fostering or promoting change in your school district, in light of probable resistance from both teachers and students? What techniques would you use for overcoming resistance?

REFERENCES

Alfonso, R. J., Firth, G. R., and Neville, R. F. (1981). *Instructional supervision: A behavior system* (2nd ed.). Boston: Allyn and Bacon.

Cohen, M. D., March, J. G., and Olson, J. A. (March 1972). A garbage can model of organizational choice. *Administrative Science Quarterly,* 1–25.

Corbett, H. D., and D'Amico, J. J. (1986). No more heroes: Creating systems to support change. *Educational Leadership, 44,* 1, 70–72.

Draft, R. (1986). Organizational theory and design. San Francisco: West.

Gorton, R. A. (1987). *School leadership and administration.* Dubuque, Iowa: Wm. C. Brown.

Havelock, R. G., Huber, J. C., and Zimmerman, S. (1970). *A guide to innovation in education.* Ann Arbor: University of Michigan Center for Research on the Utilization of Scientific Knowledge.

Herriott, R. E., and Gross, N., Eds. (1979). *The dynamics of planned educational change.* Berkeley, Calif.: McCutchan.

Hord, S. M., et al. (1987). *Taking charge of change.* Alexandria, Va.: Association for Supervision and Curriculum Development.

Knezevich, S. J. (1984). *Administration of public education* (4th ed.). New York: Harper & Row.

Lipham, J., and Furth, M. L. (1976). *The principal and individually guided education.* Reading, Mass.: Addison-Wesley.

Lovell, J. T., and Wiles, K. (1983). *Supervision for better schools* (5th ed.). Englewood Cliffs, N.J.: Prentice-Hall.

Mort, P. R., and Ross, D. H. (1957). *Principles of school administration.* New York: McGraw-Hill.

Owens, R. G. (1970). *Organizational behaviors in schools.* Englewood Cliffs, N.J.: Prentice-Hall.

Pfeiffer, I. L., and Dunlap, J. B. (1982). *Supervision of teachers: A guide to improving instruction.* Phoenix: Oryx Press.

Parish, R., and Arends, R. (1983). Why innovative programs are discontinued. *Educational Leadership, 40,* 4, 62–65.

Rogers, E. M. (1965). What are innovators like? In R. O. Carlson, et al. (Eds.), *Change processes in the public schools.* Eugene, Ore.: Center for the Advanced Study of Educational Administration.

Author Index

Acheson, K. A., 186, 192
Alexander, L. T., 124, 127, 142
Alexander, W. M., 114
Alfonso, R. J., 7, 15, 16, 18, 19, 21,
    22, 32, 34, 48, 64, 65, 87, 153,
    255, 263, 265, 268, 272
Amidon, E. J., 194, 195, 196
Amidon, P., 195, 196
Anastos, J., 256
Ancowitz, R., 256
Anderson, L. M., 130
Anderson, R. H., 159
Andrews, R., 53
Andrews, T. E., 232, 240
Arends, R., 273
Argyris, C., 43

Baden, D. J., 237
Bailey, G. D., 167
Baker, E. L., 99, 100
Barell, J., 131
Barker, L. L., 132, 144
Barnard, C. I., 34
Barnes, S., 131
Barr, D., 75, 77, 78, 80, 82

Beach, D. M., 24, 26, 70, 108, 114,
    125, 158, 167, 168, 169, 170, 171,
    176, 222, 234
Bennett, B., 233, 237
Bennis, W. G., 45
Bents, R. H., 155, 243
Berelson, B., 88
Berliner, D., 128
Berlo, D. K., 76
Bessent, W., 7
Biddle, B. J., 192, 193
Bigge, M. L., 107
Blake, R. R., 57, 58, 59
Blanchard, K., 24, 43, 59, 250, 252,
    253
Bloom, B. S., 107, 109, 111
Bolin, F., 21, 23
Bondi, J., 7, 8, 20, 21, 22, 23, 24, 33,
    37, 39, 42, 43, 45, 47, 54, 60, 102,
    140, 220
Bowell, M., 131
Bowlby, J., 55
Boyan, N. J., 4, 78, 80, 83, 160, 161,
    233
Brandt, R., 211, 237

Subject Index

About the Authors

Don M. Beach is currently professor of education at Tarleton State University of the Texas A&M University system. He received his Ph.D. from George Peabody College of Vanderbilt University in curriculum and educational foundations. He has taught at both the elementary and secondary levels in the schools of Texas and Tennessee and served in numerous supervisory positions in education. He is an active teacher, researcher, and writer and is active in numerous professional organizations including the Association of Supervision and Curriculum Development and the Council of Professors of Instructional Supervision. His varied background and nearly 20 years of experience at all levels of education bring a unique perspective to this text. He has conducted numerous workshops at the state and national levels and has published many articles in professional journals, prepared papers for presentation at professional meetings, and published numerous books and monographs.

Judy Reinhartz is currently the assistant director and associate professor of the Center for Professional Teacher Education at the University of Texas at Arlington. She received her doctorate from the University of New Mexico, majoring in curriculum and instruction. Her master's degree in educational foundations was conferred by Seton Hall University. During the last 23 years of experience, Dr. Reinhartz has served in various teaching assignments and supervisory and leadership positions in New Jersey, Virginia, and Texas at all levels of education. In 1985, she was the recipient of the University of Texas at Arlington's Outstanding Teaching Award sponsored by the Amoco Foundation. Dr. Reinhartz is actively involved in professional organizations, namely, Association of Supervision and Curriculum Development, Council of Professors of Instructional Supervision, and the Association of Teacher Educators. Because of her varied educational experience, she frequently serves as a consultant to a number of school districts on such topics as teaching, supervision, and evaluation. During the past 14 years, Dr. Reinhartz has conducted several workshops for teachers and supervisors, has presented many papers at several professional meetings, and has published numerous articles and several books and monographs in the field of education.